RESHAPING THE TAIWAN STRAIT

RESHAPING THE TAIWAN STRAIT

Edited by John J. Tkacik, Jr.

214 Massachusetts Avenue, NE
Washington, DC 20002-4999
202.546.4400 • heritage.org

Printed in the United States of America

ISBN: 978-0-89195-275-6

cover photos by Andrew Blasko and John Tkacik
cover design by Elizabeth Brewer

In memory of Eleanor Sullivan Wainstein,
a national security professional, a pillar of the community,
and a loving neighbor and to Leonard Wainstein,
whose friendship—and library—inspired
their high school babysitter decades ago
to seek a life in foreign affairs.

Contents

Contents

1

Introduction: The Permanent Crisis in the Taiwan Strait

John J. Tkacik, Jr.

Friday, November 26, 1971, was a holiday for official Americans. It was the day after Thanksgiving, and Ambassador Walter P. McConaughy planned to relax for the day at his colonial-era Victorian walled residence on bustling and noisy Chung-Shan North Road, Taipei's main street; but his morning coffee was interrupted by a phone call from the vice minister at the Foreign Ministry, who had vital business that could not wait. Ambassador McConaughy no doubt suggested that the minister come around to his residence for lunch. It was a convenient 15-minute limo ride from the Foreign Ministry. Surely, a casual lunch would be convenient.

The vice minister, however, demurred. He would meet the ambassador just after noon at a discreet restaurant (we don't know which one) where they could talk privately. In hindsight, it seems likely that Vice Minister Yang Hsi-kun was attentive to the likelihood that chit-chat in the American ambassador's parlor was quite audible to the listening devices of Taiwan's security agencies. Instead, he preferred a less public venue—one of the private dining chambers of a fashionable downtown restaurant, perhaps.[1]

---

[1] The substance of the McConaughy–Yang meeting comes from Department of State Telegram 71 Taipei 5869 from the Ambassador in Taipei to the Secretary of State, "Subject: Conversation of Vice Minister Yang Hsi-kun with Ambassador," November 30, 1971, classified "Secret/Nodis/Eyes Only for the Secretary and Assistant Secretary Green." The colorful details are literary embellishment, based on the author's recollection of his own service at the U.S. Embassy in Taipei in that era, to enhance readability. For the text of the McConaughy telegram, see Appendix A in this volume.

Ambassador McConaughy sensed that H. K. Yang's voice carried more than the usual insistence for such meetings. Just one month before, on October 25, the United Nations voted to expel the representatives of the Republic of China on Taiwan (ROC) and seat the People's Republic of China despite what Henry Kissinger called "valiant efforts" by the United States to pursue "dual representation" for both Taipei and Beijing.[2]

Expulsion from the United Nations was a dash of cold water on Generalissimo Chiang Kai-shek's hopes that his "Republic of China," operating in Taipei, would ever again return victorious to mainland China. With the expulsion, Chiang's top foreign policy aides immediately foresaw the diplomatic imperative of splitting Taiwan from China in the international context.

This was what Vice Minister H. K. Yang needed to press upon the U.S. ambassador. The minister did not waste time on niceties as he entered the dining chamber alone with Ambassador McConaughy. "Almost immediately," the ambassador reported, the minister launched "into a discussion of the critical situation." Taiwan's expulsion was an essential element of Beijing's relentless "drive to isolate the GRC [Government of the Republic of China] internationally and force general recognition of the ChiCom right to take over Taiwan as an integral part of China."

Yang had been present in New York when the fateful vote was tallied and watched in horror as the Tanzanians danced in the aisles, the Algerians embraced, and the Albanians quietly shook hands when China's victory was announced.[3] He wasted no time exiting the building and returning to Taipei for conferences with Chiang Kai-shek and his advisers. Yang confided to McConaughy that he told Chiang "it is of paramount importance" that Chiang issue a formal "declaration to the world that the government on Taiwan is entirely separate and apart from the government on the Mainland."

Yang drew a breath and, according to McConaughy, described the declaration of Taiwan independence. The declaration, he began, should prescribe a new designation for the government: "The Chinese Republic of Taiwan." It would be stipulated that the term "Chinese" did not have any political connotation but was used merely as a generic term stemming from the Chinese ethnic origin of the populace on Taiwan. It would be used in a way similar to the manner in which the various Arab countries use "Arab" in their official governmental titles.

---

[2] Henry Kissinger, *White House Years* (Boston: Little, Brown, 1979), p. 784.

[3] *The New York Times*, October 26, 1971, p. 6, cited in Kissinger, *White House Years*, p. 784.

Yang had considered the legalities of such a declaration, McConaughy recalled:

> The President in making the sort of declaration described should concurrently, or very soon thereafter, use his emergency powers to set aside the constitution and dissolve all of the parliamentary type bodies. He should then set up a new unicameral provisional representative body to be composed of two-thirds Taiwanese and one-third mainlanders. A new cabinet should be formed with some Taiwanese and some younger men included. He said a new image needed to be created with the government freed of the outworn trappings, encumbrances and shibboleths of the [Kuomintang] Party and the establishment. He said the emergency decree of the President should provide for an island-wide referendum with universal suffrage to determine the future status of Taiwan and provide for a constituent body.

This was not a far-fetched idea, the minister reassured the ambassador. Retired Foreign Minister George K. C. Yeh and future premier Y. S. Tsiang supported him. Moreover, said Yang, he had spoken "very privately" with Chiang Kai-shek and found the President "impressively open-minded and willing to listen."

This was not true, however, of most others in Chiang's immediate circle. Madame Chiang, Yang ruminated, "seems determined not to budge an inch from the old claims, pretensions and 'return to the mainland' slogans," and Madame's "malign" nephew, H. L. Kung, "from the security of his New York residence, is waging a reactionary campaign for the GRC to stand absolutely rigid." Inertia would prevent movement, and this was at the crux of Yang's plea to McConaughy.

While Yang believed that President Chiang "is increasingly convinced of the imperative requirement for some early and radical action," he was even more certain that Chiang would not "move without the application of a powerful persuasive effort by the U.S. government." Chiang had already been softened up by the Japanese, Yang revealed. In the summer of 1971, while Beijing's support in the United Nations metastasized across the General Assembly, Chiang's top aide, Presidential Office Secretary General Chang Chun, conferred in Tokyo with Prime Minister Eisaku Sato and former Prime Minister Nobusuke Kishi. (The late Mr. Kishi, by the way, was the grandfather of Japan's current prime minister, Shinzo Abe). The advice from two of Japan's most powerful politicians was blunt: "the only hope for the future of the Republic of China was to adopt a course of separation, giving up all Mainland claims and pretensions."

Understandably, the blandishments of the Japanese—Taiwan's former colonial overlords—were unpersuasive to Chiang, who himself had battled Japanese armies on the Chinese mainland during nine years of bloodshed and atrocity. But a similar jolt from the United States, especially if it came in the form of a top U.S. statesman like Vice President Spiro Agnew, or someone Chiang trusted, like former Congressman Walter Judd or retired General Albert C. Wedemeyer, could generate momentum and legitimize the advocacy of separatist policies among Chiang's more progressive advisers.

Taiwan's "Catch-22"

Of course, nothing ever came of Minister Yang's overtures to the United States about pressuring Chiang to "set aside the constitution" and establish a "Chinese Republic of Taiwan." Henry Kissinger had already made a secret pledge to Chinese Premier Zhou Enlai earlier that summer that the Nixon Administration would not support such a policy. For the following seven years, the United States followed a modality that Kissinger described to Zhou, saying "this is temporarily one China, one Taiwan."[4]

There is ample evidence that, had the United States not opened channels to China in 1971, the United States would have continued to push its "dual representation" model for Beijing and Taipei in the United Nations. The international community would have welcomed it: Certainly Japan was supportive, as were a number of other major nations. Beijing would have resisted but no doubt in the end would have accepted a U.N. seat under protest.

Like so much in history, however, if one thing had happened, another would not have, and the "Catch-22" for a "Chinese Republic of Taiwan" was that President Chiang in Taipei would have accepted it only if he had actually been expelled from the U.N.; but if the ROC was supplanted in the United Nations by the PRC, then Taiwan was never going to get back in.

Five years later, when he was President Gerald Ford's Secretary of State, Dr. Kissinger had a chance to muse over the risks inherent in a policy that accepted that Taiwan is "part of China." On October 29, 1976, Secretary of State Henry Kissinger asked his top China aides: "If Taiwan is recognized by us as part of China, then it may become irresistible to them. Our saying we

---

[4] See "Memorandum of Conversation" between Kissinger and Zhou Enlai *et al.*, July 11, 1971, 10:35 a.m.–11:55 a.m., The White House, classified "Top Secret/Sensitive/Exclusively Eyes Only," p. 12, at *www.gwu.edu/~nsarchiv/NSAEBB/NSAEBB66/ch-38.pdf*.

want a peaceful solution has no force: it is Chinese territory. What are we going to do about it?" Arthur Hummel, then Assistant Secretary of State and later ambassador to Beijing, responded, "Down the road, perhaps the only solution would be an independent Taiwan."[5]

The international context of the 1970s was such that China remained a minor strategic power and an even more diminutive trade power whose global diplomatic footprint was faint. Constitutional changes along the lines of H. K. Yang's vision would no doubt have caused apoplexy in Beijing but only minor heartburn in Washington. It would have been secretly cheered in Tokyo and shrugged off in the rest of the world, which at the time simply didn't care.

The Current International Context

At the opening of the 21st century, the "international context" is much different. Although "democracy" writ large has triumphed in most of the world since the collapse of the Soviet Union, it has been singularly unsuccessful in post-Tiananmen China. Instead, in the 15 years of economic reform since the June 4, 1989, Tiananmen crackdown, China has emerged as the world's second largest economy as measured by the "purchasing power parity" scale favored by the Central Intelligence Agency.[6] By the same scale, at an estimated $105 billion in 2006, China's military spending is second only to that of the United States,[7] and China is officially listed as the world's fourth largest trading nation after the United States, Germany, and Japan.[8]

---

[5] William Burr, ed., *The Kissinger Transcripts: The Top Secret Talks with Beijing and Moscow* (New York: New Press, 1999), p. 464.

[6] In terms of "purchasing power parity" (a quantitative measure of equivalent goods and services rather than nominal dollar values at official exchange rates), China is listed as second largest national economy behind the United States in *CIA World Factbook 2005*, at *www.cia.gov/cia/publications/factbook/rankorder/2001rank.html*.

[7] The Defense Department classes China's defense spending as third after the U.S. and the Russian Federation, but a purchasing power parity model would no doubt push China's spending into second place. See U.S. Department of Defense, *Annual Report to Congress: The Military Power of the People's Republic of China 2006*, May 23, 2006, p. 28, at *www.defenselink.mil/pubs/pdfs/China%Report%202006.pdf*.

[8] 2006 data now indicate that China's is the world's fourth largest economy (after the U.S., Japan, and Germany) if new revised figures for China's service sector and Hong Kong's GDP are included. See Joe McDonald, "China Says Economy Much Bigger Than Thought," Associated Press, December 20, 2005.

Let us posit that China's massive trade presence, its mushrooming defense spending, and the relative decline of the United States as a Pacific power as it faces increasing challenges in Iraq, Afghanistan, the war on terrorism, and a host of other crises, has given China's *totalitarian*[9] rulers undue influence among the world's democracies, including the United States.

Of course, the international community should applaud the development of constitutional democracy in Taiwan; but it doesn't, because it fears China, and that is the extent of the international community's objection to an independent Taiwan. Taipei cannot simply resolve the matter by declaring to Beijing, "That's it: You won the civil war. You're China, and we're not" and then go its peaceful way. This might have been possible in 1971 when Minister Yang Hsi-kun begged for American help in changing Taiwan's constitution, but the international situation as it has developed in the intervening decades now restrains Taiwan from moving unilaterally or without broad international approbation.

The Essays in This Volume

Many of the essays collected in this volume emerged from a September 27, 2005, symposium at The Heritage Foundation, "Reshaping the Taiwan Strait: Are There Realistic Alternatives to 'One China'?" that sought to reframe the policymaking context in a way that might avoid the missteps of 1971.[10] Others were submitted by scholars who have novel and imaginative insights into the Taiwan Strait conundrum, including two by eminent Australian scholars. Chapter 3, by Jim Auer of Vanderbilt University and a team of security policy experts (which included myself), gave special attention to the Taiwan factor in the U.S.–Japan alliance.

The operating assumption of the panel discussions was that, although the fundamental precepts of U.S. relations with Taiwan are viable in substance, the articulation of those policies is muddled, and policy implementation is

---

[9] I use "totalitarian" rather than "authoritarian" because China seems to fit better into the totalitarian classification under the Friedrich–Brzezinski theoretical model's six key tests: (1) an official ideology to which general adherence is demanded and which is intended to achieve a "perfect final stage of mankind"; (2) a single mass party, hierarchically organized, closely interwoven with the state bureaucracy, and typically led by one man; (3) monopolistic control of the armed forces; (4) a similar monopoly of the means of effective mass communication; (5) a system of terroristic police control; and (6) central control and direction of the entire economy. See Carl J. Friedrich and Zbigniew K. Brzezinski, *Totalitarian Dictatorship and Autocracy*, 2nd Edition (New York: Frederick A. Praeger, 1956, 1965), pp. 22–23.

[10] For the proceedings of this conference, see *www.heritage.org/Press/Events/archive.cfm?startdate=12/31/2005&days=364*.

therefore conflicted. Panelists were asked to point out the disconnects between precepts, articulation, and implementation and to consider "realistic" options that might help policymakers think through the thickets of jargon and misunderstanding that envelop Taiwan policy. They were also asked to propose policy initiatives that could both bolster Taiwan's status as a valuable member of the community of Asian democracies and discourage Chinese belligerence.

Because so much of America's policy toward the confrontation in the Taiwan Strait is formulaic, the key to a sustainable and successful policy will be in framing the issues clearly and pursuing policy initiatives consistent with the articulated policy. Alas, Washington policymakers have, over the years, ceded the agenda to China. Beijing now frames the issue. Beijing in turn insists that Washington use Beijing's language and demands that Washington accept Beijing's frames of reference. Thus, "reshaping" the agenda for the Taiwan Strait has become the essential first step in bringing coherence to U.S. policy in the Strait.

To do so, the panelists and other contributors to this effort had to resolve the fundamental tension internal to Taiwan Strait policy: that the United States has taken upon itself a security commitment to "resist the use of force" against Taiwan by China, but that Washington's "one China" policy is seen, in Beijing at least, as America's acknowledgement that China has the right under international law to use force against Taiwan. The panelists and contributors here see this contradiction as immanent in the curious relationship that the United States has with Taiwan.

On the one hand, Taiwan is a vibrant democracy, a major trading nation, a geopolitical "friend" (more aptly described as a "quasi-ally"), and a fairly valuable piece of strategic real estate on the Western Pacific island rim of Asia. In short, Taiwan is naturally aligned with the United States.

The United States has maintained a commitment to Taiwan's security from China for over half a century. In 1979, Congress passed the Taiwan Relations Act, which enshrined that commitment in law and pledged to treat Taiwan, for the purposes of domestic law, exactly as it treats any other independent state.[11] In the Asia–Pacific region, America's commitment to Taiwan in the face of Chinese irritation has been reassuring. All Asia has been transfixed by the rise of the new Chinese superpower, and for many, Taiwan has become a bellwether of America's presence in the Western Pacific.

On the other hand, irritation with Taiwan has been a chronic nuisance among Washington policymakers ever since Taiwan's democratic system first began its evolution into an entity that looks, for all the world, like an

[11]For the text of the Taiwan Relations Act, see Appendix B in this volume.

"independent Taiwan." Taiwan is now the focus of nationalistic fevers in Beijing. The Chinese Communist Party—which now rules China, having defeated the Nationalist Party in 1949–1950 after a bitter civil war—had long resented the fact that the Nationalists were able to establish a rival "Chinese" state on Taiwan. The very existence of the Nationalist "Republic of China" seated in Taipei had threatened the legitimacy of the Communist "People's Republic of China" seated in Beijing.

Now, ironically, Taiwan's rival "Republic of China" is welcomed by Beijing because its very name suggests that Taiwan is "part of China." No longer does Beijing take the ROC seriously as a threat to its legitimacy as a government. Instead, Beijing is now threatened by Taiwan's democracy. As Beijing's "White Paper on Democracy"[12] reflects, the word "democracy" is a powerful legitimizer, and the Chinese Communist regime frequently invokes it for that purpose. Chinese leader Hu Jintao referred to democracy six times during a speech in Washington, D.C., and averred to reporters at a White House press availability that "What I can tell you is that we've always believed in China that if there is no democracy, there will be no modernization."[13]

A measure of the threat of Taiwan's democracy to the Beijing regime can be seen in the pseudo-legalities with which Beijing surrounds the Taiwan issue. For example, the "Preamble of the Constitution of the People's Republic of China" makes no reference at all to the territorial extent of the nation except to say that "Taiwan is part of the sacred territory of the People's Republic of China." Not Beijing, not the Yangtze Basin, not Mongolia or Tibet, not Manchuria (ruled by the non-Chinese Manchus who, themselves, ruled all China until 1911): Strictly speaking, the *only* part of the People's Republic of China that the PRC constitution says is part of its "sacred territory" is Taiwan.

The PRC constitution declares that "it is the lofty duty of the entire Chinese people, including our compatriots in Taiwan, to accomplish the great task of reunifying the motherland." China's "Anti-secession Law" of March 14, 2005, mandates war (delicately termed "nonpeaceful means") should Taiwan "under any name or by any means" undergo "secession from China." The

---

[12]"The Building of Political Democracy in China," Information Office of the State Council of the People's Republic of China, issued October 2005, at *www.china.com.cn/english/features/book/145877.htm*.

[13]See text of "Remarks by Chinese President Hu Jintao to the U.S.–China Business Council, the U.S. Chamber of Commerce, and the National Committee on U.S.–China Relations," transcribed by Federal News Service, April 20, 2006, at *www.ncuscr.org/HU%20JINTAO%20REMARKS%204.20.06.pdf*. Also see "President Bush Meets with President Hu of the People's Republic of China," Office of the White House Press Secretary, April 20, 2006, at *www.whitehouse.gov/news/releases/2006/04/20060420-1.html*.

contradiction between the "great task of unifying the motherland" and the idea that Taiwan is already "united" and cannot "secede" is a continuation of the Beijing regime's ideological doublespeak that beclouds the core of the Taiwan issue: Words do not matter, and what Beijing wants, Beijing gets. Liberating Taiwan has now been established by the Chinese Communist Party regime as a touchstone of its legitimacy.

Therein lies the curiosity of America's "China policy." In Washington, democratic Taiwan is seen as an irritant which must be restrained, while Communist China is seen as a rising superpower that must be humored. Washington is horrified when Taiwan's democratic process produces leaders who want nothing less than acknowledgment of their right to exist as a polity separate from China—which is what they have, in fact, been since 1895 (except for the four years immediately following World War II). But China's abysmal record on political, civil, religious, labor, and other human rights is old news in Washington, and the fact that the human rights situation in China has actually deteriorated since the Tiananmen suppression barely elicits a ho-hum or a not-that-again reaction from American political leaders.

Most of America's political leaders are content to humor China's irredentist claims on Taiwan, if simply to avoid Chinese ill will; but for Washington, humoring China's Taiwan pretensions and adopting soothing rhetoric seems only to have intensified the ill will.

None of this confronts the crucial strategic challenge of the 21st century: an authoritarian-totalitarian Chinese regime poised for preeminence in Asia. Thus, in *Reshaping the Taiwan Strait*, we hope to provide constructive criticism of existing policies, offer useful policy alternatives, and examine where the Taiwan Strait conundrum fits into the China challenge.

2

Strategy Deficit: U.S. Security in the Pacific and the Future of Taiwan

John J. Tkacik, Jr.

> "Would you tell me, please, which way I ought to walk from here?" asked Alice.
>
> "That depends a good deal on where you want to get to," said the Cat. "I don't much care where," said Alice. "Then it doesn't matter which way you walk," said the Cat.
>
> Lewis Carroll,
> *Through the Looking-Glass*

I*F YOU DON'T KNOW WHERE YOU'RE GOING, ANY ROAD WILL GET YOU THERE*. If only there were a Cheshire Cat to give a similar jolt to America's foreign policy establishment as it ponders the unfolding geopolitical realignment in the Western Pacific.

Washington has no idea what kind of a 21st century it wants to see in the Asia–Pacific region. Consequently, it has no road map for achieving it. Our China–Taiwan policy is a singular example of this conceptual lacuna. Normally intelligent U.S. diplomats intone with straight faces that the United States "takes no position" on differences between Taiwan and China and that "our only concern is that they be resolved peacefully"—the ultimate triumph of process over outcome.[1] Recall that the American ambassador in Baghdad said the same thing about "Arab–Arab territorial disputes" to Saddam Hussein in July 1990 as dozens of Iraqi mechanized divisions lined up on the highway leading to the Kuwait border.[2]

One does not need Basil Fawlty's "doctorate in the bleedin' obvious" to know that the United States certainly *does* have an interest in keeping democratic Taiwan out of the hands of totalitarian China. America also has an interest in keeping our ninth largest trading partner beyond the control of our second largest. And Washington should also consider the fact that Taiwan remains an important defense and intelligence partner.

To claim otherwise—that is, to say that we have no interest in an end-state for Taiwan—is the diplomatic equivalent of not caring where you're going so long as the road is paved, and maybe you'll go even if it isn't paved: You just haven't decided yet.

A Lack of Strategy

It is a matter of historical record that the United States has not had a coherent strategic vision for Asia—much less a strategy for China, and still less any idea of what to do with Taiwan—at least since the end of the Cold War. Describing his 12 years of China policy work in the intelligence community staff and the White House, Robert L. Suettinger writes, "the notion that American policy is directly driven by strategic considerations, or that explanations can be found for specific American policies in theoretical speculation about the actions of nation-states in certain circumstances, is grossly inaccurate." How true. Mr. Suettinger's book describes a policy process that was chaotic, reactive, and marked by an acute attention deficit, even if Mr. Suettinger admits only that it was "politicized and changeable."[3]

My own 20 years of experience in China policy is proof enough to me that the policy was indeed bereft of "strategic considerations." "Strategy" was something the State Department talked about, but not since the Reagan years had any denizen of Foggy Bottom ever done anything about it. At least

---

[1] "The United States' main effort—and this is bipartisan in the United States—has been to prevent conflict in the Taiwan Straits. Our overwhelming concern is for resolution of this question peacefully. How it is resolved is less important to us than that it is resolved peacefully." See "Transcript: Armitage Reaffirms U.S.–Australian Ties (August 17 remarks in Sydney media roundtable)," August 17, 2001, at *http://canberra.usembassy.gov/hyper/2001/0817/epf505.htm*.

[2] See "Excerpts from Iraqi Document on Meeting with U.S. Envoy," *The New York Times*, September 23, 1990, a version of which is available at *www.chss.montclair.edu/english/furr/glaspie.html*.

[3] Robert L. Suettinger, *Beyond Tiananmen: The Politics of US–China Relations 1989–2000* (Washington, D.C.: Brookings Institution, 2003), p. 420.

in the 1980s, there existed a strategy to enlist China to help balance Soviet expansion, particularly in Afghanistan.[4] China even gave up its first chance to compete in the international Olympic Games when it joined President Jimmy Carter's boycott of the Moscow games in protest of the Soviet invasion of Afghanistan. Through the 1980s, the U.S. and China jointly collected strategic intelligence on the Soviet Union via secret mountain listing posts in Xinjiang Province—listening posts for which, I understand, the Central Intelligence Agency still pays several million dollars a year and from which the CIA gets very little useful intelligence.

The U.S.–China strategic cooperation of the 1980s was certainly one of the major factors in precipitating the Soviet withdrawal from Afghanistan in February 1989. In addition, up to the spring of 1989, China's remarkable economic reforms were accompanied by a steady loosening of political repression. Americans in general were comforted by the impression that economic and political reforms went metaphysically hand in hand.

In June 1989, 400,000 Chinese troops in heavy tanks, armored vehicles, and trucks crushed pro-democracy demonstrations in Beijing's Tiananmen Square, ushering in a period of steadily tightening political repression that has become even more ruthless in recent years. America's citizens who watched the Tiananmen Square events unfold on satellite television were unsettled by the realization that China's Communist leaders were not nice people. But Tiananmen was not the turning point in the U.S.–China strategic partnership that it should have been. Perhaps the Chinese leadership did not share American values, but there was still the Soviet Union to contend with. For all practical purposes, however, the collapse of the Soviet Union marked the end of the partnership. With it, the grand organizing principle of U.S.–China relations evaporated. By 1992, it was clear that the United States and China shared neither moral values nor strategic interests.

Incredible as it seems, the empty momentum of the partnership continued to impel the policy prescriptions of American officialdom, precisely because the United States had no strategic framework for a China

---

[4] See *National Security Decision Directive* Number 75, "U.S. Relations with the USSR," classified "SECRET/SENSITIVE," signed by President Ronald Reagan on January 17, 1983, esp. p. 5: "4. China: China continues to support U.S. efforts to strengthen the world's defenses against Soviet expansionism. The U.S. should over time seek to achieve enhanced strategic cooperation and policy coordination with China, and to reduce the possibility of a Sino–Soviet rapprochement. The U.S. will continue to pursue a policy of substantially liberalized technology transfer and sale of military equipment to China on a case-by-case basis within the parameters of the policy approved by the President in 1981, and defined further in 1982."

policy. Beijing, on the other hand, had a very coherent strategy. Beijing's immediate goal was, and remains, the subjugation of Taiwan. Its ultimate goal is to assume the mantle of Asia's preeminent power and the removal of the United States from its new sphere of influence in the Asia–Pacific region.

Taiwan, too, had a strategic vision: to remove itself firmly from all taint of Chinese identity in the way envisioned by H. K. Yang in 1971.[5] In the 1990s, Taiwan underwent its own political transformation and metamorphosed from the mild authoritarian state it had been during the early 1980s (a continuation of its evolution from a rather rigid dictatorship in the 1950s–1970s period) into a vibrant democracy, part of a regional phenomenon that saw democracies supplant dictatorships in South Korea, the Philippines, Mongolia, and, by 1999, even Indonesia. This democratic renaissance in Asia was the direct result of a Reagan–Bush policy of supporting freedom around the world as a matter of national strategy.

That strategy survives somewhat in President George W. Bush's National Security Strategy of the United States of America, which proclaims it "the policy of the United States to seek and support democratic movements and institutions in every nation and culture, with the ultimate goal of ending tyranny in our world"[6] and to preserve America's continuing role as the sole superpower as the primary force for achieving that goal.[7]

Having a grand national security strategy on paper may be a necessary element in animating Washington's China policy, but it is certainly also insufficient. The "China policy" pursued by the past three Administrations does not remotely reflect the primacy either of global democratization or of democratic America's unique post–Cold War power position.

What passes for "Asia strategy" in Washington these days is the vague vision of a democratic end-state for China.[8] But the China policy

---

[5] See Chapter 1, *supra*.

[6] *The National Security Strategy of the United States of America*, The White House, March 16, 2006, p. 6, at *www.whitehouse.gov/nsc/nss/2006/nss2006.pdf*. Cited hereafter as National Security Strategy 2006.

[7] In March 2006, President Bush urged: "We must build and maintain our defenses beyond challenge." See National Security Strategy 2006, p. 1. In November 2003, the President declared "the global expansion of democracy" to be one of the three pillars of his foreign policy. See "President Bush Discusses Iraq Policy at Whitehall Palace in London," Office of the White House Press Secretary, November 19, 2003, at *www.whitehouse.gov/news/releases/2003/11/20031119-1.html*.

[8] "The United States encourages China to continue down the road of reform and openness, because in this way China's leaders can meet the legitimate needs and aspirations of the Chinese people for liberty, stability, and prosperity." See National Security Strategy 2006, p. 41.

bureaucracy in Washington acts as though it does not believe that vision needs to inform or animate policy. Indeed, Administration policy pronouncements that use the words "democracy" and "China" in the same sentence usually imply that democracy will emerge in China all by itself without any prodding or pressure from abroad.[9]

Instead, policymakers in Washington have focused lately on America's trade relationship with China as the driver of Taiwan policy. Their view is that Americans consume so much cheap Chinese output, and China has soaked up so much U.S. Treasury debt in payment for those goods, that matters of national security and global strategic interests must be subordinated to maintaining a continuing supply of Chinese goods. Hence, their lack of interest in pursuing policies that might actually bolster democracy in China. It is a "China = Big, Taiwan = Small, *ergo* China = Important, Taiwan = Not Important" argument.

America's stake in Taiwan is substantial, so why does the U.S. national security bureaucracy keep advocating policies that push Taiwan toward an *Anschluss* with China? The answer seems obvious to many policymakers and academics who view China as an unstoppable force of nature. As Deputy Secretary of State Robert Zoellick put it after an intense grilling by the House International Relations Committee on May 10, 2006:

> [W]e have to be very careful, you see. And this is the balance, is that we want to be supportive of Taiwan while we're not encouraging those that try to move towards independence. Because let me be very clear: independence means war. And that means American soldiers....[10]

---

[9] In November 2003, for example, President Bush admitted that "our commitment to democracy is tested in China. That nation now has a sliver, a fragment of liberty. Yet, China's people will eventually want their liberty pure and whole.... Eventually, men and women who are allowed to control their own wealth will insist on controlling their own lives and their own country." See "President Bush Discusses Freedom in Iraq and Middle East: Remarks by the President at the 20th Anniversary of the National Endowment for Democracy," Washington, D.C., November 6, 2003, at *www.whitehouse.gov/news/releases/2003/11/20031106-2.html*. In March 2004, Secretary of State Colin Powell observed that "China has seen the virtues of market economics. China's political system hasn't yet followed suit. But our understanding of politics and human nature suggests it eventually will." See Secretary Colin L. Powell, "Partnership at Work in Asia," The Tenth Annual B.C. Lee Lecture, The Heritage Foundation, at *www.heritage.org/Research/AsiaandthePacific/bclee10.cfm*.

In saying that "independence means war," Zoellick apparently gave no thought to the fact that he had repeated Chinese policy word for word as U.S. policy.[11] One might just as well have asked him what would happen if Beijing were to say "Mongolia's independence meant war"? Or South Korea's? Or "Japan's continued occupation of the Senkaku Islands means war"? Would those threats also warrant American timidity?

China, Taiwan, and the Democratic Imperative

In the broad matrix of America's geostrategic stake in the Asia–Pacific region, Taiwan may indeed be "small" compared to China; but as an East Asian power, it most emphatically is not "small" at all. It is a very substantial member of the community of Asian democracies in its own right.

Taiwan is a crucial element in the new geostrategic structure of the Asia–Pacific as the magnitude of China's military might catches up with its economic and trade power. Taiwan is one of democratic Asia's major nations; its exports rank third after Japan's and South Korea's, and it is one of America's top 10 export markets. It is the second largest supplier of semiconductors to the U.S. market—a fact that should make American industry more concerned about its fate.

Taiwan's population is slightly larger than Australia's. And if Taiwan were a member of the 10-nation Association of Southeast Asian Nations, it would be ASEAN's biggest economy and largest military spender.

Taiwan is a poster child for democracy in Asia; it is a long-term (albeit "unofficial") American defense partner; and it is a strategically significant piece of real estate in the Pacific Rim. The United States has provided security assurances to Taiwan against Chinese threats for over half a century.

In short, Taiwan is an important American trading partner, a model democracy, and a critical if "unofficial" security ally. An assessment of U.S.

---

[10]See testimony of Robert Zoellick in hearing, *China's Resurgence*, Committee on International Relations, U.S. House of Representatives, transcribed by Federal News Service, May 10, 2006. Ellipsis in original.

[11]Chinese military leaders first adopted this phrase when the election of pro-independence presidential candidate Chen Shui-bian seemed possible in March 2000. See "Zhang Wannian: Taidu Yiweizhe Zhan Zheng; Fenlie meiyou heping; Baiwan Xiongshi Yanzhen Yidai" [Zhang Wannian: Taiwan Independence means war; No peace in separation; a million brave troops await the order], *Hong Kong Commercial Daily*, March 6, 2000, at *http://pdf.sznews.com/hkcd/2000/0306/newsfile/n1-2.htm*.

interests in Taiwan requires a reexamination—perhaps behind closed doors and in a confidential way—of many long-held but obsolete policy assumptions about the benefits of nudging Taiwan into the embrace of China.

Aside from the obvious political interests that the United States has in ensuring the survival and success of democracy in Taiwan, there are vital economic interests as well. For example, Taiwan's semiconductor industry is the world's most important foundry producer of microchips, according to a report issued in February 2005 by the Pentagon's Defense Science Board.[12] According to that same report, the Pentagon gets a substantial volume of vital microchips from Taiwan's chip "fabs." Meanwhile, the report adds, America's microchip production capacity is diminished, with only one U.S. chip fab able to produce "trusted and classified" chips for U.S. defense needs.[13]

If, in fact, Americans see their own national success and survival in the global expansion of democracy, perhaps a "Taiwan = Democracy, China = Dictatorship, *ergo* Taiwan = Friend, China = Not a Friend" paradigm is more consonant with America's interests. It's a simple model and certainly more useful than the alternative that Mr. Zoellick contemplated.

In a rapidly rising China, a totalitarian regime that does not suffer external pressures to change will not change. Instead, the regime that abandoned "socialism" as its ideology in 1992 now seeks to legitimate its rule by stressing that its ideology "increases the comprehensive strength of the nation."[14]

---

[12]See Defense Science Board Task Force on High Performance Microchip Supply, *Final Report*, U.S. Department of Defense, Office of the Under Secretary of Defense for Acquisition, Technology, and Logistics, February 2005, p. 22, at *www.acq.osd.mil/dsb/reports/2005-02-HPMS_Report_Final.pdf.*

[13]*Ibid.*, p. 28.

[14]A fascinating account of the ideological battle within the Chinese Communist Party that resulted in abandoning "Marxism–Leninism and Mao Zedong Thought" in favor of "increasing the comprehensive strength of the nation" is chronicled in Ma Licheng and Ling Zhihui, eds., *Jiaofeng: Dangshi Zhongguo San Ci Sixiang Jiefang Shilyu* [*Crossed Swords: A True Account of the Three Emancipations of Thought in Contemporary China*] (Beijing: Jinri Zhongguo Publishers, 1998), esp. pp. 160–204. See also "Liu Huaqing kaocha Guangzhou Junqu shi qiangdiao Liyong Gaige Kaifang youli tiaojian quanmian jiaqiang budui zhiliang jianshe" [During an inspection tour of the Guangzhou military region, Liu Huaqing stresses the need to utilize the beneficial conditions of Reform and Opening to establish a strengthened quality among the troops], *Nanfang Ribao*, January 29, 1992, p. 1.

China is a power driven by an ideology of "nationalism," committed to changing the *status quo*. The Chinese Communist Party now "opposes hegemonism and power politics" (i.e., the United States) and seeks to "boost world multipolarization" (i.e., opposing America's role as the sole superpower).[15] Moreover, it equates "terrorism" and "hegemonism" as equal threats.[16] China's pressure on its Central Asian neighbors to demand a timetable for U.S. withdrawal from Afghan border areas is only the most recent example of China's lack of enthusiasm for fighting global terrorism.[17] In an earlier incarnation as adviser to presidential candidate George W. Bush, Condoleezza Rice wrote, "China is not a 'status quo' power but one that would like to alter Asia's balance of power in its own favor"[18]—an assessment that, seven years later, seems preternaturally prescient. Moreover, this assessment makes it essential that the United States catalogue both its interests in the "*status quo*" and its strategic objectives in Asia.

There is no question that today the United States faces a new great power competitor. Secretary of State Rice admits that China is becoming a "military superpower" and that "it is crucial for the U.S. to help integrate China into an international, rules-based economy" before that happens.[19] Former Deputy Secretary of State Zoellick said that "the focus now" is to make China a "stakeholder" in these systems, as if to say that China has not been one up to now.[20] In a September 2005 speech, Zoellick asked, "For the United States and the world, the essential question is—how will China use its influence?" To answer that question, he said, "we need to urge China to become a responsible stakeholder in that system."[21] American disappoint-

---

[15]Chinese leader Jiang Zemin told the Congress: "However, the old international political and economic order, which is unfair and irrational, has yet to be changed fundamentally. Uncertainties affecting peace and development are on the rise. The harm resulting from terrorism is increasing. Hegemonism and power politics have new manifestations." See "Text of report delivered by Jiang Zemin at the opening of the 16th CCP National Congress at the Great Hall of the People," Chinese Central TV, transcribed by BBC Monitoring, November 8, 2002.

[16]Jiang was also quoted by a senior Chinese political scientist as saying: "The elements of traditional and nontraditional security threats are interwoven, with terrorism rising in harm and hegemonism and power politics having a new manifestation." The author explains that "it is very difficult to discern whether hegemonism or terrorism is the principal threat in the long run; instead, the two elements of threat are interwoven and rise alternately." See Liu Jianfei, "Grasp Relation Between Antiterrorism and Anti-Hegemonism" [Renqing Fankong yu fanbade guanxi]; *Liaowang* [*Outlook*], Beijing, February 24, 2003, pp. 54–56. English translation by Foreign Broadcast Information Service (FBIS) at FBIS–CHI–2003–0307.

ment in China's trade, financial, diplomatic, proliferation, human rights, and Taiwan policies is reflected in the poignant question mark in the title of Zoellick's speech, "Whither China—From Membership to Responsibility?" Indeed, China hasn't been, and there is little likelihood that China wants to be, a "stakeholder" in a *status quo* that it is intent on changing.

There appears to be a glimmering of appreciation among America's top foreign policy officials that China is a grave and gathering challenge, but there simply isn't any evidence that this appreciation is being translated into "policy." In 1945, President Harry Truman declared that a "strong, united and democratic China" was in "the most vital interests of the United States."[22] But is two out of three good enough? Is a "strong and united" China in U.S. interests at all? Unless China is also a reliable democracy, might it just be a greater challenge to U.S. interests than a weak, unstable, and disunited China?

Chinese leaders certainly think so. Chinese leader Hu Jintao and his chief ally, Vice President Zeng Qinghong, are reliably reported to have given "back-to-back" speeches in May 2005 at a secret party meeting that attacked "liberal elements" in society who were supposedly supported by the United States. The two top leaders, Hu and Mr. Zeng, argued that during 2004 and 2005 the United States had fostered social unrest in Ukraine's "Orange Revolution," Georgia's "Rose Revolution," and Kyrgyzstan's "Tulip Revolution" and had similar designs on China.[23]

I, for one, sincerely doubt that there is any such coordinated U.S. policy to support democratic reforms in China—other than giving large monetary

---

[17]See "Beijing Shiya Jiguo guan Mei Jidi, Fangzhi Meijun Jiankong Dalu xibu, Jizhengfu ju cong" [Beijing pressures Kyrgyzstan to close US bases, seek to avoid US reconnaissance in China's west, Kyrgyz government refuses], *World Journal* (in Chinese), New York, August 4, 2005, p. A8. For more information, see C. J. Chivers, "Central Asians Call on U.S. to Set a Timetable for Closing Bases," *The New York Times*, July 6, 2005, p. A12, at *www.nytimes.com/2005/07/06/international/asia/06kazakhstan.html.*

[18]Condoleezza Rice, "Promoting the National Interest," *Foreign Affairs*, Vol. 79, No. 1 (January/February 2000), p. 56.

[19]Neil King, Jr., "Rice Wants U.S. To Help China Be Positive Force," *The Wall Street Journal*, June 29, 2005, p. A13, at *http://online.wsj.com/article/0,,SB112001578322872628,00.html.*

[20]See Robert Zoellick, Deputy Secretary of State, "Zoellick Remarks at U.S. Embassy Beijing," August 2, 2005, at *www.state.gov/s/d/rem/50498.htm.*

[21]Robert B. Zoellick, "Whither China—From Membership to Responsibility?" Remarks to National Committee on U.S.–China Relations, New York City, September 21, 2005, at *http://www.state.gov/s/d/rem/53682.htm.*

grants to Chinese Communist Party and government delegations for academic exchanges. However, if fostering a clamor for freedom in China indeed is a strategic objective of the United States, one has to ask how belittling democracy in Taiwan promotes that objective, because belittling Taiwan's democracy has become the default mode for U.S. policy toward Taiwan.

I blame inept American diplomacy for beginning the efforts to nudge Taiwan's politicians into the Chinese orbit after 1993 just at the time when China began to plan in earnest for the takeover of the island. President Bill Clinton did not have to disinvite Lee Teng-hui from the Asia–Pacific Economic Cooperation (APEC) forum leaders' meeting in Seattle in 1993—the APEC Charter demands that all member economies be treated equally[24]—and we didn't have to pressure Lee to pull back from his "interim two Chinas policy" that same year or his two-states theory in 1999.

We did not have to snub President Lee's request for an overnight transit of Hawaii in May of 1994 or make a litmus test of denying President Lee permission to address an audience at Cornell University in 1995; or to pressure President Lee on his "special state to state" doctrine of 1999; or to pressure Chen Shui-bian for his skepticism about the benefits of "One China" under Communism.

President Chen had two successful trips to the United States (Houston in 2001 and New York in 2003), but since then, U.S. policymakers have seemed intent on making President Chen's visits needlessly inconvenient, uncomfortable, and complicated. As Hurricane Rita roared past Florida in September 2005, the State Department apparently denied President Chen's

---

[22]See President Truman's instructions to General George C. Marshall in U.S. Department of State, *United States Relations with China, with Special Reference to the Period 1944–49* (Washington, D.C.: U.S. Government Printing Office, 1949), p. 133. This document is also known as the "China White Paper."

[23]Joseph Kahn, "China's Leader, Ex-Rival at Side, Solidifies Power," *The New York Times*, September 25, 2005, at *www.nytimes.com/2005/09/25/international/asia/25jintao.html.*

[24]APEC was founded on the principle of "a commitment to open dialogue and consensus-building, with equal respect for the views of all participants." See "Seol APEC Declaration, Seol, Korea," November 12–14, 1991. Spelling as in original. "[W]e believe that the entire APEC enterprise should be conducted in the spirit of mutual respect and equality, informed by the understanding that different societies are at different stages, have different perspectives, different capabilities and different priorities." See Executive Summary in "Achieving the APEC Vision: Free And Open Trade in the Asia Pacific," Second Report of the Eminent Persons Group, APEC–94–EP–01, August 1994.

request for an extra six hours on the ground in Miami. And when President Chen petitioned to layover in New York or San Francisco for a few days *en route* to state visits to Costa Rica and Paraguay in May 2006, the State Department limited him to refueling stops at the Honolulu and/or Anchorage airports, where he would be confined to the VIP lounges for a few hours before proceeding on his way.

Perhaps the most egregious example of belittling Taiwan's democracy came on December 9, 2003, when President Bush chastised "Taiwan's Leader" for making comments that "indicate that he may be willing to make decisions unilaterally that change the status quo, which we oppose." The Taiwanese leader's comments that had upset President Bush involved a democratic referendum on Taiwan that would express Taiwanese indignation at being the target, at the time, of 350 Chinese short-range ballistic missiles.

Unfortunately, President Bush made these comments in the presence of Chinese Premier Wen Jiabao without equally chiding China for attempting to "change the status quo" with its missile deployments against Taiwan—which have since more than doubled to 820 as of mid-2006.[25] Yet very little is heard from the U.S. Administration about China's massive ballistic missile buildup as a rather egregious change in the *status quo*.[26]

This behavior leads China's leaders to believe that the United States government will denigrate Taiwan's democracy if China makes enough of a stink. Consequently, the more American officials belittle Taiwan's democracy, the more China's leaders will demand it, and the more they demand it, the more sensitive America's leaders are to China's demands…and so it goes.

The effect in Taiwan is even more insidious. It leads Taiwan's people to believe that the American leaders don't truly care what happens to Taiwan, whether peacefully or by force. It also leads China to expend a great amount of money on developing a military force that can give the U.S. a face-saving

---

[25]The Pentagon estimates that 710–790 SRBMs were deployed against Taiwan as of December 2005. See U.S. Department of Defense, *Annual Report to Congress: Military Power of the People's Republic of China, 2006*, p. 3, at *www.globalsecurity.org/military/library/report/2006/2006-prc-military-power.htm.* In private conversations, I learned that the estimate was about 810 as of May 2006.

[26]The only record of such an expression of sentiment came from Assistant Secretary of Defense Peter Rodman, who observed: "When you go from zero missiles opposite [Taiwan in] the Taiwan Strait, and a few years later there are 700, that's a change in the status quo." See Charles Snyder, "US Official Accuses China over Build-up," *Taipei Times*, March 18, 2006, p. 1, at *www.taipeitimes.com/News/front/archives/2006/03/18/2003297913.*

excuse—i.e., "avoiding war"—for not intervening in a Taiwan conflict. And if Taiwan does finally go peacefully into the warm embrace of the motherland, China has a modern military force that can be used elsewhere.

Yet, on its face, American policy toward Taiwan clearly contemplates China's ultimate absorption of the island. Since 1992, successive U.S. Administrations have called our policy toward Taiwan "our one China policy," apparently hoping to convey the signal to China that the U.S. agrees with China's contention that Taiwan is sovereign Chinese territory.

Taiwan's people, who had hoped to maintain their separation from China indefinitely as one of America's democratic friends in Asia, are now being led to believe that the United States does not want or need their friendship. This is a profound mistake, but it does not have to be so. Washington can craft its Taiwan policy in ways that minimize antagonizing Beijing, maximize support for Taiwan, and protect America's vital interests in the Western Pacific from Chinese predation.

Understanding the Formal China–Taiwan Policy

Three things American political leaders must first understand are what U.S. policy toward Taiwan actually is, how calling it "our one China policy" undermines its effectiveness, and what animates a bureaucratic antipathy toward Taiwan in the face of China's pressures against Taiwan and the United States.

The formal diplomatic stance of the United States toward Taiwan is to "take no position on the question of Taiwan's sovereignty."[27] Of course, in a rather Zen-like way, to "take no position" is indeed to take a position because having no position cedes the argument to those that do have a position. That aside, it should be obvious that the United States certainly does have very important strategic, political, economic, and defense interests in preventing one of Asia's most successful democracies—and one of America's traditional allies in Asia—from being threatened and pressured by Asia's most successful dictatorship into an annexation that it does not want.

Thus, a political union between Taiwan and China cannot possibly be in America's interests on any level. Unhappily for democratic Taiwan, China's Communist regime claims sovereignty over the island and threatens catastrophic war should Taiwan's people formally and democratically repudiate Beijing's claim. Washington accommodates the Chinese regime by assiduously ignoring the issue—and by pressuring Taiwan's leaders not to make too much of it either. The incoherence of this stance lies in its conflict with U.S. policy as clearly mandated in the Taiwan Relations Act of 1979.[28]

To the credit of President George W. Bush's Administration, it has tried to rearticulate a somewhat conditioned position which insists that the United

States is committed to "our one-China policy" and "opposes" any move by China or Taiwan to "change unilaterally" the "status quo *as we define it.*"[29] On April 21, 2004, a faint allusion to this position came in a public statement by Assistant Secretary of State for East Asia and Pacific Affairs James Kelly, who enumerated for the House International Relations Committee the "core principles" of U.S. policy in the Taiwan Strait:

- The United States remains committed to *our* one-China policy based on the three Joint Communiqués and the Taiwan Relations Act;

- The U.S. does not support independence for Taiwan or unilateral moves that would change the status quo *as we define it*;

- For Beijing, this means no use of force or threat to use force against Taiwan. For Taipei, it means exercising prudence in managing all aspects of cross-Strait relations. For both sides, it means no statements or actions that would unilaterally alter Taiwan's status;

---

[27]This is at least the public position whenever anyone can actually squeeze a position out of an executive branch spokesperson. In a letter from the State Department to Senator John East (R–NC), the department answered the direct and simple question "what is the United States' position on the matter of sovereignty over Taiwan?" by saying that "The United States takes no position on the question of Taiwan's sovereignty. We view this as a matter the Chinese themselves must resolve." See hearings, *The Taiwan Communiqué and the Separation of Powers*, Subcommittee on the Separation of Powers, Committee on the Judiciary, U.S. Senate, 97th Cong., 2nd Sess., September 17 and 27, 1982, p. 140. In July 1982, President Reagan gave personal assurances to Taiwan's President Chiang Ching-kuo that, among other things, "The United States has not changed its long-standing position on the matter of Taiwan's sovereignty." For a longer discussion of President Reagan's "Six Assurances," see testimony of Assistant Secretary of State for East Asia and Pacific Affairs John H. Holdridge in hearing, *China–Taiwan: United States Policy*, Committee on Foreign Affairs, U.S. House of Representatives, 97th Cong., 2nd Sess., August 18, 1982, pp. 15–16. Holdridge also described the "Six Assurances" in his memoir, *Crossing the Divide: An Insider's Account of Normalization of U.S.–China Relations* (Lanham, Md.: Rowan and Littlefield, 1997), p. 232.

[28]Public Law 96–8, United States Code, Title 22, Chapter 48, Sections 3301–3316, enacted April 10, 1979. For the text of the Taiwan Relations Act, see Appendix B in this volume.

- The U.S. will continue the sale of appropriate defensive military equipment to Taiwan in accordance with the Taiwan Relations Act; and

- Viewing any use of force against Taiwan with grave concern, we will maintain the capacity of the United States to resist any resort to force or other forms of coercion against Taiwan.[30]

Indeed, Secretary Kelly admitted at the April 21 hearings that when it came to "our" one-China policy, he was "not sure [he] very easily could define it." Nonetheless:

> I can tell you what it is not. *It is not the One-China policy or the One-China principle that Beijing suggests*, and it may not be the definition that some would have in Taiwan. But it does convey a meaning of solidarity of a kind among the people on both sides of the Strait that has been our policy for a very long time.[31]

Sadly, this is as close as a State Department official has ever come to defining "our one China policy," in private or in public. Nor, as it happens, has any U.S. official ever "defined" the "status quo *as we define it*."[32]

One part of the Taiwan Policy canon that also received Kelly's special mention was President Ronald Reagan's "six assurances":

> Our position continues to be embodied in the so-called "six assurances" offered to Taiwan by President Reagan. We will neither seek to mediate between the P.R.C. and Taiwan, nor

---

[29]Emphasis added. In a prepared statement for testimony before the House International Relations Committee on April 21, 2004, Assistant Secretary of State James Kelly declared that "The U.S. does not support independence for Taiwan or unilateral moves that would change the status quo as we define it" and that this was among the "core principles" of the Administration's China policy. See "House International Relations Committee Hearing on Taiwan: Statement of Assistant Secretary of State James Kelly," April 21, 2004, at *http://wwwa.house.gov/international_relations/108/Kel042104.htm*.

[30]*Ibid.* Emphasis added.

[31]*Ibid.* Emphasis added. For a transcript of the hearing, see *The Taiwan Relations Act: The Next Twenty-Five Years*," Committee on International Relations, U.S. House of Representatives, 108th Cong., 2nd Sess., April 21, 2004, at *http://commdocs.house.gov/committees/intlrel/hfa93229.000/hfa93229_0f.htm*.

> will we exert pressure on Taiwan to come to the bargaining table. Of course, the United States is also committed to make available defensive arms and defensive services to Taiwan in order to help Taiwan meet its self-defense needs. We believe a secure and self-confident Taiwan is a Taiwan that is more capable of engaging in political interaction and dialogue with the PRC....[33]

But Kelly lost count of the Reagan "six assurances" when he neglected to mention the fifth assurance—that "the U.S. has not altered its position regarding sovereignty over Taiwan"—and the sixth, which promised that "the U.S. will not exert pressure on the Republic of China to enter into negotiations with the PRC."[34] Instead, Kelly continued: "and we expect Taiwan will not interpret our support as a blank check to resist such dialogue."[35] Kelly's last phrase, however, ran counter to the Reagan assurances that the United States will not "exert pressure on Taiwan to come to the bargaining table" with the Chinese Communists. Why would the U.S. expect Taiwan to "interpret" the Reagan assurances as anything *but* a "blank check" to resist dialogue if the democratically elected leaders of the people of Taiwan choose to resist dialogue?

Congressional suspicion about an undefined "our one China policy" and "status quo as we define it" is straightforward. Both reflect a deep uneasiness in Congress and among the American public with an executive branch policy that, on its face, seems to concede that democratic Taiwan should be "one" with China's dictatorship. The prototypically "diplomatic" replies from State Department officials were equally revealing. There is no policy—at least not that they could speak of, no doubt for fear of antagonizing Beijing.

---

[32]On February 27, 2006, for example, State Department spokesman Adam Ereli was asked: "Do you think Chen Shui-bian's move is a change of the status quo, and what is the U.S. definition of...the status quo?" Ereli tried to turn the question around: "President Chen has said that he is committed to the status quo and that he is committed to the pledges in his inaugural speech." But the questions persisted: "I just want to get this right. So you don't consider this as a change of status quo?" To which the cornered Ereli could only admit: "You know, I'm not going to define it further than I already have." Needless to say, he hadn't defined it at all. For a transcript of the February 27 briefing, see Adam Ereli, Deputy Spokesman, U.S. Department of State, "Daily Press Briefing," February 27, 2006, at *www.state.gov/r/pa/prs/dpb/2006/62221.htm*.

[33]"Statement of Assistant Secretary of State James Kelly," April 21, 2004.

Twentieth century history is replete with examples of democracies that feared to antagonize dictatorships. The Western democracies' silence during the Austrian *Anschluss* in March 1938 and the aversion of their eyes during the Czechoslovakian crisis that September come to mind. More recently, Saddam Hussein's claims in 1990 that Kuwait was Iraq's "nineteenth province" brought the State Department comment that "we have no opinion on the Arab–Arab conflicts, like your border disagreement with Kuwait."[36] Given the fact that whichever side controls the terminology and terms of

---

[34]The U.S. government never formally issued the "Six Assurances" that were conveyed by President Reagan to Taiwan's President Chiang Ching-kuo on July 14, 1982, but Reagan did authorize President Chiang to release the text of the assurances on the day of the announcement of the "August 17, 1982 Communiqué" with China. That same day, then-Assistant Secretary of State John H. Holdridge repeated these assurances to the Senate Foreign Relations Committee, and Holdridge's successor, Paul Wolfowitz, later repeated the substance of the "Six Assurances" to the Senate Committee on the Judiciary. See hearing, *Taiwan Communiqué and Separation of Powers*, Subcommittee on the Separation of Powers, Committee on the Judiciary, U.S. Senate, March 10, 1983. Wolfowitz said, "it is important to bear in mind some things that we did not agree to in the communiqué. We have not agreed to consult in advance with the PRC on arms sales to Taiwan, nor shall we do so. We have not changed our position that the Taiwan question is a matter for the Chinese on both sides of the strait to resolve, and we will not interfere in this matter or pressure Taiwan to inter into negotiations. *We have not changed our longstanding position on the issue of sovereignty over Taiwan*. We do not seek any of these changes nor should we seek to change the protection of the Taiwan Relations Act itself." Emphasis added. In his memoirs, Holdridge claimed that Taipei was alerted to the August communiqué negotiations and suggested the six points as "guidelines in conducting [U.S.] relations with Taiwan." My own memory is that the "six assurances" were drafted by Dr. Gaston Sigur, then at the National Security Council. Holdridge also claims that the fifth point regarding the U.S. position on sovereignty was that the U.S. "would continue to regard Taiwan as part of China, [and] the question of reunification would be left to the Chinese themselves." See Holdridge, *Crossing the Divide*, pp. 231–232. In fact, when presented to President Chiang on July 14, 1982, the fifth point said simply that "we have not agreed to take any position regarding sovereignty over Taiwan"—a position that was later modified for public consumption to read: "The U.S. has not altered its position regarding sovereignty over Taiwan." These "six assurances" have been embraced by all subsequent U.S. Administrations as part of the canon of U.S. policy toward Taiwan. Secretary of State Colin Powell reiterated this during testimony before the Senate Foreign Relations Committee on March 8, 2001, confirming that the Assurances "remain the usual and official policy of the United States." See "Hearing on the Fiscal Year 2002 Foreign Operations Budget," Committee on Foreign Relations, U.S. Senate, transcribed by Federal News Service, March 8, 2001.

reference also controls a policy debate, these State Department responses were proof positive that the United States has ceded control of the Taiwan policy agenda to Beijing.

China's Calculus for War over Taiwan

China, unlike the United States, is quite forceful in asserting its agenda. China's irredentist rhetoric of "unification" has become alarmingly bellicose since the late Marshal Ye Jianying pronounced a "fundamental policy of striving for peaceful reunification" in September 1981.[37] On August 31, 1993, just in case anyone was under any illusions that Beijing had accepted the Cold War *status quo*, the Chinese State Council issued a white paper, which asserted flatly:

- That "there is only one China in the world, Taiwan is an inalienable part of China, and the seat of China's central government is in Beijing";
- That wishes for Taiwan's reunification with China "have not come to fruition for reasons such as interference by some foreign forces";
- That, in fact, "the Taiwan question is the responsibility of the United States"; and
- That "the Chinese Communist Party is ready to establish contact with the Chinese Kuomintang [KMT] at the earliest possible date to create conditions for talks on officially ending the state of hostility between the two sides of the Taiwan Straits and gradually realizing peaceful reunification."[38]

The repository of true authority over Taiwan, the CCP believed, was not the people of Taiwan, and still less the government of the "Republic of

---

[35]"Statement of Assistant Secretary of State James Kelly," April 21, 2004.

[36]See "Excerpts from Iraqi Document on Meeting with U.S. Envoy," *The New York Times*, September 23, 1990.

[37]See "Marshal Ye Jianying's Nine-Point Proposal," Xinhua News Agency, Beijing, September 30, 1981.

[38]"The Taiwan Question and the Reunification of China," issued by the Taiwan Affairs Office and the Information Office under the State Council of the People's Republic of China, August 31, 1993.

China," but rather the "Chinese Kuomintang Party." The white paper also stated that:

> Peaceful reunification is a set policy of the Chinese Government. However, any sovereign state is entitled to use any means it deems necessary, including military ones, to uphold its sovereignty and territorial integrity. The Chinese Government is under no obligation to undertake any commitment to any foreign power or people intending to split China as to what means it might use to handle its own domestic affairs.[39]

By February 2000, the Beijing regime sensed a need to be a bit more categorical about the status of Taiwan's "ruling clique":

> Since the KMT ruling clique retreated to Taiwan, although its regime has continued to use the designations "Republic of China" and "government of the Republic of China," it has long since completely forfeited its right to exercise state sovereignty on behalf of China and, in reality, has always remained only a local authority in Chinese territory.[40]

But Beijing was quite a bit more strident, not to say hysterical, as it pondered the possibility that in less than a month, Taiwan's voters could elect a pro-independence president. The new white paper dismissed the idea of "so-called controversy about democracy" as "an excuse for obstructing the reunification of China" and a "scheme to deceive compatriots in Taiwan and world opinion."[41] And to make certain Taiwan's voters got the message, the white paper drew its red lines defining the circumstances under which China would use armed force against Taiwan:

> [I]f a grave turn of events occurs leading to the separation of Taiwan from China in any name, or if Taiwan is invaded and occupied by foreign countries, or if the Taiwan authorities refuse, *sine die* [which is Latin for "wu xianqi" or, in English, "without a date certain"], the peaceful settlement

[39] *Ibid.*

[40] "The One-China Principle and the Taiwan Issue," issued by the Taiwan Affairs Office and the Information Office of the State Council of the People's Republic of China, February 21, 2000.

[41] *Ibid.*

> of cross-Straits reunification through negotiations, then the Chinese government will only be forced to adopt all drastic measures possible, including the use of force, to safeguard China's sovereignty and territorial integrity and fulfill the great cause of reunification.[42]

The operative word, of course, was "drastic." Four days before the Taiwan election in March 2000, Chinese Premier Zhu Rongji heatedly advised Taiwan voters to cast their ballots in the presidential election with a "cool head" or risk "not getting a second chance." The normally staid, sober-minded Chinese premier said that "Taiwan Independence Forces" were gaining strength daily as the election neared and was "unusually direct" in serving notice that "we cannot accept Taiwan independence, that's our bottom line, and it's the heartfelt demand of China's 1.2 billion people." Working himself into near hysterics in a briefing for foreign reporters on March 14, the Chinese premier warned that those who argued that China did not have the missiles, ships, or aircraft to invade the island had misread history, and the Chinese were ready to "shed blood" to prevent Taiwan from breaking away.[43] In all likelihood, Premier Zhu was under severe pressure from elements within the Chinese leadership that were willing to sacrifice China's trade relations with the West—especially the United States—on the Taiwan issue, and Zhu's emotions were more likely a reflection of his alarm at the economic costs of rash behavior of the Chinese Politburo than they were a manifestation of any concern over the political costs of rash decisions by the Taiwanese electorate.

In the end, Chen Shui-bian was elected, and China had to put up with it. There ensued four more years of Chinese histrionics, and in March 2004, Chen was re-elected. Three days before Chen's second inauguration, on May 17, 2004, China's Foreign Ministry proclaimed that China would "crush" Taiwanese independence moves "at any cost"[44] in comments that the White House spokesman declared "have no place in civilized international discourse."[45]

---

[42]*Ibid.*

[43]Paul Eckert, "China PM Warns Taiwan Voters on Chen," Reuters, March 15, 2000.

[44]"Putting a Check on 'Taiwan Independence' a Pressing Task," *China Daily*, Beijing, May 17, 2004, p. 1, at *www.chinadaily.com.cn/english/doc/2004-05/17/content_331143.htm.*

[45]White House Daily Briefing, May 19, 2004, Press Secretary Scott McClellan, at *www.whitehouse.gov/news/releases/2004/05/200405 19-8.html.*

A year later, on July 14, 2005, Chinese Major General Zhu Chenghu, dean of foreign students at the People's Liberation Army (PLA) National Defense University, at the request of China's Foreign Ministry, briefed a group of foreign journalists, all of whom had their voice recorders humming on the table before them, saying that "if the Americans are determined to interfere [then] we will be determined to respond" and adding that "we Chinese will prepare ourselves for the destruction of all of the cities east of Xi'an. Of course the Americans will have to be prepared that hundreds…of cities will be destroyed by the Chinese."[46]

General Zhu's comments were the culmination of Chinese threats that had built up over the previous several months. The 2006 Pentagon report on China's military power points out that General Zhu's views are widely shared in the PLA and, at the very least, emblematic of an ongoing debate on nuclear strategy within the military.[47] One of my colleagues at The Heritage Foundation (and now chairman of the U.S.–China Economic and Security Review Commission) who has known Gen. Zhu for more than a decade, Dr. Larry Wortzel, observed that one objective of the Chinese leadership "is to put enough doubt in the minds of the American public that they will think it's not worth going to war over Taiwan."[48]

---

[46]This was described to me first-hand by a correspondent that was in the meeting. For other reporting, see Danny Gittings, "General Zhu Goes Ballistic," *The Wall Street Journal*, July 18, 2005, p. A13, at *http://online.wsj.com/article/0,,SB112165176626988025,00.html*, and Jason Dean, "Chinese General Lays Nuclear Card on U.S.'s Table," *The Wall Street Journal*, July 15, 2005, at *http://online.wsj.com/article/0,,SB112135825292585833,00.html*. See also Alexandra Harney, "China 'Ready to Use N-Weapons Against US," *Financial Times*, July 14, 2005, at *http://news.ft.com/cms/s/28cfe55a-f4a7-11d9-9dd1-00000e2511c8,ft_acl=,s01=1.html*; Joe McDonald, "Chinese General Threatens U.S. over Taiwan; Response Might Be with Nuclear Weapons, Reporters Told," Associated Press, July 15, 2005; and Joseph Kahn, "Chinese General Threatens Use of A-Bombs If U.S. Intrudes," *The New York Times*, July 15, 2005, at *www.nytimes.com/2005/07/15/international/asia/15china.html*.

[47]See *Annual Report to Congress: Military Power of the People's Republic of China, 2006*, p. 20.

[48]Supposedly, General Zhu was "punished" for his indiscretion before a gaggle of foreign reporters with tape recorders humming, but as one unidentified Chinese source put it, "the punishment could not be too harsh or we would be seen as too weak toward the United States." See "China Punished General for Talk of Strike at U.S.," Reuters, December 22, 2005.

A few months before General Zhu's threats, in March 2005, China's National People's Congress had passed "The Statute Against Splitting the Nation," Article 8 of which declares:

> In the event that the "Taiwan independence" secessionist forces should act under any name or by any means to cause the fact of Taiwan's secession from China, or that major incidents entailing Taiwan's secession from China should occur, or that possibilities for a peaceful reunification should be completely exhausted, the state *shall* [*dei*] employ non-peaceful means and other necessary measures to protect China's sovereignty and territorial integrity.[49]

The use of the word "shall" (*dei*) in the last sentence is a mandate to act. Article 8 also directs that "the State Council and the Central Military Commission shall decide on and execute the non-peaceful means and other necessary measures" without the need for further reference to the National People's Congress. Nowhere in the legislative history of the statute, however, is there any clue as to the meaning of "splitting the nation" or "incidents entailing Taiwan's secession," or just what might be an example of "incidents entailing Taiwan's secession," or how anyone would know when the "possibilities for a peaceful reunification" were "exhausted." This is a problem because Taiwan has already functioned for over half a century as a political entity independent from China and already considers itself *de jure* separate from the People's Republic of China.

It is difficult to imagine a situation in which Taiwan could engage in any more substantive "incidents entailing secession" than it already has. Therefore, the "statute" in effect proclaims that a *casus belli* already exists without requiring further action by Taiwan. In short, this "statute" is not any kind of law that is recognizable in the Western democracies.

"War Avoidance": A Sensible Strategic Objective for Washington?

Although the United States has never had a reputation for cringing in the face of war threats from strategic adversaries who seek to dominate America's friends and allies—or anyone else, for that matter—there has arisen over the past decade a "China exception" in American doctrine about

---

[49]Emphasis added. This is the literal translation "*Fan Fenlie Guojia Fa*," more commonly known in English as the "Anti-Secession Law." For a full text, see *http://news.xinhuanet.com/english/2005-03/14/content_2694180.htm*.

nuclear war. Apparently, American policymakers who understood during the Cold War that "mutual assured destruction" was the price to pay should the Soviet Union attempt similar adventurism now believe that China's military leadership, as personified by General Zhu Chenghu, is completely psychotic. Under General Zhu's scenarios, the very rapid and drastic escalation of a war with China over Taiwan would be very difficult to control, yet many in the Washington foreign policy bureaucracy are persuaded that China will, in fact, risk nuclear war. If it were otherwise, such threats from China would have no more effect on them than Soviet threats had on America's Cold Warriors.

Many thoughtful (but perhaps naïve) commentators point out that the Taiwan issue could become a *casus belli* in a Chinese war against the United States.[50] They argue that nothing is worth the risk of getting into a war with China and that, consequently, the United States should abandon any security commitments to Taiwan save to provide Taiwan arms should the Taiwanese feel like fighting China all by themselves. What would they have said to Stalin in 1948 during the Berlin blockade if Stalin had threatened war unless Berlin was surrendered? Or to Khrushchev in 1961 as the Berlin Wall was erected and West Berlin was further isolated from the West? How would that have been different from Beijing's current demands about Taiwan? China's claims to sovereignty over Taiwan are virtually identical to the German Democratic Republic's claims to Berlin or to National Socialist Germany's claims to the Rhineland in 1936 and to Austria and the Sudetenland in 1938. "Taiwan independence means war" is not a threat that should matter if America's leaders truly consider the "global expansion of democracy" a national strategic objective.

I am often told that America's paramount national interest in the Taiwan Strait area is to "avoid a war." Taiwanese strategists have a similar view. A former Taiwan vice minister of national defense used to begin his PowerPoint briefings with the statement that "Taiwan's overarching defense policy is the prevention of war." To which I would point out, to both my American and my Taiwan colleagues, that if that's your "overarching defense policy," then the cheapest way to implement that policy is to surrender.

International relations scholars and bureaucrats alike tend to forget their academic training. Modern "war avoidance" theory centers on the proposition that democracies do not make war on each other, but rather are themselves the targets of aggression.[51] Henry Kissinger pointed out in his first published book, *A World Restored*, that in an international system where "peace" is made the highest priority, the system is at the mercy of its most

---

[50]See, for example, Ted Galen Carpenter, *America's Coming War with China: A Collision Course over Taiwan* (New York: Palgrave Macmillan, 2005).

ruthless member, and there is an overwhelming incentive to appease the demands of the most ruthless member regardless of how unreasonable they are.[52] Kissinger's model predicts that China will use its constant threats of war over Taiwan as a means to an end because it recognizes that there are influential forces in the U.S. and other nations that value "peace" more than they value democracy in Taiwan.

When one considers how much China has enmeshed itself in the international manufacturing supply chain, however, it is clear that war is no more in the interests of the Chinese Communist Party's leadership than it is in America's interests. It is inconceivable that the Beijing regime would ever challenge the United States in Taiwan unless, of course, it was absolutely convinced that the United States would back down. Consequently, its strategy in the Taiwan Strait is a multi-dimensional one—military, political, economic, and psychological—that is designed to induce America to back down.

China is financing a very rapid expansion of its military, particularly its navy, in order to give the appearance that it will soon be in a position to inflict heavy pain on the U.S. Navy in the Pacific. With a certain amount of huffing and puffing, Beijing believes that it can present Washington with a calculus that says, "The pain I could suffer from a Chinese naval strike is greater than the pain I would suffer from the loss of Taiwan; hence, I will cut my losses and quit ahead of time." Presented in this way, "Taiwan Independence = War" is an unpalatable policy equation.

One logical U.S. counter-response would be to present China with a similar calculus with an added disincentive: something that says, "The pain that China will suffer from increasing threats or even military action against Taiwan will be far greater than leaving Taiwan alone, independent or not independent." Simply put, the U.S. should posit a new strategic equation on the Taiwan issue: "(War = Economic Devastation) + (War = Taiwan Independence)."

For this response to be effective, of course, Beijing must believe that Washington is prepared to sanction China severely for military action. In addition, if Washington were also to proffer the likelihood that the United

---

[51]For a short review of "war avoidance" theory, see Steven Geoffrey Gieseler, "Debate on the 'Democratic Peace': A Review," in *American Diplomacy*, University of North Carolina at Chapel Hill, January 3, 2004, at *www.unc.edu/depts/diplomat/archives_roll/2004_01-03/gieseler_debate/gieseler_debate.html.*

[52]Stephen Richards Graubard makes this point in *Kissinger: Portrait of a Mind* (New York: W. W. Norton & Company, 1973), p. 17. Kissinger's book, *A World Restored: Metternich, Castlereagh and the Problems of Peace 1812–1822*, was republished in paperback by Weidenfeld & Nicholson, London, on October 19, 2000.

States would actually, in the end, recognize the *de jure* independence of an invaded Taiwan, Beijing would be faced with an even more unpalatable conundrum: How could it be sure that threatening military action against Taiwan would not itself ultimately result in an internationally recognized independent Taiwan?

Private conversations I had between March and May 2004 with Administration officials and Foreign Service officers around the time of Vice President Richard Cheney's April 15 visit to Beijing indicated that some thought was actually being given to this scenario. "We have told the Chinese that a Taiwan declaration of independence would be meaningless. It would just be words on paper. It wouldn't change anything, and no country on earth would change its diplomatic recognition of Taiwan one way or the other because of it," said one U.S. diplomat. When I pressed him about the message that statement was supposed to send, he replied, "We do not consider a Taiwan declaration of independence to be a legitimate cause for war."

It is possible that this is indeed the internal, confidential view of the Bush Administration. Assistant Secretary Kelly told the House International Relations Committee in 2004 that:

> A unilateral move toward independence will avail Taiwan of nothing it does not already enjoy in terms of democratic freedom, autonomy, prosperity and security. Realistically, such moves carry the potential for a response from the PRC—a dangerous, objectionable, and foolish response—that could destroy much of what Taiwan has built and crush its hopes for the future. It would damage China, too.[53]

Kelly's statement stopped short of declaring for the record that the United States considered a Chinese attack on Taiwan to be an illegitimate response under international law to a Taiwan declaration of independence, and Beijing continued its "war" threats. Beijing quickly followed the re-election of Taiwan President Chen Shui-bian on May 17, 2004, with a threat that the Taiwanese would "in the end, meet their own destruction by playing with fire."[54] One could read the rather intemperate Chinese statement as a reflection of Beijing's belief that Washington was indeed pushing Taiwan to

---

[53]"Statement of Assistant Secretary of State James Kelly," April 21, 2004.

[54]"China Denounces Taiwan's Chen, Warns Against Independence Moves," Associated Press, May 17, 2004, at *http://online.wsj.com/article/0,,SB108478661502913242,00.html.*

the bargaining table and that Beijing wanted to help move things along. It was a warning meant for the State Department, not the Pentagon.

Moreover, the Chinese statement pointed out the lack of coherence and consistency among the various U.S. policy statements about the specific reasons why the United States has taken on a security responsibility for Taiwan. This lack of consistency is especially evident in policy statements from the U.S. Department of State as contrasted with those from the Department of Defense.

Assistant Secretary of State Kelly's April 21, 2004, statement to the congressional hearing was quite different in tone from that of Assistant Secretary of Defense Peter Rodman, who testified immediately after Kelly. Kelly offered faint praise for Taiwan's democracy ("Taiwan is a most complex and, in some ways, inconsistent polity") and placed it as an interest secondary to the more important "sparing the region the dangers of war." And Kelly darkly warned Taiwan's leaders (not China's) that, "as Taiwan proceeds with efforts to deepen democracy, we will speak clearly and bluntly if we feel as though those efforts carry the potential to adversely impact U.S. security interests."[55]

The Pentagon's Rodman, pointedly, was more sympathetic to Taiwan's democratic achievements:

> The United States takes these obligations [under the Taiwan Relations Act] very seriously. The President's National Security Strategy, published in September 2002, calls for "building a balance of power that favors freedom." Taiwan's evolution into a true multi-party democracy over the past decade is proof of the importance of America's commitment to Taiwan's defense. It strengthens American resolve to see Taiwan's democracy grow and prosper.[56]

The Kelly and Rodman statements would have been more effective in moderating Chinese assertiveness on the Taiwan issue if Kelly had been a bit more supportive of Taiwan's democracy and explicated—as Rodman did—the reasons why America "takes these obligations very seriously." Unfortunately, the State Department's habit has been to insist that America's commitment to Taiwan is no more than a "responsibility under the Taiwan

---

[55]"Statement of Assistant Secretary of State James Kelly," April 21, 2004.

[56]"The Taiwan Relations Act: The Next 25 Years," Prepared Statement of Peter W. Rodman, Assistant Secretary of Defense for International Security Affairs, before the House International Relations Committee, April 21, 2004, at *http://wwwa.house.gov/international_relations/108/Rod042104.htm*.

Relations Act."[57] As a result, two years of careless statements by various senior U.S. officials have given Taiwan's people the impression that Washington foresees Taiwan as eventually shoved into the suffocating embrace of the Chinese motherland, to suffer the same fate as Hong Kong.[58]

Taiwan in America's Asia Strategy

Then there is General Douglas MacArthur's dictum to keep "island Asia" out of the hands of "mainland Asia."[59] The United States is the globe's preeminent naval power, and security of the sea-lanes is essential to its national security. Taiwan sits astride major sea-lanes between the West Coast of the United States and East Asia and Japan's sea-lanes to the Middle East. America's alliances with nations in the island chain along the Asian mainland provide the surveillance capabilities essential to protecting U.S. naval forces in the Pacific. Taiwan is a link in that "island-Asia" chain. American naval planners closely monitor Chinese ship movements through Japanese and Taiwan waters reportedly because they "consider Taiwan as part of the 'First Island Chain' of defense."[60] New phased-array radar stations on Taiwan will also be integrated into the U.S. missile defense network in the Western Pacific.

In addition, as will be discussed in subsequent chapters, the United States has a robust intelligence-sharing relationship with Taiwan. Clearly, a future Taiwan regime forced into Beijing's suzerainty would break that relationship.

While times have changed since MacArthur's era, the geography of the Pacific has not. It now seems that history has replaced one set of mainland

---

[57]State and NSC policy-level spokespersons rarely, if ever, describe America's interest in the survival of a democratic Taiwan. Instead, they couch U.S. support in terms of "obligations under the TRA." For example, when asked by the Chinese-language press about U.S. arms sales to Taiwan, Secretary of State Colin Powell said only that the U.S. "completely understands Chinese concern about the arms-sales issue" but that the U.S. "also has responsibilities under the Taiwan Relations Act. When selling arms to Taiwan, the US considers all factors." See Secretary Colin L. Powell, "Interview With Phoenix TV," Washington, D.C., February 19, 2003 at *www.state.gov/secretary/former/powell/remarks/2003/17806.htm*. Dr. Condoleezza Rice told reporters that "the U.S. is very clear on our policies about Taiwan, one China policy. We are basing our policy on the three communiqués. And we, of course, always remind people that we also have obligations under the Taiwan Relations Act to help China—to help Taiwan defend itself." See "Dr. Rice Previews President's Trip to Asia and Australia," Press Briefing by National Security Adviser Dr. Condoleezza Rice, October 14, 2003, at *www.whitehouse.gov/news/releases/2003/10/20031014-4.html*.

Eurasian non–*status quo* powers with—perhaps to no one's surprise—the same set; only this time, instead of Moscow, Beijing is the leader. Thus, keeping "island Asia" out of the hands of "mainland Asia" continues to be a compelling strategic objective even today, and within that construct we can start addressing the increasing complexities of Taiwan's domestic politics.

Taiwan's Definition of Itself

A crucial element in keeping "island" Taiwan out of Beijing's hands is understanding how Taiwan's people view themselves and supporting them in that view. For the years between 1988, when Taiwan President Lee Teng-hui came to power, and 2000, when he retired (and his presumed successor was defeated in that year's presidential elections), Taiwan's people had formed a substantial consensus on their future as a country separate from China. Since then, that consensus has been strained by external pressures from China, as well as from the United States and other fellow democracies, that have been exacerbated by internal pressures against resisting the pressure brought to bear externally by China.

One thing that the vast majority of Taiwanese believe is that Taiwan is independent from the People's Republic China and has been since 1949. This infelicitous fact has been a burr under the saddle of America's China policy for 30 years, and no doubt will continue to be for years to come, precisely because few American officials in authority have devoted any thought to a desirable end-state of the Taiwan–China calculus—or, if they have done so, have kept it to themselves.

---

[58]For example, Secretary Powell opined *ex tempore* that Taiwan "does not enjoy sovereignty as a nation" and suggested that Taiwan and China "look for ways of improving dialogue across the Straits and move forward toward that day when we will see a peaceful unification." See Secretary Colin L. Powell, "Interview With Anthony Yuen of Phoenix TV," China World Hotel, Beijing, October 25, 2004, at *www.state.gov/secretary/former/powell/remarks/37361.htm*. Both these remarks were later recanted by the State Department spokesman, who explained that "I don't think you should read that any prejudging or hinting or departure from our long-standing position" and added that "I think the Secretary is very outspoken and very emphatic about encouraging an intensification of that dialogue. And that's where we think the focus ought to be." See Adam Ereli, Deputy Spokesman, U.S. Department of State, "Daily Press Briefing," October 25, 2004, at *www.state.gov/r/pa/prs/dpb/2004/37401.htm*.

[59]This paraphrases MacArthur's strategy. See General Douglas MacArthur's "Farewell Address to Congress," delivered April 19, 1951, in the *Congressional Record* for that date, a version of which is available at *www.americanrhetoric.com/speeches/douglasmacarthurfarewelladdress.htm*.

China considers Taiwan to have been deeded over to Chiang Kai-shek's regime in 1945, and that, since the People's Republic succeeded Chiang's regime in 1949 (and in the United Nations in 1971), Taiwan's real estate is therefore Communist property. Taiwan's "Republic of China," on the other hand, has always considered itself to be, both *de facto* and *de jure*, separate from the "People's Republic of China" and since 1992 has constitutionally cut itself off from the People's Republic by statutorily disenfranchising all residents of the mainland who otherwise would have "Republic of China" citizenship.

In 2000, a pro-independence candidate was elected Taiwan's president by nearly 40 percent of the popular vote (in a three-way race), and the same candidate was re-elected with a shade more than 50 percent of the popular vote in 2004. Taiwan's long-standing official description of its own status is that it and the People's Republic are "two sovereign, independent and mutually non-subordinate nations."[61] In 1999, Taiwan's previous president described his country's relations with China as "special state-to-state

---

[60]The Chinese navy's maritime strategy envisions an American containment of China with the domination of the "first island chain" in the Western Pacific. See Bernard D. Cole, "The PLA Navy and 'Active Defense'" in Stephen J. Flanagan and Michael E. Marti, eds., *The People's Liberation Army and China in Transition* (Washington, D.C.: National Defense University Press, 2003), pp. 129–138, at *www.ndu.edu/inss/books/Books_2003/China/PLA_and_China_Transition.pdf*. The Defense Department asserts that "China also has an expressed interest in developing capabilities that could hold at risk maritime targets out to the 'second island chain' some 1,000 miles from the Chinese coast." See U.S. Department of Defense, *Annual Report to Congress: Military Power of the People's Republic of China, 2006*, pp. 11, 15, 16, and 25. The term "island chain" was coined by then Special Adviser to the Secretary of State Dean Rusk during the first year of the Korean War, apparently to describe a system of security alliances in the Western Pacific stretching from Japan through New Zealand. Rusk said "There was perhaps a need for a chain of regional pacts based on global plan. He stressed that the United States would not take the initiative with regard to the pact, that they would not wish an exclusively 'white' association and regarded participation of Asiatics as essential." See Australian diplomatic dispatches and "Cablegram from Embassy in Washington to Spender," Cablegram 622, Washington, August 3, 1950, at *www.info.dfat.gov.au/info/historical/HistDocs.nsf/vVolume/57F02E3B63827320CA256CD90074E9A2*, and "Cablegram from External Affairs Office, London to Department of External Affairs," Cablegram 1448, London, March 13, 1951, at *www.info.dfat.gov.au/info/historical/HistDocs.nsf/(LookupVolNoNumber)/17~60)*. "Island chain" as a strategic concept was first articulated by General Douglas MacArthur, who explained: "From this island chain we can dominate with sea and air power every Asiatic port from Vladivostok to Singapore…and prevent any hostile movement into the Pacific." See MacArthur, "Farewell Address to Congress."

relations,"[62] and the current president said in August 2002 that "there is one nation on each side of the Taiwan Strait."[63]

As of August 2005, Taiwan's official description of itself was "The Republic of China *is* Taiwan."[64] On May 18, 2006, Taiwan's President Chen told visiting European legislators that:

> Over the past 50 years, the "status quo" across the Taiwan Strait has been that on one side, there is a democratic Taiwan, and on the other, there is an authoritarian China. Neither of the two countries are subordinate to each other, because they are two independent sovereignties. Both sides have their own national title, national flag, national anthem, legislature, judicial system and military.[65]

Unlike the leadership of Communist China, Taiwan's political leadership is not monolithic. Democratic Taiwan's political leaders on both sides of the "Green–Blue" divide[66] are getting progressively anxious as China's military expansion builds steam, as China begins to use its economic clout to deepen Taiwan's economic dependence on China, and as China's Communist Party ratchets up pressure on Taiwanese businessmen with investments in China.

---

[61]Chen Fengxing, "Jiang Bingkun: Liangan shi liangge zhuquan guojia; Qiangdiao woguo zhengce wei 'yi yige zhongguo wei zhixiangde jieduanxingde liangge Zhongguo zhengce'" [PK Chiang: There are two sovereign nations on either side of the Strait; stresses that Taiwan's policy is 'an interim two China's policy with One China as its conceptual guide'], *United Daily News*, Taipei, November 22, 1993, p. 1.

[62]Meng Ronghua, "Li Zongtong: Liangan dingwei teshu guo yu guo guanxi" [President Lee: The two sides of the Strait are defined as special state-to-state relations], *Central Daily News*, Taipei, July 10, 1999, p. 1, at *www.cdn.com.tw/daily/1999/07/10/text/880710a1.htm.*

[63]Zongtong yi shixun zhibo fangshi yu Shijie Taiwan Tongxiang Lianhe Hui du ershijiu jie nian hui shang zhici" [President delivers remarks by live television feed to the twenty-ninth annual meeting of the Joint World Congress of Taiwanese Associations], Press Release, Office of the President, August 3, 2002.

[64]See "President Chen Receives the Youth Friendship Ambassadors of the Formosa Foundation in the United States," Press Release, Office of the President, August 2, 2005. See also "Taiwan People Want to Be Their Own Masters: President," Central News Agency, Taipei, August 13, 2005.

[65]Ko Shu-ling, "'Status Quo' Is Two Independent Countries: Chen," *Taipei Times*, May 18, 2006, p. 3, at *www.taipeitimes.com/News/taiwan/archives/2006/05/18/2003308785.*

Taiwan's pro-independence "Greens," led by President Chen Shui-bian, are nervous that China's military power will further weaken support in Washington for Taiwan. In their agitation, they believe they must trumpet ever more loudly Taiwan's democratic identity separate from China. That identity, for them, has become a fundamental element of state legitimacy. Hence, their sense of urgency in abolishing governmental institutions, like the National Unification Council and the National Unification Guidelines, that imply that unification with China is Taiwan's state doctrine.

For the moderates in the "Blue" camp, however, their "state legitimacy" rests on a claim that Taiwan's "Republic of China," not the Communists' "People's Republic," has sovereignty over all of China from the Pacific coast to the western deserts of Xinjiang. Their vision of a future China is one where the democratic "ROC" eventually supplants the totalitarian "PRC"—or that the PRC regime democratizes and the ROC can then unify with it. In the decades or centuries until China's democratic millennium, however, they are content to acquiesce to Beijing's claim that the PRC (as "China") is sovereign over Taiwan.[67] Moreover, because they have no intention of challenging Beijing's assertion that Taiwan cannot be "independent," some "Deep-Blue" politicians question the need for a robust defense and seem willing to entrust Taiwan's security to Beijing's goodwill.

---

[66]Taiwan's "Green" camp comprises President Chen Shui-bian's left-of-center, labor/environment-oriented Democratic Progressive Party (DPP) and the solidly pro-independence Taiwan Solidarity Union (TSU). The "Blue" camp is dominated by the right-of-center, pro-business Kuomintang (Nationalist) party (KMT) and includes the smaller pro-China People First Party (PFP).

[67]For an authoritative statement of the KMT's position on Taiwan, see KMT Chairman Ma Ying-jeou, "Bridging the Divide: A Vision for Peace in Asia," speech delivered at the London School of Economics, February 13, 2006. Mr. Ma noted that "insofar as the political question is concerned, should the Kuomintang regain power in 2008, we will try to resume the disrupted cross-Strait talks under the so-called 'Consensus of 1992.' This is a tacit consensus reached by the two sides in 1992 in Hong Kong accepting the 'one-China principle' but allowing different interpretations by each side, in order to find the common ground and cement mutual trust in the first place. For us, the 'China' is Republic of China; for them, it is the People's Republic of China." He added: "But as the ROC Constitution is a one-China constitution, it does not rule out the option of eventual reunification between Taiwan and Mainland China if the overall conditions across the Taiwan Strait are ripe, that is to say, when the developments in Mainland China reach a stage when its political democracy, economic prosperity and social well-being become congruent with those of Taiwan."

Taiwan and Asia in the 21st Century

At the beginning of 2006, new worries began to arise about the direction of Taiwan and the corrosive effect that incoherent U.S. policies are having on the resolve of Taiwan's people.

On January 29, Taiwan's President Chen Shui-bian made some unscripted comments about the continued utility of the National Unification Council (a public council designed to consider possible modes of future unification of democratic Taiwan with Communist China). President Chen told a Lunar New Year's gathering that "everyone now calls for, encourages, demands to know whether the national unification council and the guidelines should or should not be dismantled (*feichu*)" and opined that the "principle of 'one China'...is profoundly problematic (*feichang you wentide*)."[68] Specifically:

> [E]veryone knows the National Unification Council has become just a name on a sign, and if a store not only has a sign that no one can see, and moreover has nothing to sell, then what kind of "common unification" shall such an establishment, such a National Unification Council, such a set of National Unification Guidelines, be able to achieve?[69]

Since mid-2002, the Bush Administration had tried to gain Chinese acquiescence for U.S. moves on North Korea, Iraq, Afghanistan, and the war on terrorism by trying to keep the Taiwan issue out of sight. For Bush National Security Council aides and the State Department, this meant leaning on Taiwan's president to keep silent when China touted claims of sovereignty over the island.

In his first inaugural address on May 20, 2000, at the suggestion (if not the insistence) of the United States, President Chen made five pledges, one of them being that "abolition of the National Reunification Council or the National Reunification Guidelines will not be an issue."[70] The first blowup over these pledges came when President Chen outlined a new "One Country on Either Side of the Strait" (*yibian yiguo*) formulation on August 3, 2002, just as the United States was courting Chinese support (or at least non-opposition) in the United Nations Security Council.[71]

---

[68]"Zongtong yu Tainan Xiangqin Huanzhong Xinnian Tuanyuan Canxu" [President's Dinner Remarks to Tainan Kinsmen New Year Gathering], Central News Agency, Taipei, January 29, 2006. President Chen announced the "cessation" (*zhongzhi*) of the council on February 27, 2006.

[69]*Ibid.*

From that point on, the White House and State Department viewed the Taiwanese leader's penchant for publicizing the objective fact that Taiwan was indeed independent as a nuisance. Whenever top Beijing leaders were thrust into near proximity to an American leader, it was regularly hinted that "Taiwan" was the reason why China found it inconvenient to cooperate with the United States.[72] So American bureaucrats got into the habit of calling on the Taiwan president to refrain from publicly questioning the "one China" principle because his pronouncements had roiled the waters of the Taiwan Strait, thereby causing *mal-de-mer* in Washington.[73] Washington, of course, gets anxious any time President Chen opens his mouth: His words, they believe, could be seen in Beijing as a *casus belli* against Taiwan and precipitate an American military confrontation with China.

These concerns, however, are misplaced. Beijing, after all, is the *real* problem. Beijing's so-called Anti-Secession Law was itself an open-ended declaration of a *casus belli* against Taiwan. Unfortunately, the official U.S.

---

[70]Chen was clear that his speech would "satisfy" the Americans. See Zheng Renwen and Huang Qianyu, "Bian ti Jiuzhi Yanshuo San Yuanze" [Chen Shui-bian raises three principles for inauguration speech], *Central Daily News*, Taipei, May 4, 2000, p. 1. Those three principles were: (1) The U.S. will be satisfied (*zuo dao rang Meiguo manyi*); (2) it will be accepted by the international community (*rang guoji shehui kending*); and (3) the Chinese communists will find no excuse to say Taiwan is provocative (*Zhonggong zhaobudao jiekou lai shuo Taiwan tiaochi*). At his regular press briefing on May 15, 2000, State Department spokesman Richard Boucher was asked, "Q: Let me come back to Taiwan. The same Post article indicated that Raymond Burghardt, the AIT director in Taiwan, has tried to exert influence in the writing of President-elect Chen's inaugural speech. Would you confirm or deny that, or..." Boucher replied, "No, I'm not going to talk about—I'm not going to talk about that. We have meetings with a lot of people a lot of times and we don't get into every single one and try to talk about it." When pressed on whether the U.S. representative in Taipei had "been given any talking points on his speech," Boucher demurred: "I am not going to try to characterize it one way or the other." See Richard Boucher, Spokesman, U.S. Department of State, "Daily Press briefing," May 25, 2000, at *www.usembassy-israel.org.il/publish/peace/archives/2000/may/me0515a.html*. The so-called Five Noes were in a part of the speech that read: "Therefore, as long as the CCP regime has no intention to use military force against Taiwan, I pledge that during my term in office, I will not declare independence, I will not change the national title, I will not push forth the inclusion of the so-called 'state-to-state' description in the Constitution, and I will not promote a referendum to change the status quo in regards to the question of independence or unification. Furthermore, the abolition of the National Reunification Council or the National Reunification Guidelines will not be an issue." See President Chen Shui-bian's inauguration speech, "Taiwan Stands Up," Office of the President, Republic of China, May 20, 2000.

reaction, at least in public, was muted. The most the State Department spokesman could say was that "we believe it to be unhelpful."[74] "Unhelpful," indeed. Yet Washington's reaction to Beijing's "law" was far milder than its abuse of Taiwan's leader for far less serious transgressions.

When it comes to sincere attempts to ease strains across the Taiwan Strait, President Chen Shui-bian is the champion. Starting on New Year's Day 2001, he has proffered an unending string of compromises, outreach, and unilateral openings to China. Taiwan has opened direct links between China and the offshore islands of Kinmen (known more familiarly to Americans as "Quemoy") and Matsu, licensed direct charter flights to China, relaxed investment rules, and begged for military-to-military "confidence-building measures."

China has rebuffed every call from Taiwan for cross-Strait dialogue. Instead, it has deployed over 800 ballistic missiles targeted on Taiwan and is increasing that number at a rate of 75–100 a year. Beijing threatens both Taiwanese who support President Chen and U.S. businessmen who support Taiwan's government—behavior that is in direct contravention of U.S. anti-boycott legislation.[75] Rebuffing pleas from the U.S. government to open a dialogue with "Taiwan's elected leaders,"[76] Beijing deals only with opposition parties in Taiwan that "adhere" to the "one China principle" and oppose Taiwan's defense spending. Beijing even refused to allow a Taiwan

---

[71]For a discussion of the "yibian yiguo" controversy, see John J. Tkacik, Jr., "Taiwan Hornets Nest," *The Asian Wall Street Journal*, August 5, 2005, p. A12, at *http://online.wsj.com/article/SB102849972251391704 0.html.*

[72]This was especially true at the time of the September 11, 2001, terrorist attacks on the United States. Foreign Ministry spokesman Zhu Bangzao made clear that China would expect U.S. cooperation in return for its support. "The United States has asked China to provide assistance in the fight against terrorism," Zhu told a news conference. "China, by the same token, has reasons to ask the United States to give its support and understanding in the fight against terrorism and separatists," he said. "We should not have double standards." See John Pomfret, "China Also Wants U.S. Help Against 'Separatists;' Seeks U.S. Support on Taiwan, Tibet, Missile Defense," *The Washington Post*, September 19, 2001, p. A11.

[73]The Bush Administration believes it has an understanding with Taipei that there should be close communication on any Taiwan initiative that might upset the political "status quo as we define it" in the Taiwan Strait. Historically, however, any comments by Taiwanese leaders even hinting that Taiwan has lost interest in some future unification with Communist China have caused successive U.S. Administrations considerable jumpiness. Caught off-guard by the Taiwanese leader's comments, a State Department spokesman said on January 30, 2006, that "we certainly weren't expecting [President Chen's statement] and we weren't consulted about it. So I'd say it was a surprise."

representative to attend the December 30, 2005, funeral of Wang Daohan, Beijing's eminent Taiwan negotiator.

It is vital that the U.S. Administration, and particularly President Bush himself and his successors, sympathize with the existential challenge facing Taiwan when it harangues Taiwan's leaders about their precious, yet undefined, "*status quo*." The one thing that Taiwan's democratically elected leaders at either end of the political spectrum simply cannot, and will not, do is to compromise the legitimacy of their own governance. Sovereignty over Taiwan, they insist, belongs solely to the people of Taiwan—not to the "sole legal government of China" in Beijing. The United States government must also understand that so long as Taiwan refuses to acknowledge Beijing's sovereignty, Beijing's long-term strategy is to isolate Taiwan in the international community to the most extreme extent possible.

In short, China has done nothing—and intends to do nothing—to requite Taiwan's outreach. By the time of his November 2005 visits to Japan and China, President Bush is said to have become so dismayed by Beijing's sustained hostility toward Taiwan's leaders that he inserted a paragraph praising Taiwan's democracy into his Asia policy speech in Kyoto[77]—a paragraph that surprised every China watcher in Washington, including those in the White House.[78]

The receptivity of Taipei's "elected leaders" to a dialogue with Beijing's unelected ones is unquestioned. Beijing, however, simply refuses to engage in any meaningful dialogue.

Crucial Questions

Before moving on to specific questions about the direction of Taiwan policy, the U.S. Administration must reach a consensus on whether "war

---

[74]See Richard Boucher, Spokesman, U.S. Department of State, "Daily Press Briefing," March 14, 2005, at *www.state.gov/r/pa/prs/dpb/2005/43404.htm*: "Mr. Boucher: The decision by the Chinese leaders to have the National People's Congress adopt an anti-secession law today is—it's unfortunate. It really does not serve the cause of peace and stability on the Taiwan Strait and for that reason we believe it to be unhelpful." Assistant Secretary of State-designate for East Asian and Pacific Affairs Christopher Hill told Senators during his confirmation hearings that "We don't believe there is any justification for making these unhelpful statements that suggest that there are other options out there that the Chinese can use beside peaceful dialogue" and added: "It is unthinkable to resort to military means to solve [cross-Strait issues]. So clearly any Anti-Secession Law that alludes to the legality of military means is simply not helpful." See Charles Snyder, "Rice to Tell Beijing US Upset over Law," *Taipei Times*, March 17, 2005, p. 1, at *www.taipeitimes.com/News/front/archives/2005/03/17/2003246563*.

avoidance" by itself makes sense as a strategic objective of the United States: on whether China or any other totalitarian regime can ever be deterred from ultimately using military force except through unified and firm push-back from the democracies of the world, presumably bolstered by coherent American leadership. If firmness and unity among the nations of the international community of democracies are needed, do American policies regarding the Taiwan Strait have the perverse effect of encouraging China's bellicosity rather than assuaging it?

If Washington hopes even to begin addressing these issues, it should undertake a bottom-up reassessment of America's stake in Taiwan within the broad strategic context of the emergence of China as a "military superpower" and likely "peer competitor" in Asia.[79] By some measures, China is already the world's second largest economy and is now rising as a new "military superpower" and "peer competitor" to the United States in the Asia–Pacific.

In counterpoint, the United States and Taiwan have had a remarkable security partnership in the Western Pacific for over a half-century, but it is a partnership in peril. The Bush Administration must reexamine its strategic position in Asia and what it would look like without a robust U.S.–Taiwan relationship—or, worse still, with Taiwan under the military sway of the People's Republic of China. If U.S. policymakers do not like what they see, they must craft a strategy to prevent it and implement policies consistent with that strategy.

At the very least, the U.S. must counter Beijing's relentless campaign to isolate Taiwan economically and politically by strengthening U.S.–Taiwan trade ties and strongly encouraging allies and other democracies to include Taiwan in international efforts on health, transportation, nonproliferation, counterterrorism, and disaster relief. A U.S. free trade agreement with Taiwan would be a good place to start. Membership, even as an "observer," in other formal and informal international organizations like the World

---

[75]See Wang Zhuozhong, "Renzhi Taishang Yingxiang, Zhonggong Lalong Fandu" [Mindful of Taiwan business's influence, China Coerces them to oppose Taiwan Independence], *China Times*, Taipei, May 3, 2006. For a discussion of this, see John J. Tkacik, Jr., "Needed: A Strong Response to Beijing's Boycott of Foreign Businesses Dealing with Taiwan," Heritage Foundation *Executive Memorandum* No. 773, September 7, 2001, at *www.heritage.org/Research/AsiaandthePacific/EM773.cfm*. Section 4(b)(8) of the Taiwan Relations Act "makes clear that Taiwan will be treated as a 'friendly' country for the purposes of United States Laws. The anti-boycott provisions of the Export Administration Act, for example, are made applicable with respect to Taiwan by these sections." See *Taiwan Relations Act Conference Report*, Report No. 96–71, U.S. House of Representatives, March 24, 1979, p. 13.

Health Organization, the International Civil Aviation Organization, the International Maritime Organization, the various informal nonproliferation groups like the Australia Group (on chemical weapons) and the Missile Technology Control Regime, and refugee and relief "core groups" would benefit the international community and provide Taiwan with enhanced international legitimacy. In turn, this enhanced legitimacy would provide extra deterrence against China's constant threats of force against Taiwan.

Within this context, does it still make sense for the United States or any other democracy to humor China's claims to "sovereignty" over Taiwan? If Beijing is successful in persuading Washington to back away from its support of democratic Taiwan, would Asia see in this a signal that the United States is withdrawing from the Western Pacific? How would a Chinese-aligned Taiwan affect America's strategic position in Asia?

Taiwan's legal status, as a matter of international law, has gone unratified since 1945. Japan formally renounced "right, title and claim" to the island in its instrument of surrender at the end of the Second World War. Taiwan was occupied by the Chinese Nationalist Army in October 1945 and became a haven for the Nationalists' government in exile after their defeat in China's civil war. Taiwan was saved from certain Chinese Communist occupation by the Korean War, which obliged President Harry S. Truman to position the U.S. Seventh Fleet in the Taiwan Strait. In the absence of an international treaty formally transferring sovereignty from a defeated Japan to anyone else, the question of who "owns" Taiwan has been in diplomatic limbo since 1945.[80]

---

[76]It is an established mantra of U.S. policy that Beijing should talk directly with the democratically "elected leadership" on Taiwan. See Richard Boucher, Spokesman, U.S. Department of State, "Daily Press Briefing," May 2, 2005, at *www.state.gov/r/pa/prs/dpb/2005/45505.htm*. Mr. Boucher emphasized that "a long-term cross-strait solution will require dialogue between representatives of the duly elected leadership in Taiwan and the authorities on the mainland." On February 27, 2006, White House spokesman Scott McClellan said that "the United States continues to also stress the need for Beijing to open a meaningful dialogue with the duly elected leadership in Taiwan that leads to a peaceful resolution of their differences." See "Press Briefing by Scott McClellan," The White House, February 27, 2006, at *www.whitehouse.gov/news/releases/2006/02/20060227-1.html*. Those words were echoed the same day by State Department spokesman Adam Ereli, who said that "we continue to stress the need for Beijing to open a dialogue with the elected leadership in Taiwan." See Ereli, "Daily Press Briefing," February 27, 2006.

[77]George W. Bush, "President Discusses Freedom and Democracy in Kyoto, Japan," White House press release, November 16, 2005, at *www.whitehouse.gov/news/releases/2005/11/20051116-6.html*; see also Jennifer Loven, "Bush Hails Taiwan as Model of Freedom," Associated Press, November 16, 2005.

Communist China, of course, claims sovereignty over the island of Taiwan and its people and reserves the right, under international law, to bring this *terra irredenta* under its control by force of arms. For its part, although the United States has tried under successive Administrations to evade the legal issue by claiming that "the United States takes no position on the matter of sovereignty over Taiwan," Congress has legislated a formal defense commitment to Taiwan under the Taiwan Relations Act.

These considerations lead to three overriding questions that must be answered if a coherent U.S. policy toward Taiwan and China is to be crafted.

Question One: Is Taiwan strategically important?

Does it make sense for the United States to encourage Taiwan's voters to move toward China in an effort to stave off Chinese military and economic threats? The only answer is "no." There is no indication that China's military buildup would abate with the successful absorption of Taiwan. Aside from the unassailable fact that Taiwan is a vibrant democracy and one of America's top trading partners, U.S. policymakers certainly must be able to see that Taiwan is an important defense and intelligence partner that occupies 13,000 square miles of strategic real estate in what General MacArthur called America's "littoral defense line in the western Pacific."[81]

---

[78]For a longer discussion of this, see John J. Tkacik, Jr., "Revenge of the Panda Hugger: The Bush Administration's China Policy Is Hardening," *The Weekly Standard*, Vol. 11, Issue 23 (February 27, 2006), at *www.weeklystandard.com/Content/Public/Articles/000/000/006/784vnqpk.asp*.

[79]Senior U.S. officials began to refer to China as an emerging "military superpower" as early as June 2005. In an interview with *The Wall Street Journal*, Secretary of State Condoleezza Rice used the term "military superpower." See Neil King, Jr., "Rice Wants U.S. To Help China Be Positive Force," *The Wall Street Journal*, June 29, 2005, p. A13, at *http://online.wsj.com/article/0,,SB112001578322872628,00.html*. Director of National Intelligence John Negroponte told a congressional hearing that "China is a rapidly rising power with steadily expanding global reach that may become a peer competitor to the United States at some point." See Bill Gertz, "China's Emergence as Military Power Splits Strategists on Threat to U.S.," *The Washington Times*, February 7, 2006, p. A3, at *www.washingtontimes.com/national/20060206-102324-3179r.htm*.

[80]For the State Department's official position on Taiwan's sovereignty as of July 13, 1971, see a memorandum from the Office of the Legal Advisor entitled "The Legal Status of Taiwan," a copy of which appears in John J. Tkacik, Jr., ed., *Rethinking "One China"* (Washington, D.C.: The Heritage Foundation, 2004), pp. 180–191. For an extended discussion of the Taiwan "sovereignty" issue, see Y. Frank Chiang, "One-China Policy and Taiwan," *Fordham International Law Journal*, Vol. 28 (2004).

This will be dealt with at some length in Chapter 3, but one aspect of the relationship should not be underestimated: Taiwan is an important source for advanced electronics—a strategic commodity if ever there was one.

Taiwan's semiconductor industry is the world's most advanced, and the Pentagon gets a substantial volume of vital microchips from Taiwan's chip "fabs." America's own microchip production capacity is down to near zero, with only one U.S. chip fab able to produce "trusted and classified" chips for our defense needs. Meanwhile, U.S. semiconductor manufacturing is increasingly outsourced to China, where all chip fabs are under the control of the Chinese government.[82]

Moreover, chips are not the only vital defense items supplied from Taiwan. It is clear both that Taiwan is an important U.S. security partner and that Taiwan's freedom from Beijing's control is, by itself, in America's interests.

Question Two: A Taiwan–China security partnership?

Some senior pro-China politicians in Taiwan's "Blue" camp are quietly relieved that their continuing legislative veto of defense funding for advanced U.S. anti-missile and anti-submarine weapons—the two defense capabilities that Taiwan needs most urgently and Beijing most urgently opposes[83]—achieves the dual goal of antagonizing Washington and gratifying Beijing.

On May 12, 2005, Chinese Communist Party leader Hu Jintao and Dr. James Soong, who is now chairman of one of Taiwan's small pro-China opposition parties and was very nearly elected Taiwan's vice-president in 2004, issued a "joint news communiqué" in Beijing declaring that "Military conflicts shall be effectively avoided so long as there is no possibility that Taiwan moves toward 'Taiwan independence.'"[84] Then, at a September

---

[81]MacArthur, "Farewell Address to Congress."

[82]Defense Science Board Task Force on High Performance Microchip Supply, *Final Report.*

[83]For a discussion of these systems, see Richard P. Lawless, Deputy Undersecretary of Defense, Asian and Pacific Affairs, "Keynote Dinner Address" at U.S.–Taiwan Business Council U.S. Taiwan Defense Industry Conference, Scottsdale, Arizona, October 4, 2004.

[84]"Hu Jintao yu Song Chuyu huitan dacheng liuxiang gongshi" [Hu Jintao and Song Chuyu reach a six-item consensus], *Renmin Wang* [*People's Daily Net*], Beijing, May, 12, 2005. See also "No 'Taiwan independence,' no military conflicts: communiqué," Xinhua News Agency, Beijing, May 12, 2005, at *http://news.xinhuanet.com/english/2005-05/12/content_2951496.htm.*

2005, "peace conference" in Shanghai, Soong explained that Communist Party leader Hu had given him a commitment not to attack Taiwan and that Taiwan therefore did not need to defend itself from China.[85]

Clearly, under such a formula, China must perforce assume all defense responsibilities for Taiwan—a task that Beijing's leaders would certainly relish. Under such an arrangement with China, Beijing would also reserve the right to use military or police force against any private citizens in Taiwan, as well as members of the government or legislature, who advocate Taiwan's separate identity from China—a population that includes at least 57 percent of Taiwan's people, according to a poll conducted for the U.S. Department of State's Bureau of Intelligence and Research.[86]

In other words, there will be no room in any "one China" framework between Beijing and Taipei for Taiwan's continued security relationship with the United States or other Asian democracies.[87] Indeed, Taiwan's biggest opposition party, the "Chinese Kuomintang," also supports a new cooperative relationship with China and often points to American policy statements to justify its policies.[88]

Question Three: Is Taiwan moving in China's direction?

As Washington contemplates the political debate in Taiwan, it must also consider its own strategic position in the Western Pacific. Surely, the prospect of Taiwan's embryonic democracy and advanced technological base firmly enfolded within Beijing's 21st century co-prosperity sphere should

---

[85]Soong told reporters on September 12, 2005, that "When I visited Beijing in May, China's President Hu Jintao told me that there would not be any military threat facing Taiwan as long as it does not declare independence." Later, when asked whether he would encourage his PFP legislators to pass the defense budget in return for direct air links between Taiwan and China, Soong refused to respond. A PRC Taiwan Affairs official present at the exchange, He Shizhong, warned that there was no need whatever for "a certain defense capacity" on Taiwan, and Soong did not contradict him. See "Taiwan Opposition Shoots Down Arms Package," Agence France-Presse, September 13, 2005, at *www.defensenews.com/story.php?F=1099478&C=asiapac* (February 13, 2006). See also "Song Chuyu: Liangan bubi ti Junshi huxiang jizhi, zai liangan qingying luntan changyi 'jianli jingji huxin jizhi'; Jia Qinglin ti sidian hezuo jianyi" [James Soong: Two sides do not need military mutual confidence mechanism, Calls for 'establishment of economic mutual confidence mechanism,' Jia Qinglin proposes four point cooperation agreement], *Shijie Ribao* (in Chinese), New York, September 16, 2005, and "Taishang cu Song zancheng jungou huan zhihang, dangzhe Guotaiban Guanyuande mian, tiwen jianrui" [Taiwan Businessmen Urge James Soong to trade Arms Budget for Direct Links, Slap in Face to Taiwan Affairs Officials, Questions Sharp], *Shijie Ribao* (in Chinese), New York, September 16, 2005, p. 2.

perturb America's leaders, who value the global expansion of democracy and would like, as a matter of prudent caution, to keep America's primary source of advanced semiconductors out of the hands of Asia's leading dictatorship. Even more unsettling should be the prospect of an important U.S. defense and intelligence partner on the Pacific Rim—where reliable friends of America are getting hard to find—deciding that its future lies with the illiberal, albeit powerful and wealthy, regime in Beijing.

Democracy is a wonderful thing, but democracies in foreign countries do not always work in ways that suit U.S. policies. Taiwan's opposition parties, for example, have bottled up key defense budget legislation by claiming either that the Pentagon is deliberately cheating Taiwan's taxpayers by insisting that Taiwan buy overpriced and ineffective weapons systems[89] or that Taiwan cannot afford an "arms race" with China, and buying new systems is of no use.[90] Taiwan's President Chen has argued that Taiwan can afford new weapons systems and that they will be effective in meeting the threat from China. He points out that Taiwan certainly has better finances now than it had a decade ago, yet the proportion of the national budget devoted to defense has been cut by nearly half since then.

Clearly, Washington needs some political allies in Taipei. If Taiwan's government cannot make needed changes in the island's defense posture, however, Taiwan risks becoming a defense liability to the United States.

---

[86]Robert J. Levy, "M–16–05 Opinion Analysis: Taiwan Public's Anxiety About Beijing Does Not Translate into Willingness to Spend on Defense," U.S. Department of State, Bureau of Intelligence and Research, Office of Research, February 11, 2005, Table 3. Nearly half of all Taiwan's residents do not consider themselves "Chinese" at all, and only 4.4 percent consider themselves "Chinese only," according to Taiwan Gallup Poll results reported in Jason Dean, "National Identity Grows in Taiwan: Trend Shows Economic Ties to China May Not Propel Goal of Political Unity," *The Wall Street Journal*, March 1, 2004, at *http://online.wsj.com/article/0,,SB107808014465642122,00.html.*

[87]This would include such other Asian partners as, for example, Singapore, which has elaborate military training programs in Taiwan. See Dana Dillon and John J. Tkacik, Jr., "China's Quest for Asia," *Policy Review*, No. 134 (December 2005 & January 2006), pp. 29–40, at *www.policyreview.org/134/dillon.html.*

[88]See, for example, Caroline Hong, "Lien, Paal Discussed China Visit—KMT," *Taipei Times*, April 23, 2005, p. 1, at *www.taipei-times.com/News/front/archives/2005/04/23/2003251569*, and Lawrence Chung, "US 'may be using spy scandal as warning'; Washington could be playing up incident as a way of telling Taiwan's Chen to go easy on separatist remarks, say analysts," Singapore *Straits Times*, September 23, 2004.

What the Administration and Congress Should Do

Both the Administration and Congress should reexamine their assumptions, behind closed doors and in a confidential way, about the benefits of present policies that nudge Taiwan into the embrace of China. If those policies are detrimental to America's interests, as seems likely, they must be abandoned and replaced with policies that are designed to preserve Taiwan's identity as a country separate from China. This examination should include the following.

1. Refocus U.S. policy statements.

The Administration should not be ashamed of the substance of existing policy. In other words, rather than change "our one China policy," they should simply articulate it. The process of reiterating a long-standing policy must be gradual and accretive so as to minimize a Beijing reaction.

One sequence might focus on subtle but ever more frequent reiterations of President Reagan's "six assurances," first in press briefings and in regular policy briefings to Congress in open testimony and then through the careful enfolding of a "capitalized" enumeration of the "Six Assurances" in the canon of "China Policy" along with "Our One China Policy," "Peace in the Taiwan Strait," the "Three Communiqués," and the "Taiwan Relations Act." It might be followed by appropriate explication of all six Assurances to the press, to Congress, and in public statements. Finally, rather than being left to stand alone as though they were an unwelcome reality, presidential and Cabinet-level references to America's commitments under the Taiwan Relations Act should always be accompanied by an explanation that democratic Taiwan is a friend, partner, and model for Asia.

---

[89]This is a chronic problem. See "Liyuan chengweihui 50 du fengsha, Jungou shengbian, Guomindang you chongxin diancai" [Legislative Procedure Committee kills bill for 50th time, Arms purchase changes, KMT wants a complete reorder from the menu], *China Times*, Taipei, April 5, 2006, and Chen Yingci, "Lian Zhan: Jue bu jieshou 'Yizhong Liangzhi,' ye bu zuo Meiguo de maqianzu"[Lien Chan declares absolutely no acceptance of 'One Country Two Systems,' also will not be an American pawn], *United Daily News*, Taipei, August 17, 2003.

[90]See Xiao Xucen, "Tuiyi jiangling lianshu fan jungou, Yu 200 ke xing" [Retired Generals line up against Military Budget, over 200 stars," *China Times* (in Chinese), Taipei, September 24, 2004; see also Wu Mingjie and Jiang Huizhen, "Jungou yusuan, fanlan cu chongbian zai shen" [Pan-Blue Wants Special Arms Budget Recalculated and Re-submitted], *China Times* (in Chinese), Taipei, December 14, 2004.

Similarly, while the standard U.S. position is "no support for Taiwan independence," official statements can praise the legitimacy of "Taiwan's elected leaders" that include increasingly frequent use of the word "sovereign." In the course of a State Department press briefing, for example, a sentence saying that "Taiwan's people have the sovereign right to the government of their choosing" might be one way to reinforce American (and Taiwanese, for that matter) public opinion that Taiwan's future is important to the United States.

When China gets obstreperous on the Taiwan issue, White House and Cabinet spokespersons can develop the idea that "the United States does not recognize or accept that China has any right whatsoever under international law to use or threaten the use of force against democratic Taiwan." This is indeed U.S. policy, but it has never been stated in public. In background to journalists and reporters, U.S. "senior officials" could explain that "even a Taiwan declaration of independence would just be 'words on paper' and would not change any country's behavior or affect China's security posture." This wording would make it clear that the United States does not now recognize, and never has recognized, China's territorial and sovereign claims to Taiwan.

Finally, a diplomatic deal might be struck with the "elected leaders of Taiwan" that they would refrain from verbal challenges to the so-called *status quo* in the Strait in return for authoritative expressions of support like those described above.

2. Reexamine assumptions about trends in Chinese political reforms.

In the 17 years since the June 4, 1989, suppression of China's democracy movement at Tiananmen, the Communist regime's repression of civil, political, and religious rights has grown worse, not better. Despite international concern for human rights in China, the post-Tiananmen Beijing regime remains, and in all probability will continue to be, a counter-liberal force encouraging despotism and undermining democracy in its own country as well as in Asia and across the globe.

Unfortunately, there is not the slightest evidence that the Chinese Communist Party is moving toward a democratic future.[91] To the contrary, present evidence is overwhelming that the Beijing regime is in fact returning to its old totalitarian ways rather than evolving away from them, primarily in an attempt to shore up the regime's legitimacy.[92]

Within this context, the U.S. national security bureaucracy should ask itself whether Taiwan can play a role in active measures to encourage democratic reforms in China.

3. Enhance U.S.-Taiwan trade ties.

A free trade agreement with Taiwan would not only increase U.S. exports—something very few existing American FTAs do—but also incentivize some key Taiwan advanced-technology firms to reverse their supply chains away from final assembly in China to final assembly in Taiwan. The U.S. Department of State, for example, discovered in May 2006 that hundreds of its laptop and PC computer work stations are manufactured by a Chinese government-owned firm, Lenovo.[93] This will become increasingly important as U.S. defense procurement agencies find that the only sources for high-tech computer and telecommunications systems are in China.

Finally, a U.S.–Taiwan FTA would signal China that America takes very seriously its strategic stake in Taiwan—something that Beijing does not currently believe.

4. Strengthen U.S.-Taiwan partnerships in informal international organizations.

The U.S. should examine the spectrum of non-defense cooperation relationships, including trade, finance, humanitarian reconstruction, public health, scientific, and environmental arrangements, to strengthen ties with

---

[91]One gross measure of a country's human rights progress is the U.S. Department of State's country reports on human rights. Over the past 15 years, with the exception of 1993 and 1997, the State Department has reported that China's human rights record "deteriorated," "declined," or "displayed well-documented abuses and/or violations." In 2005, the State Department judged that "the [Chinese] Government's human rights record remained poor, and the Government continued to commit numerous and serious abuses." Generally, these assessments are in the third or fourth paragraph of each year's report. Electronic versions of these reports are available at the Department of State Web site at *www.state.gov/g/drl/rls/hrrpt*. For reports from 1993–1999, see *www.state.gov/g/drl/hr/c1470.htm*.

[92]That the Chinese government's grip on civil, political, and religious rights is growing ever tighter rather than being relaxed is amply documented in the *Congressional–Executive Commission on China 2005 Annual Report at www.cecc.gov/pages/annualRpt/annualRpt05/index.php*. The report's executive summary describes "increased government restrictions" on worship, "strengthened control" over religious practice, "more aggressive" policies against Tibetan Buddhists, "curtail[ed] activities" of domestic civil society organizations, "rapid [loss of] judges," "tightened restrictions" on journalists, "exacerbated ethnic tensions," "women fac[ing] increasing risks from HIV/AIDS," population control policies that "exacerbate the [human] trafficking problem," and a worsening gender imbalance, all charting a distinct downward trend in China's human rights environment.

the island and give it a sense that the United States does in fact value its continued friendship with the island.

5. Encourage third countries to reexamine their own "one China" policies.

Several countries have "one China" policies that are identical to America's. As carryovers from the 1951 San Francisco Treaty, Canada, Australia, Japan, and the United Kingdom, for example, have resisted Chinese demands that they recognize Beijing's sovereignty over Taiwan.[94]

6. Encourage third-country diplomatic ties with Taiwan.

The Departments of State and Defense and U.S. diplomatic missions abroad should encourage the preservation of third-country diplomatic ties with Taiwan. Apparently, the State Department does so now on a limited basis.[95]

In November 2003, Taiwan's establishment of diplomatic relations with the Pacific Island nation of Kiribati led to China's hurried dismantlement of an elaborate space tracking station on Kiribati's Tarawa Atoll. China had a 15-year lease for a "secret base" station at the atoll rim of a downrange splashdown target area for American missile tests and no doubt used the base to monitor U.S. missile tests.[96]

7. Loosen self-imposed limits on U.S.–Taiwan official exchanges.

Defense cooperation is already at a high level, but the Administration should enhance it—again, quietly—by lifting the self-imposed ban on visits

---

[93]"U.S. Pulls Lenovo PCs from State Department," Agence France-Presse, May 19, 2006, at *www.washingtontimes.com/world/20060518-104316-9737r.htm*.

[94]See, for example, Frank Chiang's "One-China Policy and Taiwan," pp. 36–38.

[95]In a press interview, former Bush Administration National Security Council official Michael Green wondered aloud: "if Washington gets annoyed again, what signals will Taiwan's Central American allies begin picking up from the State Department the next time they are lobbied by Beijing to switch relations?" Presumably, they had been "picking up" sympathetic signals about Taiwan. See "Michael Green Interview—The Gambit Behind the NUC's Removal," *Taipei Times*, February 24, 2006, p. 4, at *www.taipeitimes.com/News/taiwan/archives/2006/02/24/2003294 388*.

[96]"China Rushes to Pull Down Atoll Satellite Tracker," Agence France-Presse, November 27, 2003, at *www.taipeitimes.com/News/taiwan/archives/2003/11/27/2003077400*. See also Zhu Jianling, "Zhonggong Shenmi Jidi, Zuyue 15 nian" [PRC had secret 15-year base lease], *China Times*, Taipei, November 8, 2003, p. 10.

to the island by flag-rank U.S. military and naval officers. It should encourage visits by Cabinet-level officials, a practice that was common during the Clinton Administration. Senior U.S. State Department officials up to the rank of undersecretary could visit Taiwan without undue stress to ties with Beijing.

Conclusion

China's rapid modernization is eerily similar to Japan's Meiji Restoration a century ago. Beijing's new ideology of "One China" nationalism resonates with the "One German Nation" during the first half of the 20th century. Today, in a totalitarian China, the United States, Japan, and the other Asian democracies face an eerily similar challenge. Until China is democratic, a "most vital interest" of the United States will be to maintain America's strategic posture in the Western Pacific. Taiwan is a key part of that strategy.

Some believe that America's only interest in Taiwan is to ensure that the "Taiwan issue is resolved peacefully," but this simplistic formulation places exclusive emphasis on "process" and none on "outcome." Taiwan is one of America's most important trading partners; it is a thriving, dynamic, and vibrant democracy; and it is a key American security partner in Asia. America does have important interests in the outcome of Taiwan's future, and Washington policymakers must take this into consideration in crafting America's strategy for Asia in the 21st century.

3

Reframing U.S. and Japanese Strategy in the Taiwan Strait

JAMES AUER, RUPERT HAMMOND-CHAMBERS, RANDALL G. SCHRIVER, AND JOHN J. TKACIK, JR.[1]

"WHEN FUTURE GENERATIONS READ THE HISTORY OF THESE TIMES," former U.S. Deputy Secretary of State Richard Armitage has observed, "the story may not focus on how we managed the Middle East or nuclear proliferation. Rather, the story will be about how we dealt with the defining strategic challenge of our age, of the first half of this century, and that is the emergence of China in the context of a rapidly changing Asia."[2] The strategic environment in the Asia–Pacific region is indeed undergoing a profound transformation, and this chapter is devoted to considerations of the strategic and defense effects that this transformation is having on the United States, Japan, and Taiwan.

China's emergence is unquestionably the most profound strategic development in Asia since the Second World War. To the list of significant changes, one could easily add the re-emergence of Japan, the "Asianization" of India, and Indonesia's fledgling democratic experiment in the world's most populous Muslim country; but the rapid expansion and modernization of China's army, naval, and air forces (and Beijing's increasingly proprietary approach to Asia more generally) are what generate the nervousness over

---

[1] This chapter represents the collective judgment of these scholars but not necessarily the specific views of each individual.

[2] Richard Armitage, "China the Emerging Power," *Yomiuri Shimbun*, Tokyo, August 14, 2005, unedited version at *http://taiwansecurity.org/News/2005/YS-140805.htm*.

the uncertainties looming in the Asian security environment for the United States, Japan, and Taiwan.

While Asia encompasses a variety of flash points that carry a potential for crisis, the only identifiable threat to America's existential security is a future China that opts for strategic rivalry with the United States, its allies, and its like-minded friends. Any three-way dialogue between the United States, Japan, and Taiwan that is oriented toward security issues must therefore be reframed within a context of the challenge posed by China's emergence as a superpower and peer competitor to the United States. The specific implications of China's rise in Asia for the U.S.–Japan alliance and the role Taiwan can play in shaping developments in the most positive direction—that is, toward a more benign integration of China into regional and global affairs—should be the central concern of policymakers in the three capitals.

China's "Rise" and Strategic Intentions in Asia

A report by the U.S. National Intelligence Council's 2020 project offered the analysis that the likely emergence of China is similar to the advent of a united Germany in the late 19th century and early 20th century and could transform the global geopolitical landscape in an equally dramatic way.[3] China's emergence is a story of strengthening capabilities and evolving structures of intent.

Chinese foreign policy has evolved substantially over the course of the past decade. China pursues its interests today through a more creative and proactive diplomacy than it had prior to the late 1990s. In addition, China has greater economic and trade influence, and this gives its diplomacy a new, multi-drawered "tool box" with which to pursue its foreign policy goals. The net effect is that China is choosing deeper engagement and involvement with the outside world and is increasingly effective at promoting its interests—even in the cases where its interests clash with the United States, Japan, and other established powers. This has led to widespread consternation about the so-called rise of China.

No one is more acutely aware of the alarm in Asia about China's strategic rise than the Chinese themselves. Chinese scholar Zheng Bijian, a close policy adviser to Chinese leader Hu Jintao, proposed a model of "China's Peaceful Rise" at an international economic conference in China's southern Hainan province in late 2003, but the debate about a "peaceful rise" began in earnest in 2004. In April, another scholar, Huang Renwei, published a

---

[3] *Mapping the Global Future: Report of the National Intelligence Council's 2020 Project*, NIC 2004–13, December 2004, at *www.dni.gov/nic/NIC_globaltrend2020_s2.html*.

full-page disquisition on China's "strategic choice" of a "peaceful rise" in Shanghai's *Liberation Daily* without once mentioning "Taiwan."[4] It was an inspirational and reassuring tract that outlined an altruistic vision of China's future—peaceful—interactions with Asia and stressed Beijing's sensitivities to Asia's worries that China's industrial and manufacturing mass would overwhelm its neighbors.

By May, however, it appeared that Jiang Zemin, China's reigning elder and chairman of the Central Military Commission (essentially, commander of the armed forces), objected to this peaceful look at the world. On May 17, 2004, Jiang directed that China's propaganda department levy several blasts at Taiwan, which had just reelected the pro-independence Chen Shui-bian as president. By September, the Central Party School's propaganda organ, *Study Times*, also blasted away at the idea of "Peaceful Rise," saying that the "two arguments against the idea are... the Taiwan question" and "relations with the United States, both of which are closely linked to a certain degree." The article continued: "one can't say that if China uses armed force to resolve the Taiwan Issue as a last resort, to carry out the legitimate right to use force to unify Taiwan [with the Mainland], then that isn't a 'Peaceful Rise'."[5]

When Hu Jintao finally succeeded the retiring Jiang Zemin as chairman of the Central Military Commission, he had apparently agreed to continue Jiang's policy of "Wealthy Nation, Strong Military" (*fuguo qiangbing*).[6] "Peaceful rise," it appears, does not apply to Taiwan, the United States, or any other country that would come to Taiwan's aid. Taiwan is a *sui generis* issue for China and deserves special and distinct mention.

One should not underestimate the neuralgia that seizes Chinese leaders on questions related to Taiwan and their consequent implications for Chinese foreign policy. Whereas in Washington or Tokyo there may be some vagueness on the part of some leaders regarding Beijing's overall strategic direction, within the Chinese leadership, there is complete clarity as to their specific intentions toward Taiwan. They simply will not tolerate suggestions

---

[4] Huang Renwei, "Zhongguo Heping Jueqide Daolu Xuanze he Zhanlue Guannian" [China's Choice of the road of Peaceful Rise and its Strategic Context], *Jiefang Ribao* [*Liberation Daily*], Shanghai, April 26, 2004, at *www.people.com.cn/GB/guandian/1035/2468305.html.*

[5] Chen Xiankui and Xin Xiangyang, "Zhongguo Heping Jueqi Shifo Keneng?" [Is China's Peaceful Rise Possible, or Not?], *Xuexi Shibao* [*Study Times*], Beijing, posted September 2, 2004, at *www.china.org.cn/chinese/zhuanti/xxsb/648323.htm.*

[6] See Arthur Waldron and John Tkacik, Jr., "China's Power Struggle," *The Asian Wall Street Journal*, August 13–15, 2004, p. 11, at *http://online.wsj.com/article/0,,SB109235074074490451,00.html.*

that Taiwan is anything but sovereign Chinese territory and, when pressed, insist that "Taiwan is part of the sacred territory of the People's Republic of China."[7] This animates in consequential ways both the PRC's foreign policy and its behavior in the world. Specifically, Beijing:

- Uses foreign aid to lure away countries that maintain diplomatic relations with Taiwan,

- Pressures countries with which it has diplomatic relations to abjure any positive interactions or engagement whatsoever with Taiwan's government and government entities, and

- Uses its influence in multilateral and international organizations to isolate Taiwan as much as possible.

China has been wildly successful in its campaign to isolate and coerce Taiwan, but this could also prove ultimately to be an Achilles' heel if Beijing allows its emotions over Taiwan to drive decisions that are otherwise irrational in terms of China's own interests.

The "Taiwan Question" has also served China well in another critical fashion. China's aggressive efforts at military modernization are paying off, and China is acquiring broad and advanced military capabilities. The single most important factor driving this is a single-minded focus on scenarios that operationalize the Taiwan challenge. The net result has been a remarkably consistent degree of operational coordination among the critical communities within China's military establishment that are responsible for acquisition, training, logistics, doctrine, strategy, etc.

Historically, such coordination has been a formula that has enabled other militaries to become very good very quickly, and the recipe is working for China as well. Dr. Kurt Campbell, a Deputy Assistant Secretary of Defense who specialized in Asia policy during the Clinton Administration, is

---

[7] There is some speculation among non-Chinese China specialists that Beijing is open to the idea that perhaps Taiwan and mainland China are all part of some yet-to-be-negotiated Chinese entity. Clearly, however, the Chinese leaders have never compromised on the principle that "there is only one China, and the People's Republic of China is the sole legal government of China." That Taiwan is part of the PRC and not a vague "China" was clear in the official announcements of China's "Anti Secession Law" of March 14, 2005. See National People's Congress vice chairman Wang Zhaoguo's "Guanyu 'fan fenlie guojia fa (caoan)' de shuoming [Explication regarding the 'Law Against the Separation of the Nation (Draft)'], Xinhua News Agency, Beijing, March 8, 2005, at *http://news.xinhuanet.com/newscenter/2005-03/08/con-tent_2666011.htm*.

astonished at China's incredibly rapid military modernization. "You look back on those [intelligence] studies, and it's only been a decade," he marveled in October 2005. "China has exceeded—in every area of military modernization—that which even the far-off estimates of the mid-1990s predicted." Indeed, over the past 10 to 15 years, U.S. intelligence analyses have *underestimated* the success of PLA modernization efforts at every juncture.[8]

The singular focus of the Chinese People's Liberation Army (PLA) on the Taiwan scenario is not simply a specter for Taiwan to contemplate; it is a shared challenge for the United States, its treaty allies, and virtually every other country in Asia. Of course, the implications for the United States are most obvious. America's commitments under the Taiwan Relations Act, which include the statutory requirement to maintain the "capacity to resist the use of force" in the Taiwan Strait, ensure that any Chinese attack on Taiwan will be a direct and immediate crisis for the United States.[9] The Chinese have long been expecting U.S. intervention in any Taiwan scenario and they have years of experience planning for combat operations against U.S. forces in the Pacific.

The focus on Taiwan should give others pause as well. Clearly, the capabilities that the PLA is developing to operationalize the Taiwan scenario are capabilities that are transferable to other military scenarios. In fact, planning, equipping, and training for operations against a small island nation approximately 100 nautical miles off China's east coast have immediate and direct implications for China's capabilities vis-à-vis the small Japanese islands that Beijing claims as Chinese territory; the potentially oil-rich seabeds of East China Sea waters, which are within Japan's exclusive economic zone (EEZ); and populated parts of metropolitan Japan that would host U.S. forces in a Taiwan scenario.

Tipping Points

With respect to U.S. planning, two broad factor sets will inform and guide a decision to commit forces to defend Taiwan in the event of a Chinese attack: political factors and military factors.

The political factors are extremely complex and highly scenario-dependent. Thus, they remain very difficult to evaluate in hypothetical

---

[8] See comments by former Deputy Assistant Secretary of Defense Kurt Campbell in Mike Shuster, "Growing Chinese Military Strength Stirs Debate," *Morning Edition*, National Public Radio, October 17, 2005, at *www.npr.org/templates/story/story.php?storyId=4961290.*

[9] For the text of the Taiwan Relations Act, see Appendix B in this volume.

constructs. That is, one cannot predict the myriad possible sequences of an unfolding Taiwan Strait crisis: how Chinese threats and behavior in the political, economic, information, and diplomatic areas will affect Taiwan political leaders' behavior and how responses and counter-responses across the spectrum of non-military dimensions will play out.

Military factors, on the other hand, can be calculated with greater confidence in advance of a potential political crisis—and that is where the alarm-bells are going off. One of the greatest concerns within the U.S. policymaking community is that the military trend lines in the Taiwan Strait and the seas around Japan are evolving so unfavorably that they ultimately may trump future political considerations in a manner that limits the ability of the U.S. to aid Taiwan, even if there were an overwhelming political will in the United States to do so.

There are essentially two tipping points in the military equation for the United States regarding how a potential Taiwan intervention is evaluated.

The first tipping point relates to the PLA's capacity to inflict sufficient damage on U.S. forces to significantly raise the cost of U.S. intervention. In other words, PLA force-projection capacity could move beyond a point where a political decision in the United States to intervene could be predicated on a reasonable expectation of low military cost. Many analysts believe that China's acquisition of modern cruise missiles and submarines (both of which are anti-aircraft carrier capable) already has moved beyond the first tipping point. For them, a "low-cost" U.S. intervention is no longer envisioned.

The second tipping point relates to the possibility that the PLA might develop a rapid envelopment capacity to attack Taiwan and accomplish China's political objectives so suddenly that the United States could not reasonably expect to make a political decision to engage and "get to the fight" before Taiwan's defenses are breached. Because the U.S. and Taiwan are not formal treaty allies and U.S. forces are not based in Taiwan or deployed in Taiwan waters, deploying from outside Taiwan in the event of a conflict makes the challenge of getting to the fight very real. Given developing PLA capabilities, as well as Taiwan's deteriorating defense capabilities, some analysts in the United States fear that we are on the cusp of this second tipping point. The implications for crossing the tipping point should be clear: All political considerations are rendered moot if the United States and its allies and friends lack the capability to get to the fight in time to engage.

The U.S.-Japan Alliance

In calculating these tipping points, American planners have become extremely sensitive to the Japan Factor. Indeed, while much has changed in Northeast Asia since the end of the Cold War, the one thing that has not changed at all is the role of the U.S.–Japan alliance in providing stability in the Asia–Pacific region.

While deterring the Soviet Union obviously is no longer the primary focus of the alliance, the goal never was to fight and win a war against Moscow. In addition, despite the diminution of the Soviet Russian military threat, post–Cold War East Asia is not nearly as balanced and stable as is Europe.

During the Cold War, U.S. bases in Japan and Korea were imperative because U.S. strategy rested on presenting the Soviet Union with the threat of a two-front war. In other words, if the Warsaw Pact attacked westward into Germany, American forces in Asia needed to worry the Soviets with a credible potential strike from the east. This logic of complicating Soviet military planning was behind the Nixon opening to China as well. Japan essentially got what some in Congress called a "free ride" because Japanese leaders understood that America, without access to bases in Japan, would be unable to mount a credible threat of a two-front war. Thus, Japan was able to resist U.S. pressure to "do more" within the alliance.

The fact, however, is that even during the Cold War, Japan contributed substantially and meaningfully to joint strategic objectives in Northeast Asia. The most obvious example is U.S.–Japan maritime cooperation in the Japan Sea during the 1980s. With Soviet forces visibly threatening Japan, Tokyo was willing to contemplate war-fighting in time of actual U.S.–USSR conflict and actually to pay for and man the necessary forces. Japanese and American naval pilots flew their respective submarine-hunting PC-3 Orion aircraft over the Sea of Japan on alternate days. They were fully armed and ready to fight. Thus, deterrence worked because Soviet commanders believed that Japan would fight if necessary.

From 1974 onward, a U.S. aircraft carrier battle group has been permanently home-ported in Yokosuka, the first time a U.S. carrier had ever been based outside the United States. But while U.S.–Japan maritime cooperation was effective, Japan's air and ground forces had much less interface with their American counterparts.

Even in the 21st century, the key alliance issue is still interoperability of C4ISR—command, control, communications, computers, intelligence, surveillance, and reconnaissance. American defense policymakers seek to channel their Japanese counterparts down a path of "connectivity" so that Japan's forces complement America's and do not remain so separated by walls of codes and software, which do nothing but translate data formats into intermediate data formats *ad nauseam*, that C4ISR becomes more trouble than it is worth. Significant progress is being made, especially in missile defense systems, but as the U.S. globally reconfigures its military, some difficult issues remain in relation to U.S. bases here.

True, a foreign base presence always entails social and political problems in Japan, especially in Okinawa where U.S. bases are heavily concentrated, but Japan, at modest cost and risk to itself, also obtains the services of the world's most powerful military to deter aggression—now from China. U.S. forces deployed in Okinawa include the largest composite Air Wing in the U.S. Air Force, as well as an entire U.S. Marine Corps Expeditionary Force (the "III MEF"), the only mobile, self-contained combined arms unit among some 100,000 U.S. service members in the Asia–Pacific region.

Moreover, few Japanese seem to know that the U.N. flag flies over three U.S. bases in Okinawa—Futenma, White Beach, and Kadena—as a consequence of the Korean War. Thus, the U.N. Command in Korea, whose authority derives from the 1950 U.N. Security Council resolution authorizing the defense of South Korea, would need bases in Japan to reinforce South Korea if war were to break out there again. Strategic circumstances have changed greatly since 1950, but the importance of Okinawa's location has in no way diminished.

To be sure, there are a few Japanese who complain that U.S. bases make Japan a target instead of offering security. However, the presence of 200 or more Nodong missiles in North Korea—which, though unreliable and not particularly accurate, are nonetheless theoretically capable of hitting anyplace in Japan with conventional, biological, chemical, or now plausibly nuclear weapons—persuades far more Japanese that a close alliance with the U.S. remains in Japan's national interest. Indeed, some Japanese defense officials claim that, because of the missile threat from North Korea, defense consciousness in Japan today is higher than it was during the Cold War, even when the Soviets placed several aircraft carriers in Vladivostok and a division of troops in Japan's Northern Territories.

Japan's China Challenge at Sea

For over a century and a half, Japan's economic development and prosperity have relied on seaborne trade. Secure and stable maritime transport has been at the heart of Japan's national security and national cohesion, ensured by merchant shipping among its home islands and the Ryukyus. For over a decade, however, the Japanese—citizens and bureaucracies alike—have grown progressively more anxious about the new maritime challenge from China. Southeast Asian experts were aghast when

China unilaterally declared itself to be an "archipelagic state" in 1992, greatly increasing the size of its claimed maritime "economic exclusion zone" in the vast South China Sea, one of Asia's busiest sea-lanes. The move also meant that China's newly claimed East China Sea EEZ would encroach hundreds of miles into Japan's traditional waters.

To make matters worse, China has been increasingly in the habit of poking Japan in the eye just for practice, ignoring the sage foreign policy advice of the late Deng Xiaoping, who in 1992 urged China's leaders to "keep your head down [in the world] and work hard [at home]" (*maitou kugan*). In 2004–2005, Chinese nuclear submarines began routine submerged transits of Japanese EEZ waters, and there was at least one instance in which a PLA Navy (PLAN) nuclear sub actually rattled its way through Japanese territorial waters within a few miles of Taramajima Island in Okinawa Prefecture. Despite Japan's having tracked the Chinese intruder throughout its journey, the Chinese proclaimed that the voyage demonstrated its growing naval power.[10]

With China increasingly assertive in the East China Sea, particularly in waters above the "Chunxiao" seabed gas fields near the Senkaku Islands (*Diaoyutai* in Chinese) positioned at the east end of the Ryukyu Chain north of Taiwan, Japan itself has an interest in maintaining a naval deterrent against China. China has laid territorial claims on the Senkaku islands and has steadfastly refused to negotiate demarcation lines in the area—unless, of course, it can be established beforehand that the demarcation would place the Senkakus within Chinese territorial seas.

To complicate matters further, China's claims to the islands and their waters are rather recent and apparently unsupported by historical evidence. The Chinese claims were unarticulated for all the millennia of Chinese history until the 1969 publication of a United Nations–sponsored report on ocean bottom resources that indicated possible hydrocarbon deposits in the seabed north of the Senkakus.[11] A September 2005 incursion of a Chinese naval flotilla that included an advanced Russian-built *Sovremennyy*-class

---

[10]For an expanded discussion, see Norimitsu Onishi and Howard W. French, "Japan's Rivalry With China Is Stirring a Crowded Sea," *The New York Times*, September 11, 2005, p. A3, at *www.nytimes.com/2005/09/11/international/asia/11taiwan.html*. See also Agence France-Presse, "China Sends Warships to East China Sea" September 29, 2005, at *www.defensenews.com/story.php? F=1143235&C=asia*. For the nuclear submarine incursion, see Joseph Ferguson, "Submarine Incursion Sets Sino–Japanese Relations on Edge," Jamestown Foundation *China Brief*, Vol. 4, Issue 23 (November 24, 2004), at *www.jamestown.org/publications_details.php?volume_id=395&issue_id=3152&article _id=2368904*.

destroyer in the Chunxiao waters close to the Senkakus was clearly designed to enhance China's negotiating posture in its claims.

For the past several years, China has strengthened its naval presence both in the East China Sea off Japan and in the South China Sea under a policy designed to establish China's sovereignty over the continental shelf by claiming as many offshore islands as possible.[12] In February 2003, Xinhua News Agency reported plans to expand China's "maritime surveillance and control" rights from 50 nautical miles to 100 nautical miles by the year 2010 and further expand surveillance activities across China's entire 200-nautical-mile exclusive economic zone by the year 2020. As an example of what China was talking about, the official press claimed that increased PRC maritime patrol operations in the Yellow and East China Seas had already implemented "effective supervision" against American and Japanese vessels.[13]

In January 2003, *China Youth News* quoted the Chinese Maritime Patrol Service's deputy commander, Chang Huirong, as saying that the Service had responded effectively to violations of Chinese jurisdiction in the East China Sea with patrol vessels and aircraft to meet incursions by American and Japanese ships and aircraft. Chinese Maritime Patrol ships "had warned Japanese ships which were leaking oil pollution into the territorial seas" and had also "engaged in effective supervision" against the U.S. naval vessels *Bowditch* and *Sumner*, which "were engaging in military mapping activities."[14] Earlier, Chinese media had accused U.S. naval hydrographic vessels of engaging in "criminal activities" in Chinese waters.[15]

In June 2003, China began its first major air–sea exercises in the South China Sea, calculated to demonstrate a capacity to enforce its claims in waters that control Japan's sea-lanes to the Middle East and Europe.[16] In the

---

[11]For a discussion of China's claim, see John J. Tkacik, Jr., "China's New Challenge to the U.S.–Japan Alliance," Heritage Foundation *WebMemo* No. 533, July 13, 2004, at *www.heritage.org/Research/AsiaandthePacific/wm533.cfm.*

[12]The Nautilus Institute reported new Chinese maritime regulations on offshore islands. See "PRC Uninhabited Islands Regulation," Nautilus Institute *NAPSNet Daily Report*, July 1, 2003, at *www.nautilus.org/archives/napsnet/dr/0307/JUL01-03.html#item10.*

[13]Xu Xiangli, "Zhonggong Qianghua Haishang Jiankongquan" [PRC beefs up Maritime Surveillance Capabilities], *China Times*, Taipei, February 13, 2003.

[14]*Ibid.*

[15]Tammy Kupperman, "U.S., China in New Naval Dispute, Survey Vessel in Yellow Sea Accused of Criminality," September 19, 2002, NBC News, September 19, 2002, at *www.msnbc.com/news/810165.asp?cp1=1.*

summer of 2005, Chinese warships began to haunt the waters surrounding the largest island in the South China Sea's Spratly island chain, Itu Aba (Taiping), which was occupied by a small Taiwan garrison.[17] Taiwan's Defense Ministry is exceedingly nervous, but its only response to a tightening noose around the strategic island was to "avoid war" by replacing the marines with a Taiwanese coast guard detachment.[18]

In December 2005, in an effort to cope with a prospective Chinese occupation of Itu Aba, the Taiwanese Defense Ministry announced plans to build a 1,150-meter runway and a control tower on the island that would be suitable for C-130 aircraft (but not jet fighters). The ministry insisted in public that the airport was intended for "humanitarian purposes," such as emergency rescue efforts for sick or injured merchant seamen or fishermen who might encounter difficulties in the treacherous waters, but at least one Kuomintang (KMT) party legislator, Su Chi, criticized the plan as likely to trigger controversy over sovereignty in the Spratlys.[19]

In early 2006, Beijing eventually decided to reassert itself in the Itu Aba area, claiming that it had a "tacit understanding" with Taipei on sovereignty and referring to a 1993 statement from Taiwan's defense ministry that "did not rule out joint development with China" of the island's waters.[20]

---

[16]"Guangzhou Junqu Kongjun, Nanhai Jiandui, Shoudu Shenhai Lianyan" [Guangzhou Military Region Air Force, South Sea fleet, hold first Deep Ocean Joint Military Drills], *Shijie Ribao*, New York, June 12, 2003.

[17]Wu Mingjie, "Guojun Youxin, Gongjian Pinxian Wo Taipingdao Haiyu" [Taiwan Military Alarmed, PRC Warships regularly appear in Taiwan's Spratly Island waters], *China Times*, Taipei, July 11, 2005, p. 1.

[18]Wu Mingjie, "Lixing Bizhan; Taiping Dao gai Haixunshu Zhushou" [War Avoidance is Ideal; Spratly Island garrison to be turned over to Coast Guard], *China Times*, Taipei, July 11, 2005, p. 2; Wu Mingjie, "Taipingdao Zhoubian daojiao duo cao zhanling" [Island Reefs Surrounding Spratly All Occupied by China], *China Times*, Taipei, July 11, 2005, p. 2.

[19]Wu Mingjie, "Taipingdao jian jichang, taioqi zhuquan zhengyi? Guofangbu, Haixunshu: rendao kaoliang" [Airport construction on Spratly, Does it provoke a controversy on sovereignty? Defense Ministry and Coast Guard: Humanitarian considerations], *China Times*, Taipei, December 16, 2005, p. 2; "Government Has Plans for Airstrip on Taiping Island," Central News Agency, Taipei, December 16, 2005, at *www.tro-taiwan.roc.org.uk/dc/nsl151205m.htm*.

[20]"Dalu meiti zha Tai tiaozhan Nanhai Chenji; Taiwan fangmian junbei zai Taipingdao jian jichang" [PRC Media blasts Taiwan; Challenge to Tacit Understanding in South China Sea, Taiwan plans airstrip on Itu Aba], *World Journal*, New York, January 7, 2006, p. A8.

Japan's anxieties about China's aggressive presence in the South China Sea, and Itu Aba in particular, are clearly warranted. The prospect of a Chinese military occupation of the largest island in the South China Sea should concentrate minds wonderfully in capitals on the Sea's Southeast Asian littoral as well as in Tokyo. Taiwan's occupation of the island is a strategically important factor in maintaining a stable balance of power in the Sea. Chinese military occupation of Itu Aba would give Beijing almost total control of international maritime navigation in the area.

Moreover, the Spratly Islands are the least of Japan's worries when it comes to Chinese territorial assertiveness. By August 2005, Chinese fighter aircraft were shadowing Japanese P-3 surveillance aircraft in international waters close to the home islands.[21] For the first time, the Japanese press reported several years of previous incursions into Chinese waters and airspace by "suspicious" Chinese vessels. "Secret" documents from the Japan Self Defense force reported that Chinese submarines had entered "in the area" of Japan's territorial waters at least six times in 2003.[22] Chinese incursions into the Japanese exclusive economic zone became commonplace in 2004, with at least 12 EEZ violations by Chinese hydrographic vessels by May of that year.[23] In June, the Japanese media reported that Chinese submarines had entered Japanese territorial waters the previous November and had shown themselves "very comfortable" with marine characteristics of the Japanese coastline.[24]

These claims and incursions are worrisome for the United States as well as for Japan because Washington has explicitly declared the Senkaku Islands

---

[21]"Xian Qi Zhanji Gonghai Lanzai Riben Jianchaji" [Chinese Jian-7 jet fighter intercepts Japanese Surveillance Aircraft], *World Journal*, New York, July 18, 2003; "Jiefangjun Zhanji Lanzai Fanqian Zhenchaji" [PLA Fighters shadow Japanese ASW aircraft], *World Journal*, New York, August 4, 2003.

[22]"Gongjun Qianting, Ceng Liudu Chumo Ri Linghai" [PRC submarines enter Japanese territorial waters six times], *China Times*, Taipei, January 14, 2004.

[23]"Zhonag Ri Zai Chuan Haijiang Moca, Dalu Diaochachuan dao 'Chongzhin-iao,' Dongjing Kangyi" [China Japan Again Lock Horns over Maritime Boundaries, Chinese survey vessel at *Shigaki Shima*, Tokyo Protests], *World Journal*, New York, May 15, 2004.

[24]Chen Shichang, "Dalu Qianjian Gongran Fuhang Riben Hai, Dumai Xinwen Zhiyi zai Shiwei, Xianshi Suxi Haiyu Dixing, 'Haimianxia de Shili' Chaoyue Ri Ziweidui" [Mainland Submarine Cruises in Sea of Japan for first time, *Asahi Shimbun* says significance is in its demonstration, clearly it was familiar with the maritime characteristics, 'Subsurface force' surpasses the Japanese Self Defense Forces], *World Journal*, New York, June 9, 2004.

to be within the ambit of the mutual defense treaty as "territories administered by Japan."[25]

(It should be noted, however, that the government of Taiwan has occasionally tendered claims to the Senkakus, generally at the instigation of politicians from the "Pan-Blue" Chinese nationalist parties. These claims are more grounded in PRC evidence and seem designed more to irritate Taiwan's relations with Japan than to assert "Taiwanese," as opposed to Chinese, rights to those waters. Moreover, scholarly consideration of the Beijing evidence tends toward the view that it is "fraudulent."[26] One acknowledged expert on the seabed boundary delimitations of the Senkaku Islands area is Ma Ying-jeou, now chairman of Taiwan's Kuomintang party, who very definitely believes that the Senkakus are sovereign Chinese territory.[27])

It is clear, therefore, that Japan has a direct strategic interest in assuring Taiwan's security, especially because Taiwan's geographic location is important to effective monitoring of Chinese submarine activities and because, incidentally, Taiwan's presence on Itu Aba supports at least the color of international interests along the shipping lanes in the South China Sea. Nonetheless, Tokyo is understandably keen to remain a few degrees removed from an explicit public pledge to Taiwan's security. Explicit or not, the structure of the U.S.–Japan and U.S.–Taiwan relationships is an interlocking one and apparently one that the American and Japanese publics and their elected representatives have strongly embraced.

Several days before the September 11, 2005, elections for the lower house of the Japanese Diet, the PLAN suddenly deployed several destroyers, with a Russian *Sovremennyy* as flagship, to observe Japanese seabed exploration drilling in the East China Sea. This certainly was not the major factor in Prime Minister Junichiro Koizumi's smashing victory in the elections, but it also did not go either unnoticed or unreported in Japan. Nervousness about

---

[25]See U.S. Department of State, "Daily Press Briefing," March 24, 2004, at *www.state.gov/r/pa/prs/dpb/2004/30743.htm*. The transcript reads: "MR. ERELI: The Senkaku Islands have been under the administrative control of the Government of Japan since having been returned as part of the reversion of Okinawa in 1972. Article 5 of the 1960 U.S.–Japan Treaty of Mutual Cooperation and Security states that the treaty applies to the territories under the administration of Japan; thus, Article 5 of the Mutual Security Treaty applies to the Senkaku Islands." However, the department's spokesman, Mr. Ereli, continued: "Sovereignty of the Senkaku Islands is disputed. The U.S. does not take a position on the question of the ultimate sovereignty of the Senkaku Diaoyu Islands. This has been our longstanding view. We expect the claimants will resolve this issue through peaceful means and we urge all claimants to exercise restraint."

China was a key factor in drawing overwhelming public support to his faction in the Diet election. Koizumi may even have had to restrain himself from sending a letter of thanks to Beijing.

If so, he had to restrain himself only until October 2, when news came from his naval commanders that the fire-control radar aboard the Chinese *Sovremennyy* warship in a disputed zone near the Senkaku islands had "locked-on" a Japanese P-3 patrol aircraft and that another vessel's artillery radar had targeted a Japanese coast guard vessel nearby.[28] Clearly, the Chinese were showing their teeth.

The Japanese people are becoming increasingly alarmed at China's naval assertiveness in traditional Japanese waters, and Japanese strategists are concerned that China, unrestrained, might try to seize Taiwan. The 800 (a number that is increasing) Chinese short-range ballistic missiles (SRBMs) deployed against Taiwan are now judged to be in range of Japanese targets as well. These considerations led Tokyo, for the first time since 1969, to state on February 19, 2005, that Japan and America, as security allies, share the "common strategic objective" of a peaceful solution in the Taiwan Strait.[29]

---

[26]"Diaoyutai Lieyu Shang gei Sheng Xuanhuai? Xuezhe zhi Zixi Zhaoyu xi Weizao" [Was the Senkaku Chain bequeathed to Sheng Xuanhuai? Academics say that Cixi Empress Dowager Ukaze giving Senkaku to Japan was fraudulent], *World Journal*, New York, September 28, 2003. See also Melody Chen, "Academics Waffle over Status of Tiaoyutai Islands," *Taipei Times*, September 28, 2003, p. 3, at *www.taipeitimes.com/News/taiwan/archives/2003/09/28/2003069556*, and Liu Yunxiang, "Zheng Diaoyutai, Guojifa bu Li Taiwan" [International Law not on Taiwan's side in Senkaku Diaoyutai Dispute], *China Times*, Taipei, September 28, 2003. One international legal scholar based in Taiwan says that ROC government maps dating as late as 1970 show the Senkakus as separate from China. See Lee Ming-juinn, "A Closer Look at the Tiaoyutai Debate," *Taipei Times*, October 3, 2002, p. 8, at *www.taipeitimes.com/News/edit/archives/2002/10/03/170528.*

[27]Ying-jeou Ma, *Legal Problems of Seabed Boundary Delimitation in the East China Sea* (Baltimore: University of Maryland School of Law, Occasional Papers/Reprints in Contemporary Asian Studies, 1984). The OPRSCAS series has since been changed to the Maryland Series in Contemporary Asian Studies MSCAS).

[28]"Zhong-Ri zheng youtian, Zhanjian dapao dui feiji, Jiefangjun paokou xiangxiang, Ri Dachen pi tiaoqi, jianyi buzhangje huitan jiejue," [PRC–Japan squabble over oilfield, Chinese Warships aim cannon at Japanese Aircraft and Ships, Japan PM slams Chinese provocation, Suggests Ministerial Level Summit to discuss resolving issue], *World Journal* (in Chinese), New York, October 3, 2005, p. A8.

Japan's U.N. Security Council Bid: An Affront to China's Status

In asserting Chinese preeminence in Asia, the Chinese leadership could see itself in a rivalry with Japan as Asia's leading economic and political power. Hence, China cannot abide Japan's quest for a permanent seat on the United Nations Security Council. Beijing believes that China alone is Asia's legitimate representative in the Council. It was therefore not surprising that China was a bit unhappy when Prime Minister Koizumi announced in August 2004 "the Japanese idea that there could be permanent (Security Council) members other than the current five, and that Japan could be one of them."[30]

Japan had a very good case. It is, after all, the world's second largest economy, as well as Asia's largest, and the second largest contributor to the U.N. treasury, to which points the Chinese Foreign Ministry spokesman replied:

> As to the membership fee and the historical question, first, the UN Security Council is not like a board of directors of a company. It is not composed according to the amount of contribution a country pays. Second...if a country wishes to play a responsible role in international affairs, it must have a clear understanding of the historical questions concerning itself.[31]

Japanese Chief Cabinet Secretary Hiroyuki Hosoda noted that he did not think "the other side would wait to recognize that Japan is a peaceful nation until the issue of history is resolved."[32] Regrettably, he was wrong. Yet, contrary to China's intemperate rhetoric about Japan's failure to deal with its World War II history, Japan's numerous apologies, made in numerous ways, are well documented (not to mention the facts that Japan has not threatened

---

[29]See "Joint Statement of the U.S.–Japan Security Consultative Committee," U.S. Department of State, February 19, 2005, at *www.state.gov/r/pa/prs/ps/2005/42490.htm*.

[30]Barney Jopson, "Koizumi to Step Up Campaign for Permanent Security Council Seat," *Financial Times*, August 25, 2004, p. 5.

[31]See transcript of PRC Foreign Ministry Spokesman Kong Quan's press conference, September 21, 2004, at *www.fmprc.gov.cn/eng/xwfw/2510/2511/t160214.htm*.

[32]"Japan Questions China's Raising History Over UNSC Bid," Kyodo News Agency, September 22, 2004.

anyone since 1945 and historically has earnestly sought good relations with the PRC).[33]

Attacking Japan's 20th century wartime behavior has become a central point in Beijing's propaganda offensive against a Japanese Security Council seat. By March 2005, Chinese Internet Web sites sponsored by the official Xinhua News Agency had gathered over 7 million signatures against Japan's seat—or so they claimed.[34] Ultimately, the Chinese claimed that nearly 24 million signatures had been collected by dozens of different Web sites.

The Chinese have been able to seize on Prime Minister Koizumi's repeated visits to Japan's Yasakuni Shrine, a memorial to Japan's World War II dead, as evidence of Japan's alleged "insincerity," and this has resonated with some audiences in the United States because the exhibits in a museum attached to the shrine indicate no shame whatsoever with respect to Japan's World War II record. Nonetheless, given the background of the Yasakuni visits and China's intemperate rhetoric on the matter, one cannot help but suspect that China's prime purpose is to gain leverage for propaganda purposes rather than to reflect true popular indignation in China.[35]

Rather than quietly veto the bid in the Security Council, however, the Beijing regime sought to manufacture (or at best to stir up) violent public resentment toward Japan. China's new naval aggressiveness in Japanese territorial waters throughout 2005 dovetailed neatly with its violent, state-directed anti-Japanese campaigns of March and April. Those demonstrations were complete with police-supplied buses that ferried stone-throwing crowds to the Japanese embassy in Beijing and public security officers who sat idly by while rioters smashed windows at Japanese firms in cities across China.[36] The Chinese leadership's entire anti-Japan campaign seemed animated by a feral urge to demonstrate China's new predominance over

---

[33]Senior Japanese leaders, including the emperor, prime ministers, and foreign ministers, have issued rather heartfelt expressions of apology, sorrow, remorse, and grief at least 48 times since the Japan–China normalization in 1972. On April 22, 2005, the Japanese prime minister told an audience in Indonesia that "Japan squarely faces these facts of history in a spirit of humility. And with feelings of deep remorse and heartfelt apology always engraved in mind, Japan has resolutely maintained, consistently since the end of World War II, never turning into a military power but an economic power." See Raymond Bonner and Norimitsu Onishi, "Japan's Chief Apologizes for War Misdeeds," *The New York Times*, April 23, 2005, p. A3, at *www.nytimes.com/2005/04/23/international/asia/23japan.html*.

[34]"Fan Ri 'Changren' Da chuangsheng, Dalu Wangzhan qianming dizhi, yi jin qibaiwan ren" [Outcry against Japan's 'permanent seat,' Mainland websites sign in resistance, nearly seven million signatures], *Shijie Ribao*, New York, March 28, 2005, p. A9.

Japan in Asia and, not incidentally, to test the limits of the U.S.–Japan mutual security treaty.

Confronted with Beijing's hostile reaction to what was very clearly a reasonable bid by Tokyo for a permanent U.N. Security Council seat, the Koizumi government in Japan called a halt to Tokyo's traditional solicitude toward Beijing. By mid-2006, public opinion surveys showed that over half of all Japanese supported constitutional changes that would allow Japan to play a greater role in international affairs, and a significant majority wanted Japanese troops to participate in international peacekeeping efforts.[37]

---

[35]Japanese prime ministers began visiting Yasakuni on a regular basis in 1951, and those visits continued through 1979, albeit without any mention of whether they were "official" or private. Prime Minister Miki announced on August 15, 1975, that his visits were "private in nature." No one outside of Japan took particular notice, least of all the Chinese, who had their own problems with the "Great Proletarian Cultural Revolution" and the "Gang of Four." Mysteriously, in 1978, the names of Class-A war criminals (the leading militarists who were charged with starting the war) materialized on Yasakuni rolls, although, again, there was no notice until 1979, when it was the topic of a news article. Prime Minister Ohira made a "private" visit to the shrine in 1979, and Prime Ministers Ohira and Suzuki made several visits to Yasakuni between 1979 and 1983. During 1983–1984, Prime Minister Yasuhiro Nakasone made eight visits to Yasakuni, all without drawing any notice whatsoever from China. On the morning of April 22, 1985, Nakasone made his ninth visit to Yasakuni and then had lunch with visiting Chairman of the Chinese National People's Congress (and Politburo Standing Comitteeman) Peng Zhen. Again, Nakasone's visit drew no reaction from China. On August 15, 1985, Nakasone announced that he had made an "official" visit to Yasakuni, at which point there was a Chinese protest. Behind the scenes, Chinese diplomats apparently urged Japan to tone down the visit because it was embarrassing to then-Communist Party General Secretary Hu Yaobang, who at the time was the Chinese leadership's main proponent of good ties with Japan. At this point, Japan's chief cabinet secretary pledged that the prime minister would refrain from making "official" visits to Yasakuni (specifically referring to the August 15, 1985, visit) but made no comment on "private visits" or visits on any other date. China's recent edginess about visits to Yasakuni seems to stem from Jiang Zemin's abortive visit to Japan in October 1998, when the Japanese resisted changing their Taiwan policy to include a formula similar to U.S. President Bill Clinton's "Three No's" on Taiwan, announced in July 1998. Chinese leaders launched a relentless campaign on Japan's supposed failure to face up to its history.

Taiwan's Role in U.S.–Japan Security Cooperation

Taiwan needs forces that are complementary with the naval and air forces of the United States and Japan. In particular, Taiwan needs naval and air forces that can operate and communicate in real time together with any naval and air forces of the United States and Japan that will be operating in a theater of battle. Just as Japan is becoming a "normal" nation—i.e., one with a defense force that makes sense for Japan in the 21st century post–Cold War world—Taiwan should normalize its military establishment to make it suited to an island nation that is threatened by aircraft and missile attacks and a submarine blockade.

If Taiwan's weapons systems and warfighters are not interoperable with friendly forces, Taiwan essentially will be forced to fight alone. A non-interoperable Taiwan military force alters the PLA's calculus to assume that a blitz attack could succeed. If Taiwan does little to enable interoperability and complementarity with U.S. and Japanese forces, the U.S. calculus might assume that it is not practical to join in operations with Taiwan forces. This calculus could also affect a political decision to become involved in combat in the first place. However, if Taiwan, Japan, and the U.S. are seen as having interoperational capacities, the deterrent effect on China's calculus is heightened.

Taiwan has been a central concern of the U.S.–Japan alliance at least since 1960. A confidential U.S.–Japan understanding of that year placed Taiwan within the scope of the U.S.–Japan mutual security treaty, and the 1997 U.S.–Japan joint defense guidelines certainly contemplated a confrontation with China as one of the "emergency situation[s] in areas surrounding Japan."[38] The implication was strong that Japanese self-defense forces would be used in direct support of U.S. operations against China in the event of a Chinese attack on Taiwan. On February 19, 2005, the U.S. Secretary of State and Secretary of Defense joined their Japanese counterparts in a formal declaration of "Common Strategic Objectives" of

---

[36]For an account of the Chinese government's complicity in anti-Japanese violence, see Joseph Kahn, "China Is Pushing and Scripting Anti-Japanese Protests," *The New York Times*, April 15, 2005, at *www.nytimes.com/2005/04/15/international/asia/15china.html*.

[37]"A Giant Stirs, a Region Bridles," *The Economist*, May 13, 2006, p. 26.

[38]The Japanese government has refused to define the geographical scope of "areas surrounding Japan." Instead, it has said that the term covers any location that would "seriously affect the peace and security of Japan." See "What's What in Review of Defense Guidelines," briefing sheet prepared by *The Daily Yomiuri / Yomiuri Shimbun*, September 23, 1997.

the alliance that included "[e]ncourag[ing] the peaceful resolution of issues concerning the Taiwan Strait through dialogue."[39]

America's Quasi-Alliance with Taiwan

Taiwan itself has a "quasi-alliance" with the United States by virtue of Section 2(b)(6) of America's Taiwan Relations Act, which articulates a formal defense commitment to Taiwan.[40] This commitment is arguably even more binding than the one embodied in the now-defunct U.S.–Republic of China mutual defense treaty,[41] but it is not a formal, two-way commitment, and within the context of the formal U.S.–Japan alliance, Taiwan is somewhat of an anomaly. Taiwan has no conditional obligations under the Taiwan Relations Act, unlike Japan, which is at least obliged to "act in accordance with its constitutional provisions and processes" if U.S. troops are attacked "in the territories under the administration of Japan."[42]

Facing a rising China that is emerging as a peer-competitor superpower on the Eurasian landmass, the United States and (indirectly) Japan benefit strategically from their existing relationship with Taiwan.[43] They would benefit even more from a defense and security relationship that is considerably closer and more coordinated than it is now.

There are obvious geographic advantages in having Taiwan as a "virtual ally." It sits astride the major sea-lanes between the west coast of the United

---

[39]See "Joint Statement of the U.S.–Japan Security Consultative Committee," February 19, 2005.

[40]Section 2(b)(6) of the Taiwan Relations Act (P.L. 98–6, enacted April 10, 1979) reads: "It is the Policy of the United States to maintain the capacity of the United States to resist any resort to force or other forms of coercion that would jeopardize the security, or the social or economic system, of the people of Taiwan." Section 3(c) directs that "the President and the Congress shall determine, in accordance with constitutional processes, appropriate action by the United States in response to any such danger."

[41]Mutual Defense Treaty Between the United States of America and the Republic of China, signed in Washington, D.C., December 2, 1954, at *www.taiwandocuments.org/mutual01.htm*. Article II of the MDT specifies that "the Parties separately and jointly…will maintain and develop their individual and collective capacity to resist armed attack and communist subversive activity directed from without against their territorial integrity and political stability." Article V states that each Party will "act to meet the common danger in accordance with its constitutional processes."

[42]Treaty of Mutual Cooperation and Security Between Japan and the United States of America," signed in Washington, D.C., January 19, 1960, at *www.mofa.go.jp/region/n-america/us/q&a/ref/1.html*.

States and East Asia, as well as Japan's vital sea-lanes to the Middle East. A key tenet of America's security strategy in the Western Pacific was articulated six decades ago by General Douglas MacArthur: The United States, as the world's preeminent maritime power, must be able to secure the Pacific Ocean against hostile forces, and that can be done only if America can keep "Island Asia" out of the hands of "Mainland Asia."[44]

In the year ending August 15, 2002, a total of 259,086 civilian aircraft transited the Taiwan Air Defense Identification Zone (ADIZ), while 246,015 commercial ships transited the Taiwan Strait and the East Taiwan maritime route.[45] During the same period, People's Liberation Army Air Force (PLAAF) aircraft made 1,379 sorties over the Taiwan Strait (none in East Taiwan airspace), for an average of nearly four sorties a day, while the PLA Navy conducted 6,825 sorties through the Strait and five off eastern Taiwan.[46] At the same time, a Chinese hydrographic vessel on a reconnaissance mission was sighted in Pacific Ocean waters within Taiwan's 12-mile territorial limit.[47] The same vessel reportedly had been in Taiwan's southeastern waters.

The United States already gains from Taiwan's surveillance, intelligence, and reconnaissance potential. There appears to be mature and robust intelligence collection cooperation between the two countries that in recent years has proven useful in processing real-time data on Chinese military operations.

Since the Taiwan Strait missile crisis of March 1996, the U.S. Navy has been collecting hydrographic data in the Taiwan Strait, Bashi Channel (between Taiwan and the Philippines), northern Taiwan, and the deep ocean Luzon Ridge drop off Taiwan's east coast. Apparently with Taiwan's military cooperation, the U.S. Navy utilizes a system called "NOWcast" for surface and subsea measurements that produce "range-dependent acoustic propagation profiles, sound channel positions, bottom bounce path profiles, submarine diving depth surveys and undersea terrain studies" in a three-dimensional forecast for U.S. naval operational movements. Evidently, during the 1996 crisis, the U.S. Navy found that it had little familiarity with the hydrographic environment of the Strait and vowed that it would not be blindsided in future Taiwan Strait deployments.[48]

---

[43]See Nancy Tucker, "If Taiwan Chooses Unification, Should the United States Care?" *The Washington Quarterly*, Summer 2002, p. 22. Tucker notes that Chinese control of Taiwan would alarm Japanese military planners, giving China a presence along Japan's shipping routes and abutting its Ryukyu island chain. Control of Taiwan would "in fact lead to a more significant projection of Chinese naval and air power beyond coastal waters."

Taiwan attempted its own seabed acoustic sensor network with assistance from U.S. Navy technicians in 1982. The system, called "Longyan" (Dragon Eye), was tested in Taiwan's eastern waters where its sensors would be protected somewhat from malicious damage from PRC fishing trawlers. Its mission was to detect submarines approaching Taiwan from the east. Exactly how successful the program has been is classified. Suffice it to say that it is an indicator of an ongoing and rather robust program of U.S.–Taiwan cooperation in submarine surveillance.

The same cannot be said for Taiwan–Japan intelligence cooperation. In November 2004, Taiwan's military informed Japan's quasi-official office in Taipei that they had identified a Chinese nuclear submarine in Japanese territorial waters.[49] The Taiwan media reports, however, embarrassed the Japanese government, which responded that its own Japan Defense Agency (JDA) forces had already identified the vessel and did not need Taiwan's help.[50] The fact that the Taiwan government publicized its purported intelligence cooperation with Japan underscores two things: (1) there is significant potential in such cooperation, but (2) if it exists, Taiwan cannot be trusted to keep a secret.

To the extent that there is any Taiwan–Japan intelligence, surveillance, or reconnaissance cooperation, it is indirect and through U.S. channels. Over the past several years, there have been sporadic reports in the Taiwan press

---

[44]For the definitive articulation of this strategy, see General Douglas MacArthur's "Farewell Address to Congress," delivered April 19, 1951. The relevant text reads: "The Pacific no longer represents menacing avenues of approach for a prospective invader. It assumes, instead, the friendly aspect of a peaceful lake. Our line of defense is a natural one and can be maintained with a minimum of military effort and expense. It envisions no attack against anyone, nor does it provide the bastions essential for offensive operations, but properly maintained, would be an invincible defense against aggression. The holding of this littoral defense line in the western Pacific is entirely dependent upon holding all segments thereof; for any major breach of that line by an unfriendly power would render vulnerable to determined attack every other major segment. This is a military estimate as to which I have yet to find a military leader who will take exception. For that reason, I have strongly recommended in the past, as a matter of military urgency, that under no circumstances must Formosa fall under Communist control. Such an eventuality would at once threaten the freedom of the Philippines and the loss of Japan and might well force our western frontier back to the coast of California, Oregon and Washington." The full text of the speech is available at *www.americanrhetoric.com/speeches/douglasmacarthurfarewelladdress.htm*.

[45]Briefing for members of the Trilateral Conference by the Ministry of National Defense, Taiwan, August 26, 2002, PowerPoint presentation, p. 7 of 16 pp.

[46]*Ibid.* Totals do not include fishing vessels or domestic Taiwanese aircraft.

about intelligence cooperation arrangements between the United States and Taiwan that have been in place for over 20 years, including a "major signals intelligence facility in cooperation with the US National Security Agency (NSA) on Taipei's suburban Yangmingshan Mountain" that is identified as a "data processing center." At the time of this report, the NSA had just completed a five-year upgrade and training program, "which features the development, design, implementation and operation of a variety of special-purpose telecom and data processing systems."[51]

Taiwan intelligence reportedly also supplied the United States with full data transcripts of the April 1, 2001, collision of an EP-3 with a PRC jet fighter, which reinforced American insistence that the U.S. plane was on autopilot at the time of the collision and the Chinese fighter had rammed the U.S. craft.[52] Separately, in December 2000, a secret Pentagon report recommended that the U.S. should improve its understanding of how both sides of the Taiwan Strait view the military balance. A "highly sensitive military observer"—apparently a civilian source—was reported to have "discovered" that U.S.–Taiwan military and intelligence exchanges had steadily improved since the May 20, 2000, inauguration of Taiwan President Chen Shui-bian.

In August 2000, a delegation of Pentagon specialists, advisers, and defense contractors made a low-key visit to Taiwan to review how Taiwan could best deploy a long-range radar system that the United States had

---

[47]"Spy Ship off Southern Coast," *Taipei Times* Internet edition, August 9, 2003, p. 1, at *www.taipeitimes.com/News/front/archives/2003/08/09/2003062884*.

[48]Brian Hsu, "Military Needs Better Data on Maritime Conditions," *Taipei Times*, February 18, 2003, p. 4, at *www.taipeitimes.com/News/taiwan/archives/2003/02/18/195006*.

[49]Chen Shichang, "Dalu Qianjian chuang Ri linghai, Zhuan Tai Tongbao, Fushi Dianshi Baodao, Fangweiting Fengsheng Wenji Ke duanding shi Dalu Hanji Heqianjian" [Taiwan said to have alerted Japan to presence of Chinese submarine in Japanese waters, Fuji TV reports that Self Defense could determine from profile that vessel was Chinese Han Class nuclear submarine], *World Journal*, New York, November 12, 2004, p. 3.

[50]Melody Chen, "Taiwan 'Regrets' Japan's Stance on Sub," *Taipei Times*, November 27, 2004, p. 3, at *www.taipeitimes.com/News/taiwan/archives/2004/11/27/2003212741*.

[51]Wu Chongtao, "Zhanshi Guofang Zazhi: Tai Mei Hezuo dui Zhonggong jinzing Dianzi Qingsou" [Janes Defense Magazine: Taiwan–US carry out electronic intelligence collection against the PRC], *China Times*, Taipei, January 29, 2001. See also Brian Hsu, "Taiwan and US Jointly Spying on China: Report," *Taipei Times*, January 30, 2001, at *www.taipeitimes.com/news/2001/01/30/story/0000071597*.

approved during an earlier defense consultation session in Washington. That radar system apparently would be linked with U.S. satellite data to provide additional ballistic missile launch warning, perhaps as much as seven minutes, for Taiwan's theater missile defense units, such as they are.[53]

In November 2000, in the last months of the Clinton Administration, two separate Pentagon delegations made secret visits to Taiwan, including one to Quemoy. Taiwan Ministry of National Defense (MND) officials who accompanied the Americans refused to offer any views on such sensitive questions as whether it might be "possible to withdraw garrisons from Quemoy and Matsu" and "are there any plans to deploy missiles [on the islands]?" The other Pentagon group carried out confidential consultations with Taiwan Navy Headquarters, General Staff Headquarters, and the MND. Other "reliable sources" said that U.S.–Taiwan intelligence exchanges are currently handled in two channels: one via the MND and the General Staff Headquarters (under the Bureau of Military Intelligence) and the other through the National Security Bureau under Taiwan's National Security Council (NSC). During a classified briefing of the Legislative Yuan budget committee in the winter of 2000, Taiwan National Security Bureau Director Ting Yu-chou said that "improving the capabilities of Taiwan's intelligence work in the coming fiscal year centers on two major tasks, international intelligence cooperation [and cross-Strait matters]."[54]

American defense cooperation with Taiwan is not limited to intelligence collection. The U.S. Pacific Command will also benefit (if it does not do so already) from early warning coverage of mainland China that will be available (if it is not already) from advanced radar stations in Taiwan.[55] In October 2002, the PLA Navy redeployed a *Luhu*-Class guided-missile frigate from the North Sea Fleet to the Zhanjiang base of the South Sea Fleet, ordering it for the first time to transit waters off the east coast of Taiwan,

---

[52]See Liu Ping, "Meijiyuan Baogao, Qianzheng Taiwan Qingbao" [U.S. Aviators' reports confirmed by Taiwan intelligence], *China Times*, Taipei, April 18, 2001.

[53]"US to 'Conditionally' Share Military Data with Taiwan," Agence France-Presse, October 7, 2002, at *www.taiwansecurity.org/AFP/2002/AFP-100702-1.htm*. The article states: "Once linked to the US satellite system codenamed 'Defense Support Project' (DSP), Taiwan would be able to allow up to seven more minutes in advance while its Patriot anti-missile weaponry prepared to intercept any incoming missiles." In addition, the "Taiwan military plans to set up ground stations over the next five years to plug the island's Patriot systems to the US military satellite system."

[54]See Wu Chongtao, "Wuerling zhihou, Tai Mei Junshi Jiaoliu Mingxian 'Sheng-wen'" [Post–May 20, Taiwan–US military exchanges clearly 'warm up'], *China Times*, Taipei, December 20, 2000.

maintaining a distance of about 180 nautical miles. Taiwan media reports indicated that Taiwan, Japanese, and American naval planners closely monitored the PLAN naval deployments through Japanese and Taiwan waters and consider Taiwan to be part of the "First Island Chain" of defense.[56] Two weeks later, the Chinese intelligence surveillance vessel *Xiangyanghong* No. 14, a hydrographic survey ship that belongs to China's State Oceanic Administration, loitered in Taiwan territorial waters within 10 kilometers of Orchid Island, apparently developing seabed maps for Chinese submarine operations.[57]

American defense industries, of course, benefit from the pay-as-you-go relationship with Taiwan's military, which has been America's second best customer (after Saudi Arabia) for defense equipment and services every year for the past 10 years, including $1.4 billion in deliveries in FY 2002, $592 million in FY 2003, and $962 million in FY 2004.[58] The increasing Chinese military threat to Taiwan has made it easier for the Bush Administration to justify providing Taiwan with higher and higher levels of technology, and Taiwan has become an important partner in financing American defense research and development.

Moreover, if Taiwan should ever decide to finance the 2001 arms package announced by President Bush in April 2001, the U.S. Administration would be in a position to consider more advanced defense articles and services for Taiwan, including the AEGIS destroyer system. There is every indication that the United States would welcome Taiwan's participation in the next-

---

[55]Zhang Lifang, "Yujing Leida Shenru Dalu Sanqian li" [Early Warning Radar can see 3000 km into Mainland], *Central Daily News*, Taipei, April 19, 2000. See also Wang Jionghua, "Changcheng Yujing Leida Suoxiaoxing kezaoqi Zhenze Daodan" [Long Range Radar attenuation can give early detection of guided missiles], *Central Daily News*, Taipei, April 19, 2000; "PAVE PAWS Zaoqi Yijing Leida, Mei Kongjun fandaodan Yujing Hexin Zhuangbei" [PAVE PAWS early warning radar, core equipment to US Anti-missile warning], *China Times*, Taipei, April 19, 2000; and Lyu Zhaolong "Huamei Junshou Huiyi Benzhou Dengchang" [US–Taiwan Arms Sales Meeting held here this week], *China Times*, Taipei, June 7, 2000.

[56]Lyu Zhaolong, "Zhonggong dan [sic] Jian chuangyue 'Diyi Daolian' Yi zai Shitan" [PRC ship penetrates 'First Island Chain' in exploratory move], *China Times* Internet edition, October 31, 2002.

[57]Brian Hsu, "Chinese Spy Ship in Taiwan Waters," *Taipei Times* Internet edition, November 4, 2002, at *www.taipeitimes.com/news/2002/11/04/story/000017825*.

[58]See U.S. Department of Defense, Security Assistance Agency, *Facts Book: Foreign Military Sales, Foreign Military Construction Sales and Foreign Military Assistance Facts as of September 30, 2004*, at *www.dsca.mil/programs/biz-ops/2004_facts/facts%20book%202004.pdf*.

generation Joint Strike Fighter program as a development partner.[59] Taiwan should also be in the market for a "gap-filler" fighter aircraft as its F-16 fleet ages.

There is a tremendous—but as yet unrealized—potential for Taiwan to contribute to American and Japanese strategic interests in the Western Pacific, and vice versa; but both Washington and Tokyo are hamstrung by exaggerated concerns for Beijing's "one China" sensitivities and cannot quite bring themselves to expand their intelligence, surveillance, and reconnaissance cooperation with Taiwan. For its part, Taipei has three very bad habits that compromise its standing with its American and Japanese defense partners.

First, leaks regularly reveal the extent of Taiwan's existing military and intelligence interactions with Washington and Tokyo—revelations that have the unhelpful effect of irritating Beijing and, in turn, antagonizing Taipei's partners in America and Japan.

Second, Taiwan gives the impression that it is not taking seriously its own responsibilities for defense. Coastal defense has eroded; command and control centers, submarine bases, air strips, communications nodes, fuel and supply storage facilities, and the like go unhardened; conscription terms for draftees have been shortened; and numbers of professional pilots and engineering and technical personnel have been allowed to decline.

Third, a persistent lack of consensus on defense paralyzes decisions on the procurement of key defensive items (PAC-3 air defense missiles, diesel-electric submarines, and P-3C anti–submarine warfare aircraft). This paralysis has become an irritant in Washington even as Taiwan remains one of America's top customers for defense articles and services.

Although Taiwan is the proximate beneficiary the U.S.–Japan alliance's "common strategic objective" of ensuring a "peaceful resolution of issues concerning the Taiwan Strait," both the U.S. and Japan have significant strategic interests of their own in a Taiwan that is well beyond China's political or military influence. China's increased naval assertiveness in the Taiwan Strait and the Senkaku Islands—areas that are both strategically and militarily important to all four players—is symptomatic of a widening Chinese military posture in the East China Sea.

Japan and the U.S. already engage in broad defense cooperation in weapons development (AEGIS, missile defense, fighter aircraft); in ISR (intelligence, surveillance, and reconnaissance) interface; and in Afghanistan and Iraq. Taiwan has the potential to contribute quite

---

[59]Private conversations with U.S. officials. See also Sofia Wu, "Plan to Lease AV8b Fighters Never Got off the Ground: ROC Air Force," Central News Agency, Taipei, March 11, 2002.

significantly to the U.S.–Japan effort to support freedom and democracy in Asia, and both Washington and Tokyo should let it do so. However, Taipei must not trumpet its contributions until they become significant, routine, and more valuable to its partners than Beijing's political sensitivities are. In short, Washington and Tokyo will have to toughen their hides to Beijing's complaints, and Taipei will have to remain cooperative and quiet, at least for a few years.

Taiwan Security Trends: Conflict or Consensus?

The past several decades have brought tremendous political and security changes to Taiwan, and internal forces and external pressures are pushing the island in many different directions. Taiwan's strategic planners clearly see the military threats that they face and are pressing ahead bravely, but their biggest challenge is bridging the crevasse in the underlying political—in fact, existential—consensus that undermines their struggle to strengthen their defenses and their position in Asia. Much has been accomplished in the decade since 1996, but much also remains to be done. As Taiwan's security falls into the shadow of an increasingly modernized Peoples Liberation Army, the need to adapt is ever more urgent.

Thus far, Taiwan's MND has made progress in its efforts to modernize the military. Embedded traditions and legacy ideology are giving way to a military that is increasingly adaptable, coordinated, and relevant. The transition from a posture that relies heavily on ground forces to one that embraces air and naval power is a notable accomplishment. The process of moving from a conscripted to an all-volunteer military force is also underway and should help the MND to generate a more professional, dedicated, and better-trained work force.

Additionally, the major investments being made in Taiwan's Po-Sheng Project, aimed at standardizing Taiwan's C4I (command, control, communications, computers, and intelligence) architecture to ensure multiple redundant communications nodes, mutually intelligible software codes, common transmission bandwidths and broadcast frequency standards, etc., will serve as a force multiplier. As the Po-Sheng program moves steadily toward its 2009 full operational capability (FOC) phase, Taiwan's aspiration to network-centric warfare capabilities is becoming realized. These innovations in Taiwan's fighting forces are paving the way for a smaller and more effective military and a more sharply honed defense capability.

The March 2002 implementation of Taiwan's National Defense Law and Defense Organization Law was also a positive development. These two laws helped to restructure the Ministry of National Defense and are facilitating modern defense reforms in a systematic and orderly manner. The statutory changes focused on two fundamental goals: the privatization of most production and maintenance operations, previously undertaken by the uniformed services themselves, and the encouragement of strategic alliances in order to bring in new technologies to improve Taiwan's defensive operations. The law also committed Taiwan to transforming its military into a professional and functional defense organization by dividing the defense system into three separate operational mechanisms: policy, command, and armaments. The two laws have served as a platform from which Taiwan has made significant strides toward modernization.

There has also been significant progress in military-to-military interaction, exchanges, and policy relations between the United States and Taiwan. The effort to strengthen defense relations with Taiwan began slowly and quietly in 1997 during the Clinton Administration under then-Deputy Assistant Secretary of Defense Kurt Campbell and has grown significantly since then. The establishment of the Monterey Talks in that year was an important part of the U.S.–Taiwan security partnership. The talks encompass an annual bilateral flag-officer and sub–cabinet-level review of Asia's strategic situation, Taiwan's defense needs, and overall military doctrine and theater planning by senior U.S. national security and defense officers and their Taiwanese counterparts. From these talks have sprung bilateral war games that have given focus to U.S. defense assistance for Taiwan. The replacement of retired military officials at the American Institute in Taiwan (AIT) office in Taipei with active-duty U.S. military officers is another important gesture of Washington's growing commitment to democratic Taiwan.

Over the past decade, Taiwan has made efforts to modernize its physical capabilities as well. The procurement of *Kidd*-class destroyers, F-16s, Patriot Modified Air Defense Systems (MADS) for ballistic missile defense, E-2T AWACS-type airborne warning and command aircraft, a "Pave Paws" phased-array surveillance radar program, and many other systems is a strong sign that many in Taiwan take national security very seriously.

Unfortunately, support for this type of strong defense is neither universal nor even the consensus in Taiwan. Ongoing and consistent reductions in Taiwan's annual defense budget and the obstructionist attitude toward meeting basic weapons requirements on the part of opposition parties in the Legislative Yuan present major security challenges. Political partisanship has severely compromised Taiwan's military modernization objectives, and a general lack of consensus and failure of leadership have undermined defense spending as a national priority. These shortcomings jeopardize the maintenance of an effective military balance of cross-Strait power and are serious impediments to the island's ability to control its own destiny.

For a long time, arms sales have been inexorably intertwined with U.S.–Taiwan relations. Procurement of defense systems has been a powerful factor in both military (in the operational abilities of the systems purchased) and political (as a demonstration of commitment to the U.S.–Taiwan security relationship) ties between the two countries.

The 1992 case of the F-16 fighter aircraft sale to Taiwan is an excellent example of the deliverables that come from such sales. Throughout the 1980s, Taiwan had sought a next-generation fighter to replace its obsolescent F-5s and other platforms that date from the Vietnam war era. Virtually all defense planners in Washington and Taipei agreed that the basic F-16 A/B model was an ideal weapons platform, given its durability in air combat and limited potential for offensive strikes deep into China, and fit the Taiwan Relations Act criterion "to provide Taiwan with arms of a defensive character." Even so, the approved sale of F-16s to Taiwan in 1992 was considered highly controversial at the time. Both the Reagan and Bush Administrations had resisted Taiwan's repeated requests for the F-16. The Reagan Pentagon instead supported a plan to develop an indigenous infrastructure in Taiwan so that it could build its own F-16 class of fighter interceptors, and by the early 1990s, Taiwan was producing the "Ching-kuo" indigenously developed fighter (IDF) under the supervision of General Dynamics.

However, in 1992, several new forces converged to impel President George H. W. Bush's Administration to approve Taiwan's request for the F-16: China signed an order for 48 high-performance Sukhoi-27 fighters from Russia; France promised to sell Taiwan Mirage 2000-5s as the solution to its need for a new fighter; and President Bush faced domestic business pressure in his home state of Texas, where the F-16s were assembled. Senator Lloyd Bentsen (D–TX) charged that President Bush's kowtowing to the demands of the Chinese Communists in Beijing, who were still in disfavor because of the Tiananmen Square massacre of June 4, 1989, would cost Texas thousands of jobs. The General Dynamics F-16 production line in Fort Worth was running out of back-orders. President Bush made a virtue out of necessity by approving the Taiwan F-16 sale.

Bush's decision was intended to preempt the French deal. Approval of the F-16 sale left Taiwan suddenly with an embarrassment of riches. Taiwan signed the order for 150 F-16s, which meant that the Texas production line was saved (although the decision was not enough to keep President Bush in the Oval Office), but went ahead and ordered 60 Mirage 2000-5s as well, ensuring its air superiority in fourth-generation fighter aircraft over the Taiwan Strait for another decade. It was a massive defense sale that brought with it a foreign market for U.S. goods, a renewed commitment to the TRA, stronger Taiwanese defense capabilities, and an important and positive development in U.S.–Taiwan relations, which had experienced considerable strains through much of the 1980s.

Through the 1990s, Taiwan received all of the 150 F-16 A/Bs and 60 Mirage 2000-5s that it ordered. The F-16 program brought together industry, government, and both the U.S. and Taiwan militaries in equipping, training, and deploying the Taiwan military's most sophisticated platforms at that time. (It should be noted, however, that France was unable to withstand Chinese pressure to cease all further arms sales to Taiwan and—in a diplomatic concession that Paris had not been obliged to make when it normalized relations with Beijing in 1964—even wound up signing a new communiqué with China formally recognizing that "Taiwan is part of China.")

The F-16 program provided important momentum into the late 1990s that enabled the Department of Defense to begin to expand the depth and breadth of military ties between the island and the U.S. It also demonstrated Taiwan's commitment to its own defense and recognition of the need to provide significantly for its security. Finally, it was a demonstration for Taiwan of America's ongoing commitment to act as the ultimate guarantor of Taiwan's self-determination. The 1980s had generated so many new insecurities for Taiwan that such a display of support, over significant Chinese objections, was very important. The F-16 sale is a good example of the psychic, as well as military, benefits that flow from Taiwan's procurement of U.S. defense articles and services.

The Defense Budget Deadlock

Conversely, Taiwan's more recent domestic political squabbling over the procurement of American defense items has had the opposite effect. In April 2001, faced with a Chinese military buildup in the Taiwan Strait that was much faster than expected, President George W. Bush approved a number of long-standing Taiwan requests for more advanced weapons systems and platforms.

The "Big Bang" arms package approved by President Bush was the largest single tranche of defense equipment ever approved for Taiwan. It included four *Kidd*-class destroyers, eight diesel submarines designed to counter naval blockades and seaborne invasions, 12 P–3C Orion aircraft, and Paladin self-propelled artillery systems valued at the time at $4 billion. (The cost of the submarine package alone is now considered to be over $10 billion.) Moreover, sometime in 2004 or early 2005, the White House was to have reviewed Taiwan's request for *Arleigh Burke*–class destroyers outfitted with the AEGIS system, which is able to perform search and missile-guidance functions and can track 100 or more targets simultaneously—a package that could easily top $4 billion all by itself. (Inclusion of the *Kidd* destroyers in the "Big Bang" obliged the Bush Administration to defer the AEGIS sale.)

Under its new statutory budgeting requirements, Taiwan's Defense Ministry worked overtime for two years to prepare the highly complex and detailed funding proposals for the largest "Big Bang" systems. The Ministry's overlord, the Executive Yuan, forwarded a special budget request for several of the systems to the Legislative Yuan in June of 2004. Thirty months later, in January 2007, the request still sat in the Legislative Yuan's Procedural Committee after having been rejected 67 times.

The legislature's "Pan-Green" coalition, led by President Chen Shui-bian's Democratic Progressive Party (DPP), has attempted to convince the opposition that the package is vital to Taiwan's security, but legislators of the "Pan-Blue" coalition, led by the Kuomintang party, rejected not only the package, but also the methodology of using a special budget. At the demand of key legislators, the MND has been obliged to break out the proposals and meld them into the regular fiscal submission, but there is little hope that pro-China legislators will ever approve the systems. Disappointingly, the special budget bill never even made it to the Legislative Yuan's Defense Committee for debate. Taiwan's Blue lawmakers continue to argue that the DPP is buying ineffective platforms and have used the special-budget method of funding the three major "Big Bang" procurements to avoid politically painful budget allocation decisions.

Although it is true that, for a government not used to deficit financing, a growing government debt creates a psychological environment that makes behemoth weapons systems procurement politically difficult, the DPP argues that financial sacrifices must be made when the integrity of Taiwan's security is at stake. The fact that it was the KMT itself that requested the systems in the first place when it ruled Taiwan prior to the 2000 presidential elections apparently is no longer a persuasive factor for the KMT or its Blue allies in the Legislative Yuan.

Taiwan's Struggle for Consensus on Defense

As a result of this ongoing debate, Taiwan's force modernization is under a new threat that has little to do with the superficial issues currently souring the debate over specific weapons systems. The superficial factors were such arguments as the illegality of a "defensive referendum" on missile defense that failed in March 2004, the dubious economic calculus of how much an "adequate" defense should cost, and finger-pointing about the timing of, and mechanisms for, budget requests for critical systems such as those in the proposed special budget. Instead, there is a far more profound threat to

Taiwan's defense modernization: a fundamental split between the Green and Blue sides over the underlying purpose of Taiwan's national defense.

The core of Kuomintang military strategy was the eight-decade rivalry with the Chinese Communist Party, which began with Chiang Kai-shek's purge of Communist Party members from KMT ranks in 1927. The KMT focused on ultimately defeating the Communists on the mainland of China by defending their island stronghold on the island of Taiwan. For the KMT, the Republic of China's territory encompasses all of China including Taiwan. After the KMT fled to Taiwan in 1949, its strong defense posture focused first on repelling a Communist invasion and then on the supposition that the ROC would one day reinvade the mainland, defeating the Communist armies and bringing all of China under ROC sovereignty. Through the 1980s, that history evolved into a doctrine that a strong defense was necessary to ensure that Taiwan's interests were defended and that, because weakness could result in coercion and unfavorable terms, any negotiation with Communist China over the final outcome of the Chinese civil war must be conducted from a position of military strength.

As Taiwan's democracy evolved in the 1990s and into the new century, however, a new view of Taiwan's military and of the need for a strong and credible defense for the island has emerged. The Pan-Greens agree that the role of Taiwan's military is to guarantee the viability and sovereignty of the "Republic of China," not with an eye to eventual negotiation and reconciliation with China, but as a necessity to guarantee Taiwan's *de facto* independence today and to ensure a possibility of full *de jure* independence tomorrow. Without a credible defense, the Pan-Greens understand that the window for Taiwan's survival as a democracy free of Beijing's authority is closing.

Thus, in today's debate on national security, there may be consensus among the two largest parties that Taiwan requires some defensive capacity, but the two political camps are still in opposite corners about democratic Taiwan's ultimate fate. Philosophically, this problem is particularly acute for the KMT, whose party history is intertwined with the military, whose leadership ranks are still dominated by KMT adherents. Taiwan's "independence" from China is inconceivable to the KMT's leaders, yet they recognize that Pan-Green support for military procurement, transformation, and modernization is central to the Greens' goal of Taiwan's formal independence—if not today, then at some time in the future.

As long as this gulf exists, it will be an insuperable barrier to any Blue–Green consensus on funding and support for Taiwan's legitimate defense needs. Indeed, Taiwan's people need to be better educated on defense policies, doctrine, and goals if they are ever to make informed choices or elect officials that are able to formulate a new consensus. It is, however, unrealistic to hope for a consensus on defense to coalesce until after the 2007–2008 legislative and presidential elections at the earliest.

If we are to wait another one or two years for Taiwan to reach a consensus on how best to meet its legitimate defense needs, how does Taiwan tread water in the interim? The TRA is quite specific regarding America's obligation "to maintain the capacity of the United States to resist any resort to force or other forms of coercion that would jeopardize the security, or the social or economic system, of the people on Taiwan." U.S. support, however, is predicated on Taiwan's demonstration that it takes its defense seriously. This leads us to the subject of political leadership on both sides of the Blue–Green divide.

Taiwan must sustain a concerted effort to educate its people on the hard choices facing the public purse and the need to link defense and national security to sustainable development, prosperity, and political freedom. If the effort is insufficient, the military gap across the Strait will widen, placing more pressure on the U.S. to fill that gap. This in turn will place more strain on the U.S.–Taiwan relationship.

Without a demonstrable consensus among Taiwan's leaders on the need to defend their own country, the people and government of America will finding it increasingly difficult to sustain their commitment to "maintain the capacity" to resist the use of force against the island. Many in Taiwan understand our hesitation, especially with U.S. forces engaged in combat in other parts of the world. How can the United States commit itself to defend a nation that cannot decide how to defend itself?

Taiwan's President Chen Shui-bian has heard and understood this message. In addition to the very expensive procurement programs included in the defense special budget, he has publicly stated that he is resolved to reverse the 10-year decline in Taiwan's annual defense budget. Chen's current goal is to raise the budget from its current 2.54 percent of GDP to 3 percent of GDP within three years, and eventually to the 1995 rate of 3.5 percent of GDP. A plussed-up defense budget would demonstrate Taiwan's recommitment to its own defense and would reassure the United States that Taiwan is willing to stand up for itself.

There are also many other opportunities to improve on the current situation. Military procurement not only sends a message about Taiwan's taking national defense seriously, but also creates a large political deliverable for the island. The augmentation of Taiwan's defensive capabilities engages the U.S. government, military, and industry; and by investing in defense platforms, the government of Taiwan reinvests America in the U.S.–Taiwan defense relationship, thereby further encouraging the United States government to work with Taiwan.

Could U.S. Policies Aid Consensus in Taiwan?

There are two levels at which U.S. policies affect Taiwan's defense consensus. First, as outlined in the previous chapter, is the perception in Taiwan that the United States wants democratic Taiwan eventually to unite with Communist China. This perception leads many Taiwanese voters to question the value of expending large amounts of financial and personnel resources in a quest for a separate identity from China when Taiwan's most important (if not only) ally ultimately opposes that goal.

Second is the perception that limiting Taiwan to a purely defensive posture vis-à-vis China is horrifically—and needlessly—expensive. For example, the Pentagon seems to believe that 180 Patriot PAC-3 missiles, which would cost roughly $9 million per missile launch, is an adequate response to China's 800 short-range ballistic missiles, which are estimated to cost China less than $1 million apiece to manufacture and deploy. Given a 50 percent kill rate with the PAC-3, Taiwan is expected to spend 20 times as much to kill an incoming Chinese SRBM as it costs China to produce the SRBM. While it makes eminent sense to field a defense shield for high-value Taiwan targets with the PAC-3, a calculus of deterrence requires that Taiwan also develop a limited offensive capacity to inflict serious pain on Chinese targets.[60]

Taiwan does have a capacity for research, development, and manufacture of weapons systems with an offensive capacity. The Hsiung Feng III supersonic cruise missile is one example of Taiwan's virtuosity in missile design. The missile, which has a range of several hundred miles, can hit targets on China's coast. However, the United States is said to have put considerable pressure on Taiwan not to manufacture the weapon, apparently fearing that it would somehow offend China.[61]

---

[60]These price figures are necessarily the personal estimates of the authors.

[61]Wu Mingjie, "Xiongfeng Sanxing feidan Shengji, Liangnian nei fuyi" [Hsiung Feng III Missile Progresses, to be deployed in 2 years], *China Times*, Taipei, September 1, 2002. Perhaps two years was optimistic. See Lu Zhaolong, "Tuixiu zhuanjia huiguo, 'Xiongsan' yi fei chong tian" [Retired Expert brought back, 'Hsiung Feng 3' finally flies successfully], *China Times*, Taipei, January 7, 2005, p. A2, and Lu Zhaolong, "Xiongfeng Xunyi Feidan, jijiang liangchang" [Hsiung Feng Cruise Missile to enter serial production], *China Times*, Taipei, July 20, 2005. There is evidence that the Hsiung Feng 3 is indeed ready for serial production but that pressure from the United States is preventing it. See "CSIST 'successful' in firing supersonic anti-ship missile," *Taipei Times*, January 8, 2005, p. 3, at *www.taipeitimes.com/News/front/archives/2005/01/08/2003218507*, and "Defense ministry rejects missile deployment story," *Taipei Times*, August 13, 2005, p. 3, at *www.taipeitimes.com/News/front/archives/2005/08/13/2003267-544*.

In December 1999, KMT presidential candidate Lien Chan insisted that Taiwan must establish a credible deterrent military force, specifically the development of a potential for a long-range ballistic missile force to convince China that it should not dare to attack Taiwan. At the time, Lien said China's missile threat made it imperative that Taiwan strengthen its anti-missile early warning, target acquisition, and interception. Further, an effective deterrent force would make it impossible for any foreign country to accept the cost of striking Taiwan. In order to guarantee Taiwan's national security, Taiwan must develop a "second strike" capability, Lien said.

Lien's speech, which was drafted by the Ministry of National Defense, marked the first time a senior Taiwan official openly called for an offensive missile force. The Minister of National Defense at the time "confidentially" confirmed Taiwan's progress in long-range missile development.[62] But once again, as discussed in the previous chapter, Lien Chan and his Blue allies have since completely changed their minds about Taiwan's need for a limited offensive capability, judging that the United States seemingly does not approve, and China certainly does not, and that such deployments would irritate Beijing, foster an arms race in the Taiwan Strait, and delay or even block the ultimate unification of China.

Electoral considerations among Taiwan's Blue camp, however, could be influenced if there were a stronger domestic constituency for defense production. If the United States would work to give Taiwan "ownership" in the procurement of certain weapons systems, that constituency would be enhanced. The creation of a strong indigenous defense industry has been the goal of many on the island, and that goal could be facilitated through cooperative programs with U.S. defense industries. A prime example can be found when reviewing Taiwan's MiTAC-Synnex Group and their contribution to the American-led Po-Sheng program. The U.S. is also interested in helping Taiwan to privatize state-owned enterprises (SOEs) affiliated with Taiwan's military–industrial complex. American support in reorganizing these types of industries could help Taiwan increase its ability to defend itself by bringing U.S. experts into partnership with their Taiwanese counterparts.

Growth in the domestic defense sector also has an important role to play in meeting Taiwan's national security needs. While it is not likely that Taiwan is capable of developing systems and platforms that operate at the level of those developed by the U.S., Taiwan does have niche areas that could be useful to U.S. defense companies as well as to the Pentagon. As with the Po-Sheng program, there is no reason that some of Taiwan's leading

---

[62]This story appeared on p. 1 of Taipei's *United Daily News* on December 9, 1999, according to authors' notes.

technology companies cannot be relied upon to develop components for a complete system and perhaps for systems that are not just used by Taiwan's military customers, but also have a global market. By partnering with America's defense companies, Taiwan businesses could open up new opportunities for themselves and bring their ability to design and manufacture—and their globally competitive prices—into play.

The creation of an increasingly large domestic constituency vested in the national security choices of Taiwan and its principal ally could only have a positive impact on the security choices that Taiwan's local politicians make. Growth of that constituency becomes important if a more robust base of support among Taiwan's voters and, through them, their elected representatives in the legislature is to emerge. Direct purchases of full-up defense systems from the U.S. makes the Taiwan "deliverable" much tougher to articulate.

Finally, as pressure on its own defense budget grows, the U.S. seeks ways to reduce its own procurement budgets by procuring items off-the-shelf as opposed to underwriting expensive processes of research, development, and manufacturing specifically for military means. A Pentagon delegation that visited Taiwan in 2005 sought items as varied as ammunition and batteries, GPS receivers, and floodlights for the U.S. military. The proven ability of Taiwan companies to manufacture at low cost and high quality under original equipment manufacturing contracts allows customers to buy quantities of a product quickly and with little overhead. Taiwan is well placed to become a significant vendor to U.S. defense component consumers and their principal customer, the Pentagon.

In a growing threat environment, Taiwan has risen to the challenge only halfheartedly. By pushing aside partisan politics and embracing and funding effective force modernization, the island could not only contribute to its own ability to defend itself, but also send a message, both to the United States and to those who would do the island harm, that Taiwan is a strong partner in democratic East Asia against the forces of despotism. This is essential if America's political leadership hopes to justify its ongoing commitment to the island.

The direction in which Taiwan's military is headed presents a spectrum of opportunities and challenges. Taiwan's Ministry of National Defense is attempting to convince the nation's leadership that the threats the island faces from across the Strait are clear, present, and growing by the day. Without inter-party cooperation, consensus, and strong leadership, Taiwan will continue to erode both its ability to protect itself and the will of the United States to help it do so.

Conclusion

A profound transformation has occurred in Chinese foreign policy. What is observable verifies that China is growing in terms of its comprehensive national power and is quite willing and able to promote its interests through the exploitation of this power. What cannot be observed or quantified with specificity is China's global strategy. This may be either the result of intentional Chinese obfuscation or a reflection of China's lack of a strategy. Nonetheless, we can observe that China is infused with the notion of acquiring more power and influence, even in the absence of a fully formed view as to the ends for which its influence may ultimately be used.

Taiwan is undeniably a focal point of China's immediate strategy, particularly as it orients its military modernization efforts. This mere fact places Taiwan in a position from which it can either further complicate the strategic challenges for America, as well as the rest of democratic Asia, or play a constructive role in encouraging China to move away from the pursuit of military preeminence toward a peaceful, benign integration into regional and global affairs.

China will continue to face discrete decision points in the global arena that will affect U.S. interests and the interests of its friends and allies. It is important that China be incentivized to make choices that lead it down a path of peaceful integration and benign competition. The United States, Japan, and other countries have an opportunity—through engagement with China, through shaping Asia's strategic environment, and through appropriate security planning—to persuade China's leaders to make the right decisions.

4

A Cross-Strait Policy Based on Democracy and Mutual Consent

DANIEL BLUMENTHAL

WHILE THE BUSH ADMINISTRATION HAS DONE AN ADMIRABLE JOB taking on many of American foreign policy's sacred cows, the "One China" policy, based on a series of joint communiqués issued by Beijing and Washington in 1972, 1979, and 1982, remains America's stance toward China and Taiwan. Given the profound changes in the geopolitical environment since it was first crafted, the policy is anachronistic. Worse yet, it has become dangerous as what was once considered its most clever characteristic—ambiguity—may now lead to the kind of misperceptions that cause war.

The basic source of this ambiguity is a circumlocutory statement in the 1972 Shanghai Communiqué:

> The United States acknowledges that all Chinese on either side of the Taiwan Strait maintain there is but "One China" and that Taiwan is a part of China. The United States Government does not challenge that position. It reaffirms its interest in a peaceful settlement of the Taiwan question by the Chinese themselves.[1]

---

[1] For a Chinese-language version of the Shanghai Communiqué, "Zhongghua Renmin Gongheguo he Meilijian Hezhongguo Lianhe Gongbao," February 28, 1972, see the Chinese Foreign Ministry Web site at *www.fmprc.gov.cn/chn/wjb/zzjg/bmdyzs/gjlb/1948/1950/t7513.htm*.

In 1978, the two countries issued a second communiqué announcing the mutual establishment of diplomatic relations. The Normalization Communiqué stated: "The U.S. side acknowledges the Chinese position that there is one China and Taiwan is part of China."[2]

Beijing interprets the word "acknowledges" differently in these two communiqués but insists in both cases that Washington had "accepted"[3] its claim that Taiwan is part of China and that "reunification" will be the final resolution to the "Taiwan issue." But that is not what Washington meant. The United States position was only to accept any outcome that is peacefully negotiated between the two sides. Washington claims not to "support independence" for Taiwan, but by that it means that it is not supporting either outcome—independence or reunification. And Washington restates time and again its commitment to Taiwan's self-defense as stipulated in the Taiwan Relations Act.[4]

To Beijing, this policy perhaps seems duplicitous: America on the one hand "accepts" its claims that Taiwan is part of China while on the other it conducts *de facto* independent diplomatic and security relations with Taipei. What is more, selling arms and helping Taiwan to improve its defense posture against Taipei's only threat—the Chinese armed forces—would appear to contradict the U.S. stance that it "accepts" Chinese claims to Taiwan.

For Taipei, the policy is even more frustrating. Washington expresses pride that Taiwan has become a democratic *de facto* state but then chides Taipei's elected leaders when they take the next logical steps in their democratic consolidation. Taiwan's President Chen Shui-bian is deemed "provocative" when he unveils plans to reform a constitution that was written when Taiwan and its government still claimed to rule all of China and was not yet a democracy. When Taiwan's president makes statements of

---

[2] For the 1979 Normalization Communiqué, "Zhongghua Renmin Gongheguo he Meilijian Hezhongguo guanyu Jianli Waijiao Guanxide Lianhe Gongbao," dated January 1, 1979, but announced in Beijing on December 16, 1978, see the Foreign Ministry Web site at *www.fmprc.gov.cn/chn/wjb/zzjg/bmdyzs/gjlb/1948/1950/t7509.htm*.

[3] The Chinese and English texts of the 1972 Shanghai Communiqué were carefully negotiated, and the English term "acknowledges" was rendered "renshidao," a neutral term that implies the "observance of a fact" without any formal or legal connotation. There was no such rectification of translations for the 1979 "Normalization Communiqué," in which the U.S. side "acknowledges the Chinese position that there is One China and Taiwan is part of China." In that document, the verb "acknowledges" was rendered in the Chinese text with the verb "chengren," which Beijing interprets to have the stronger legal meaning of "accepts" or "recognizes."

[4] For the text of the Taiwan Relations Act, see Appendix B in this volume.

the obvious—that Taiwan is an independent, sovereign state—or launches diplomacy to secure more international recognition, he is also blamed for provoking China. Washington's hypersensitivity to the democratic noise coming out of Taipei must seem all the more hypocritical in an age when the Bush Administration is advancing a muscular version of America's long-standing grand strategy of global democracy promotion.

The "One China" policy is thus dangerous because we do not mean what we tell Beijing. Those in the American policy community who really believe that Taiwan is part of China are outside the mainstream. But when policymakers ritualistically repeat their fidelity to "One China," they encourage Beijing to coerce Taiwan. By hinting that we will not defend Taiwan if Beijing is "provoked," we make our defense commitment appear conditional and provide Beijing with the incentive to accuse Taiwan of provocations that could easily become a pretext for war.

Moreover, America's policy is still governed by internal staff memoranda interpreting how America would conduct unofficial relations with Taiwan that were written in 1979. Thus, we restrict ourselves from helping Taiwan to improve its defense capabilities—including its ability to operate with our armed forces should the need arise. Though America has an implicit commitment to Taiwan's defense, not a single general or flag officer has visited Taiwan in over two decades. And though Taiwan is an advanced industrial democracy and our eighth largest trading partner, no standing U.S. President has met with his Taiwanese counterpart in decades.[5]

Given the vast changes in Taiwan and China, it is high time to formulate a new policy that helps to secure Taiwan and make clear to China that it will not resolve the issue by force, coercion, or intimidation.

How We Got Here

The "One China" policy has been remarkably durable despite the vast changes in international politics, the East Asian security environment, and Washington's relations with Taiwan and China since the last communiqué was issued in 1982. The history of its formulation, as well as the excitement that the opening to China sparked, helps to explain that endurance.

The policy was authored by President Richard Nixon and National Security Adviser Henry Kissinger in 1971–1972, a period marked by vastly different strategic circumstances. America was looking for Beijing's help in extracting itself from the Vietnam war and seeking to increase pressure on

---

[5] This is despite the fact that leaders of other "non-countries" such as the Dalai Lama, Yasser Arafat, Mahmoud Abbas, and Gerry Adams have met repeatedly with U.S. Presidents.

its chief geopolitical rival, the Soviet Union. In addition, Taiwan's government then was led by an autocratic clique of mainlanders who, after losing the Chinese civil war, seized power over Taiwan and claimed to be the rightful rulers of all of China.

None of these conditions exists today. The Soviet Union is gone, America has long been out of Vietnam, and the current Taiwanese leadership has gained power through democratic elections. Democracy in Taiwan has ended the bitter Chinese civil war: Taipei no longer claims to rule China. Equally important, the legitimacy of Taiwan's government is no longer based on its Cold War alliance with the United States against Communism; instead, it is based on competitive democratic elections and a liberal democratic political order. For its part, and as some predicted in the 1970s, China is still an authoritarian, one-party state but is now economically, politically, and militarily powerful and able to challenge U.S. leadership in Asia. Yet the "One China" policy remains.

The "One China" policy was conceived in secrecy and clouded in ambiguity. Nixon and Kissinger had much to hide in order to sell the policy to a skeptical Congress and public. Beijing made clear from the outset that the price of its cooperation was the breaking of Washington's mutual defense treaty with Taiwan. At the time, this was easier to do than it would be today. Nixon could get away with "acknowledging" that the Chinese on both sides of the Strait believed in "One China" and that Taiwan was part of China—if what one meant by "Chinese in Taiwan" was the ruling Kuomintang (KMT) party. The KMT (also known as the "Chinese Nationalist Party" or, to Americans, simply as the "Nationalists") kept the majority Taiwanese out of the political process and did indeed adhere to its own "One China" policy.

The existence of a majority Taiwanese population was acknowledged by the Americans—Nixon stated that he opposed the "Taiwanese Independence Movement"—but merely as an afterthought or as a potential obstacle to a new China policy. America looked at Taiwan and China through the geopolitical prism of the Cold War. In the minds of Nixon and Kissinger, it was not a question of abandoning a democracy to a dictatorship, but a question of recognizing one dictatorial regime as a partner and the "sole representative" of China at the expense of another.

The success of this policy was premised on two prospective outcomes for Taiwan: Either it would remain under the rule of an authoritarian KMT, committed to "One China," that would negotiate unification with the Communists on the mainland, or it would eventually be absorbed by China against its will. A democratic Taiwan ruled by Taiwanese that did not claim to be the "sole representative" of China was not anticipated.

Recognizing that important segments of the American public would not support the abandonment of a Cold War ally, Kissinger and Nixon conducted much of their business with China in secret, through back channels, and with a highly personalized style of diplomacy that relied heavily on the two men's relationships with their Chinese counterparts. They said one thing in private to the Chinese and other things for public consumption. In his talks with Zhou Enlai, President Nixon pointed to the need to deceive the U.S. public:

> [W]hat we are trying to find is language which will meet the Prime Minister's need, but language which will not give [the] strong coalition of opponents to the initiative we have made the opportunity to gang up and say in effect that the American President went to Peking and sold Taiwan down the river.[6]

China diplomacy as practiced by Nixon and Kissinger set the precedent and tone for those who would succeed them, although Jimmy Carter and his National Security Adviser, Zbigniew Brzezinski, took Nixon's policy a step further. Brzezinski, fashioning himself a Kissingerian statesmen and grand strategist, continued Kissinger's style of highly personalized, dramatic diplomacy with China. The results were rushed decisions and unnecessary concessions on Taiwan. Brzezinski wanted to normalize relations with China ahead of the Strategic Arms Limitation (SALT II) talks to improve the U.S. position with the Soviets. The Chinese wanted normalization announced before those talks in order to destroy them altogether—but mostly to give the impression that the United States had approved of China's invasion of Vietnam, which took place the month after "normalization." The Chinese got their wish. Carter's and Brzezinski's contribution to their predecessors' China diplomacy was to begin the practice of ceding leverage to China.

As these developments unfolded, some American strategists made powerful arguments against the direction of American China policy. In 1978, for example, Edward Luttwak at the Center for Strategic and International Studies asked prophetically: "Is it our true purpose to promote the rise of the People's Republic to superpower status.... Should we become the artificers of a great power which our grandchildren may have to contend with?"[7] But Brzezinski was as uninterested in this question as he was

---

[6] "Memorandum of Conversation," Tuesday, February 22, 1972, 2:10 pm–6:00 pm, p. 6, George Washington University, National Security Archive, at *www.gwu.edu/~nsarchiv/nsa/publications/DOC_readers/kissinger/nixzhou/*.

focused on the need for Chinese cooperation in order to counter the global Soviet threat.

Ronald Reagan came into office determined to reverse what he saw as a wrongheaded China and Taiwan policy, but his Secretary of State, Alexander M. Haig, was a Kissinger disciple who continued in the tradition of his mentor. Haig's vision of U.S.–China relations, however, did vary in one respect from Kissinger's initial formulation: He saw a good relationship with China as an end in itself. As the Reagan Administration prepared to take a tougher line against the Soviets, Haig was able to prevail over China skeptics by calling upon the well-established belief that the Chinese provided an essential partner against the Soviet Union. He was thus the force behind the 1982 communiqué, which for the first time publicly set limits on U.S. arms sales to Taiwan.[8]

Reagan tried to undo his Secretary of State's work and ultimately demanded his resignation in the face of escalating policy disagreements. The President wrote a memo to contradict the principles behind the 1982 communiqué, stating that "The United States would restrict arms sales to Taiwan so long as the balance of power between China and Taiwan was preserved."[9] Implicit in Reagan's policy interpretation was the view that if China upgraded its military capabilities, the United States would have the right to upgrade its arms sales.

Both Reagan's and Haig's views have left definite legacies. Haig augmented Kissinger's China diplomacy with a view that good relations with China is an end in itself. His exaggeration both of China's importance to the United States and of the confluence of national interests is still deeply embedded in America's China policy. Reagan's understanding that the limits on arms sales to Taiwan would necessarily have to be reversed if China upgraded its military capabilities remains the implicit policy of the United States.

When Secretary of State George P. Shultz took over from the purged Haig, he and his new team thought that China's strategic importance had been exaggerated and that too much had been given away for too little. China was

---

[7] Edward N. Luttwak, "Against the China Card," *Commentary*, Vol. 66, No. 4 (October 1978), p. 43.

[8] "Joint Communique of the United States of America and the People's Republic of China" on Taiwan arms sales, announced August 17, 1982, at *http://usinfo.state.gov/eap/Archive_Index/joint_ communique _1982.html*.

[9] For the full text of this short memorandum, see James R. Lilley and Jeff Lilley, *China Hands: Nine Decades of Adventure, Espionage, and Diplomacy in Asia* (New York: PublicAffairs Books, 2004), p. 248. See also Jim Mann, *About Face: A History of America's Curious Relationship with China, From Nixon to Clinton* (New York: Alfred A. Knopf, 1999), p. 127.

the country that feared invasion by the Soviets, they reasoned, not the United States. Additionally, in 1978, when the Carter Administration had agreed privately to a moratorium on arms sales (later reversed by Reagan), it was China that desperately needed stable relations with the United States in order to invade Vietnam.[10] The Shultz team restored some balance to U.S. China policy, although with the August 17, 1982, communiqué, his predecessor had already concluded the major policy statement of the period.[11]

Inexplicably, President George H. W. Bush's Administration strove to put the policy back in the Kissinger–Brzezinski–Haig box just as historic changes on Taiwan and in China were conspiring to undermine a consensus in Taiwan about "One China." By the late 1980s, Taiwan's ruling KMT was opening up the political system. Taiwan's leadership took a series of steps that at once should have eased tensions between Beijing and Taipei but instead complicated U.S. policy.

As the Taipei government liberalized its political system, it also abandoned its policy of "retaking the mainland" and attempting to regain international recognition as the sole representative of China. In its renunciation of its claims to the mainland, Taiwan became a *de facto* separate state whose people had no further stake in the Chinese civil war. Instead, the Taiwanese wanted to focus on building a democratic nation. It was at this moment in history that the "One China" policy ceased to make sense. Contrary to the assertions in the Shanghai Communiqué, it was no longer true that "Chinese on both sides of the Strait" claimed to part of China. The Taiwan side emphatically did not.

Meanwhile, on the other side of the Strait, many Chinese began to call for freedom and democracy as well. Unlike Taipei's government, which was racing full-steam toward complete democratization, Beijing's decided to crush China's nascent democracy movement. Beijing's massacre of pro-democracy student demonstrators at Tiananmen Square in the early morning hours of Sunday, June 4, 1989, sparked outrage among the American public and deeply alienated the fast-changing Taiwanese from their hopes of reconciliation with the mainland's rulers. Up until that point, the American public had gone along with the new China policy, convinced by their leaders that China not only was an important part of America's strategy to bring down the Soviet Empire, but also was moving inexorably toward greater political openness. Tiananmen belied the latter conviction just as the former had lost its relevance.

---

[10]Mann, *About Face*, p. 129.

[11]*Ibid.*, p. 164.

Though he ordered a number of punitive sanctions against Beijing, President Bush, acting in the manner of Nixon, twice sent his National Security Adviser, Lieutenant General Brent Scowcroft, and Deputy Secretary of State Lawrence Eagleburger as secret emissaries to China to assure Deng Xiaoping that the sanctions were temporary—a necessary evil to placate a horrified American public and an overly touchy Democratic-controlled Congress.[12] But Bush misjudged the public and congressional mood toward China, aptly expressed by former U.S. Ambassador to China Winston Lord, who accused the Administration of dismissing "the Chinese as a people apart from the global winds of change."[13] Lord's words remain true today.

With Taiwan's new leaders under President Lee Teng-hui implanting democracy on one side of the Taiwan Strait and the Chinese Communist Party politburo in Beijing bloodily enforcing its dictatorship on the other, the "Taiwan issue" ceased to be about who deserved recognition as the rightful rulers of China. The "One China" policy, which had been crafted to finesse the recognition issue, no longer provided a realistic road map to resolution. It had something to say about the Chinese position in the dispute—America "acknowledged" China's position—but nothing to say about Taiwan's. Nowhere else in the world did America "acknowledge" one side's position in a dispute while altogether ignoring the other's. This was all the more awkward since the side whose position was acknowledged (China) was a dictatorship that did not govern on the basis of the "consent of the governed," while the other (Taiwan) was building a truly democratic state.

To its credit, the Administration of William Jefferson Clinton looked at the rather incongruous arrangement in the Taiwan Strait and decided in the summer of 1994 that these changed circumstances called for a review of Taiwan policy. However, the results of the review, issued in September 1994, disappointed nearly everyone. The legacy of Kissinger, Brzezinski, and Haig was too deeply imbedded to bend to common sense. Their acolytes in the State Department, in charge of China affairs, were unwilling to challenge a decade of self-imposed protocolary practices: Taiwan officials would not be allowed to visit the Pentagon or the State Department, and top-level Taiwan officials would not be granted visas to visit America.

Even so, Beijing was upset with the slight concessions to Taiwan offered by the review: Taiwanese officials would be allowed to transit the United States, and top American economic officials, even Cabinet officers, would be allowed to visit Taiwan. The new Republican Congress, with Tiananmen still much on its mind and with growing bipartisan support for Taiwan's

---

[12]*Ibid.*, p. 221.

[13]Quoted in Mann, *About Face*, p. 224.

infant democracy, felt that the Clinton Administration had caved in to Beijing.

There are many possible explanations for why the Clinton Administration held fast to a policy that was increasingly out of touch with reality. The Kissinger–Brzezinski–Haig legacies and a powerful business lobby that was at the peak of its "China fever" are two possible reasons. But another, probably decisive factor for the Clinton team was its worldview. Philosophically, the Clinton Administration was as committed to promoting democracy as is the current Bush Administration. The Clinton Administration believed that a policy of engagement would transform China into a responsible democratic player that accepted the international rules of the game. The idea was to enmesh China in a web of bilateral and international agreements that would force it to play by the same rules that the world's democracies obeyed. It also would have to change its domestic system to become a member of the World Trade Organization.

As is often the case with "engagement" policies, however, engaging China became an end unto itself.[14] For the Clinton Administration, part of the logic of engagement seemed to oblige Clinton to inch closer to China's Taiwan policy. Under this logic, in order to empower "moderates" in Beijing who supposedly wanted political reform in China, America had to make concessions on Taiwan—a "core issue" of regime legitimacy, according to the American architects of engagement.

Administration China hands should have been shaken when Clinton was obliged to send two carrier battle groups into the Taiwan Strait area in response to Beijing's provocative missile "tests" in March 1996, which closed the Strait to commercial shipping for the weeks surrounding Taiwan's first-ever presidential election. Chinese brinkmanship proved that Beijing indeed was prepared to use force to "settle" the Taiwan issue, and the Clinton Administration wanted to avoid a military showdown over the island. Clinton was very uncomfortable with shows of force anywhere, and immediately following the departure of the U.S. battle group from the Strait, he dispatched National Security Adviser Anthony Lake to Beijing to try to smooth things over with the Chinese. It was dispiriting that an Administration that had come to office determined to put human rights at the top of its China agenda ended by accepting China's position on Taiwan in Clinton's infamous "Three No's" speech in June 1998.[15]

At the same time, China and Taiwan were changing rapidly in opposite directions and in ways that increased the tension between them. As should have been expected, the sudden preeminence of the native Taiwanese in the

---

[14]Peter Feaver, "I Love Zhu, Zhu Loves Me: Clinton's China Policy," *The Weekly Standard*, April 26, 1999, pp. 27 and 29.

political process following the 1992 constitutional revisions resulted in an electorate that abjured their government's claims that Taiwan was part of China. For a majority of Taiwanese, their ties to China were much like Louisianans' ties to France: Their families had emigrated abroad centuries before, and they retained cultural and linguistic similarities to the old country, but Taiwanese families had lived on the island for centuries and had undergone cultural and linguistic transformations during the half-century of Japanese colonization.

The Chinese Nationalists' occupying force in Taiwan following the Japanese surrender in 1945 was oppressive, corrupt, and arrogant. After a year of malfeasance and misgovernment, an island-wide rebellion erupted on February 28, 1947, and lasted a week. Chiang Kai-shek's army landed in Taiwan to quell the uprising, and in the six months that ensued, Nationalist Chinese army and secret police executed 18,000 Taiwanese and imprisoned many more. By 1988, after four decades of police-state repression, the majority of ethnic Taiwanese had developed a strong distaste for anything having to do with mainland China, first chafing under the rule of the mainlander-dominated KMT and then being humiliated during the 1990s by the Chinese Communists' relentless campaign to suppress their international identity.

Meanwhile, the balance of military power in the Taiwan Strait was fast tipping toward the mainland as China used its growing wealth to finance an ambitious military modernization program that was aimed in large part at bringing Taiwan back into the fold of the "motherland." The Taiwan issue became more important ideologically to China in these years as the basis of its legitimacy shifted from its Maoist–Marxist roots to a form of Chinese hypernationalism. Holding onto and regaining the territorial possessions of the old Manchu empire was a critical element of a "One China" ideology.

The Question of Taiwanese Identity

Any new policy toward China and Taiwan must do something that successive U.S. governments over the past two decades have failed to do: take into account the wishes of the inhabitants of Taiwan. This is not just the right thing to do; it is the only realistic thing to do. During China policy deliberations at the beginning of the Cold War, Secretary of State Dean

---

[15]"I had a chance to reiterate our Taiwan policy, which is that we don't support independence for Taiwan, or two Chinas, or one Taiwan–one China. And we don't believe that Taiwan should be a member in any organization for which statehood is a requirement. So I think we have a consistent policy." See "President's Comments at the Shanghai Library," Office of the White House Press Secretary, June 30, 1998.

Acheson had decided that the Taiwanese were not "mature" enough to hold the line against the Communists. After the mutual defense treaty was signed in 1954,[16] Washington let Generalissimo Chiang Kai-shek rule as he wished over the island's inhabitants.

Over the decades from the 1950s through the 1970s, many thousands of ethnic Taiwanese students came to the United States for advanced studies and in the process became political dissidents in exile. Consequently, there was some awareness in America of the so-called Taiwan Independence Movement—enough that Nixon felt obliged to assure Mao that he would not support it.[17] But there was little indication that the Nixon Administration ever took the Taiwanese sentiments about political reform into consideration.[18]

Paradoxically, the Nixon–Carter derecognition of Taiwan spurred the growth of the Taiwan Independence Movement. With the announcement of derecognition on December 16, 1978, the KMT lost a crucial pillar of its legitimacy as it was no longer recognized by its last significant ally as the sole representative of China. Within a year, on December 10, 1979, KMT police clashed with about 10,000 protesters, who marched in the southern Taiwan city of Kaohsiung demanding political reforms, and arrested several of the reform movement's leaders. Martial law trials of the *Formosa Magazine* defendants in military tribunals only increased international demands that the KMT respect civil and political freedoms, and it became increasingly difficult for the KMT to justify the continued oppression and exclusion of Taiwanese from the political system.[19]

For decades, Chiang Kai-shek and his son and successor Chiang Ching-kuo had used the organs of their "Republic of China" government to indoctrinate their island subjects that they were part of a great Chinese

---

[16]Mutual Defense Treaty Between the United States of America and the Republic of China, signed at Washington, D.C., December 2, 1954, at *www.taiwandocuments.org/mutual01.htm.*

[17]"Memorandum of Conversation," Tuesday, February 22, 1972, 2:10 pm–6:00 pm, p. 5.

[18]The United States clearly knew this was a possibility. In his first meetings with Chinese premier Zhou Enlai in July 1971, National Security Adviser Henry Kissinger cautioned that "if the Taiwan Independence Movement develops without us, that is not in our control." See "Memorandum of Conversation," July 11, 1971, pp. 10–11, George Washington University, National Security Archive, at *www.gwu.edu/~nsarchiv/NSAEBB/NSAEBB66/ch-38.pdf.*

[19]For an excellent summary of the incident, see John Kaplan, *The Court-Martial of the Kaohsiung Defendants* (Berkeley: University of California, Institute of East Asian Studies, 1981).

nation that ultimately would be restored to the rule of the KMT–Nationalists. Just how forced and artificial this coerced cultural assimilation was became apparent as Taiwan became free. According to scholar Stephen Phillips:

> As important as what islanders experienced is what they missed: the key events that shaped the national consciousness of the Chinese, including the collapse of the [Manchu dynasty], Sun Yat-sen's revolutionary efforts, warlord depredations, the literary revolution of the May 4th Movement, the glory of the Northern Expedition, and the myth of national unity during the War of Resistance.[20]

The majority of ethnic Taiwanese had developed their own political identity, much of it in opposition to their mainlander leaders. Brutal acts of KMT suppression since the beginning of the postwar occupation, the imprisonment of political opponents, and the experience of exile for many activists crystallized into a shared national consciousness for a new generation of Taiwan's political and opinion leaders. Many Taiwanese elites in exile abroad had experienced the freshness and freedom of studying and working in two liberal democracies: Japan and the United States. Their experiences during the Cold War were so diametrically divergent from those of the Chinese masses on the mainland that they simply did not regard themselves as part of the same country.

In addition, as the KMT began to relinquish control and open up the political system, the Taiwanese politicians who took power focused on the task of building a democratic state. This democratic state-building process has made the most salient and important contribution to the formation of a separate "Taiwanese" identity for Taiwan's people. Taiwan's new elites and public have the shared experience of forming a democracy. They have a highly developed sense of identity as citizens of a liberal democratic polity. It is this part of their identity that they most contrast to the still-totalitarian People's Republic of China (PRC).

This is borne out in some of the extensive polling conducted in Taiwan on issues of identity and policy preference: unification or independence. Dr. Emerson Niou, for example, has illustrated that in terms of identity, what matters most to the Taiwanese is that they are citizens of a liberal, advanced industrial, *de facto* state. He shows this by identifying the strong trend of

---

[20]Stephen Phillips, "Building a Taiwanese Republic: The Independence Movement, 1945–Present," in Nancy Bernkopf Tucker, ed., *Dangerous Strait: The U.S.–Taiwan–China Crisis* (New York: Columbia University Press, 2005), p. 47.

"pragmatism" in Taiwanese preferences. This is defined as wanting independence if it can be achieved peacefully or unification if China attains the level of growth and democracy that Taiwan already has.[21] The Taiwanese do not want to give up their democratic Taiwanese citizenship in exchange for life in a less-advanced despotism.

Moreover, the PRC's own policy further alienates Taiwanese citizens. The 1995–1996 missile tests, "blocking UN aid after the September 1999 earthquake, denying Taipei observer status in the World Health Organization during the 2003 SARS crisis, attempting to reduce Taiwan's status in the WTO to that of Hong Kong"[22] were incidents of churlishness that cumulatively resulted in the supplanting of the Chinese Communist Party (CCP) by the Chinese Nationalist Party (KMT) as the prime bully and oppressor of Taiwanese.

The PRC's unrelenting military buildup, with some 700–800 short-range ballistic missiles pointed at Taiwan, and the Anti-Secession Law (ASL), which threatens to resolve the Taiwan Strait standoff by "nonpeaceful means," have further alienated the majority of Taiwanese from China. For the Taiwanese, who believe that the political *status quo* is the existence of a *de facto* independent country called Taiwan, the term "secession" itself seems irrelevant. Chinese attempts to reverse the damage of the ASL by inviting the discredited opposition leaders to China without so much as acknowledging President Chen's various proposals for the revival of "Cross Strait Talks" between the now-unemployed bureaucrats of China's Association for Relations Across the Taiwan Strait (ARATS) and Taipei's Strait Exchange Foundation (SEF) are a further affront to Taiwanese dignity.

Thus, a policy that attempts to freeze a *status quo* that existed in 1979 or 1982 or 1989 is utterly unrealistic. Almost no one on Taiwan believes that their island is a part of the PRC or that mainland China is a part of Taipei's Republic of China. Nor do any Chinese really believe that the Taiwanese will "reunify" without some combination of military coercion, force, economic pressure, and international political isolation. They are quite right under current circumstances, but these are factors that cause instability in the Strait, not "provocations" or moves toward independence by Taiwan's elected leaders.

---

[21]Emerson Niou, "Understanding Taiwan Independence and Its Policy Implications," *Asian Survey*, Vol. 44, No. 4 (July/August 2004), pp. 555–567.

[22]Lowell Dittmer, "Taiwan and the Issue of National Identity," *Asian Affairs*, Vol. 44, No. 4 (July/August 2004), pp. 475–483.

A New Cross-Strait Policy

In Washington, the top priority of a new cross-Strait policy must be America's interests. America's primary interest is in maintaining the hegemony of a liberal democratic order in the Asia–Pacific region. Whether American diplomats like it or not, Taiwan is viewed throughout Asia and the world as "made in America"—a textbook example of the successful transformation of a former authoritarian security ally into a flourishing democracy. America would suffer a strategic blow if Taiwan were to be coerced or intimidated into a settlement with China. America's credibility in Asia as a nation that would intercede when the region is threatened by totalitarianism would suffer if China's latest attempts to manipulate the Taiwanese political system were to succeed.

Should Asia's democracies come to see China as Asia's preeminent power—one that gets what it wants from the United States, including a democratic Taiwan that American lawmakers declared it was "the policy of the United States" to defend—the "bandwagoning" effect would be immediate. First, perhaps, the Southeast Asian countries would reach their accommodations with China, and then perhaps Australia, which now counts China as its top customer for iron ore, minerals, coal, and uranium, not to mention agricultural commodities.

The last to go would probably be Japan, which is the linchpin of America's network of security alliances in Asia. Would Japan simply bow to Chinese predominance and seek an accommodation? Or would Japan, spooked by China's vicious anti-Japanese violence of March–April 2005, begin to weigh its own nuclear options? American policymakers should consider what kind of Asia would emerge if the United States were seen to have abandoned Taiwan.

Conversely, America has a vital interest in ensuring that China's "rise" is peaceful and that China is a "cooperative and constructive" participant in what is now an American-led system of global politics. The lessons of history from the past century tell us that stable international systems can only accommodate "rising" powers which are democratic—the rising powers of postwar Japan and Germany are two good examples, while prewar Japan and Germany are two bad examples along with the Soviet Union.

In this context, a "One China" policy is inconsistent with American interests. Americans are telling the Chinese in essence: "We understand that you can't 'lose' Taiwan because that would mean a fatal blow to your regime's legitimacy." Aside from the fact that this line of thinking implies that the United States has some interest in maintaining the legitimacy of a despotic, authoritarian regime in Beijing, it has the other nasty effect of inducing many Washington policymakers to explain away the Chinese military buildup as a legitimate Chinese interest because it is merely a "deterrent" to Taiwan's independence.

China's leaders believe that their immediate task is to retake Taiwan now that the PRC has successfully absorbed Hong Kong and Macao. And once Taiwan is "reunited" with the mainland, Beijing's eyes no doubt will fall upon Mongolia, despite its treaties with the old Soviet Union respecting Mongolia's independence, not to mention the fact that China now recognizes Mongolian independence.

Clearly, America and its democratic friends and allies in Asia do not have an interest in supporting a regime that claims legitimacy in this manner. To the contrary, America and the democracies have every interest in making the point to China that, in the 21st century, political legitimacy may not be gained by conquest or intimidation: Political legitimacy arises naturally from the consent of the governed.

America's current Taiwan policy is also remarkably unrealistic. It ignores basic facts on the ground in Taiwan. Even the KMT and their Pan-Blue allies have had to shift their stated policy to one that calls for the short-term maintenance of the *status quo* and long-term unification only when the political and economic systems on both sides of the Strait converge.[23] Unsurprisingly, this policy is unacceptable to China; by definition, it means that the CCP has to accept its own demise as a condition for unification.

Furthermore, America's current policy suffers from a short-term practical danger: It encourages China to think that, one way or another, it will get Taiwan back in much the same way as it got back Hong Kong and Macao. This is not, in fact, what the U.S. means to encourage. What America really wants is a peaceful resolution of the conflict with both sides providing their assent to such a resolution through their democratically elected leaders. Of course, only one side in the dispute can now meet this criterion—Taiwan. What American policymakers seem to be doing is trying to wait it out in the hope that the issue will be resolved when China becomes a democracy.

The flaw in that plan, however, is that while we sit around waiting for China to democratize on its own, much can happen in the interim, including a Chinese military attack on Taiwan. China is clearly preparing the diplomatic groundwork for the use of force against the island. If America, Europe, and even Japan were all to declare a "One China" policy that Beijing takes as their formal recognition that Taiwan is part of China, would not Beijing be perfectly justified in using force if all other measures

---

[23]Xing Zhigang, "Experts: Pan-Blue Camp Makes Dangerous U-Turn," *China Daily*, January 8, 2004, at *www.chinadaily.com.cn/en/doc/2004-01/08/content_296 710.htm.*

fail? And is it not Beijing, after all, that has the legal authority to decide, on its own time and its own initiative, when all other measures have failed?

A new China and Taiwan policy for America should align with the Bush Administration's National Security Strategy of active promotion of democracy.[24] The Bush Administration's insight that America's security is directly correlated to the number of democracies in the world is not a new one.[25] What is new is its proactive and muscular promotion of this strategic insight in the post–September 11 world. Yet, if the Bush Administration makes a "China exception" in its cross-Strait policy, it undermines its own strategy.

U.S. cross-Strait policy should be a commitment to a peaceful outcome that is decided upon mutually by the people on both sides of the Strait through their democratically elected leaders. Two corollaries should follow:

1. We will not formally recognize a unilateral declaration of independence by Taiwan, and

2. We will work actively to promote a significant international personality for Taiwan based on its development as a *de facto* independent, democratic entity.

The first corollary might be hard for Taiwan to swallow, but given the years of propaganda that Chinese citizens have endured, if we are seen to favor a non-negotiated independence, we will likely alienate 1.2 billion people. We would be wise to take Chinese threats of force at face value.

Nonetheless, the policy should put the onus on Beijing to create the kind of country that the Taiwanese would wish to join. It is quite possible that a liberal democratic China with a per capita income equal to that of Taiwan would attract the Taiwanese into some sort of union or confederation. Of course, it is equally possible that the Taiwanese would want a state of their own. A liberal democratic China, in all likelihood, would be willing to compromise on that issue. The legitimacy that a new regime in China would bring would quickly destroy the fears of losing hold of the rest of the

---

[24]See *The National Security Strategy of the United States of America*, The White House, March 16, 2006, p. 6, at *www.whitehouse.gov/nsc/nss/2006/nss2006.pdf*.

[25]See, among many examples, Ronald Reagan, "The Evil Empire," speech delivered before the House of Commons, June 8, 1982; Anthony Lake, "From Containment to Enlargement," speech delivered before the Johns Hopkins University School of Advanced International Studies, September 21,1993; and Strobe Talbott, "Democracy and the National Interest," *Foreign Affairs*, Vol. 76, No. 6 (November/December 1996), pp. 47–63.

Chinese empire. To paraphrase Robert Kagan, China might begin to see Taiwan as the Germans see Alsace-Lorraine.

America should not pursue this policy unilaterally. Other democracies and friends, especially the Europeans, Australians, and Japanese, should be asked to support it in advance. If effected through skillful diplomacy, a cross-Strait policy that abandons the increasingly dangerous "One China" rhetoric might receive more international support than one might expect. This is especially true if such a policy is tied to a policy that energetically promotes democracy in China. As Michael McFaul has illustrated, democracy promotion is now not only an American, but also an international project.[26]

The United States should also work to establish a "Security Community of Democracies" in Asia to which China might accede if and when it ever meets the criteria. Though not an official state, Taiwan should be included, both to help break China's headlock of isolation and to give Taiwan incentives to improve its self-defense capabilities. Besides its many other benefits, such a community, with Taiwan firmly anchored in it, would leave the United States less isolated as Taiwan's sole supporter.

Critics of this policy will surely claim that it would start a war with China or forever alienate the Chinese people from us. In reality, however, the "One China" policy is bringing us closer to war with China than this alternative would. It is far better to make clear our interests *before* China makes further strides in military power and convinces itself that the world will stand by as it takes Taiwan by force.

---

[26]Michael McFaul, "Democracy Promotion as a World Value," *The Washington Quarterly*, Vol. 28, No. 1 (Winter 2004), pp. 147–163. McFaul points out that Europe devotes greater resources to the promotion of democracy than the United States does.

Eroding the "One China" Policy: A Tripartite Political-Legal Strategy for Taiwan

JACQUES DELISLE

TAIWAN HAS BEEN REMARKABLY EFFECTIVE in preserving a *status quo* in which it enjoys the functional attributes of a state in the international system despite being denied the full formal status of independent statehood. This has helped to advance the policy interest of the United States—and the vital national interest of Taiwan—in reinforcing Taiwan's stature as a robust, valuable member of the international community and, in turn, undermining the legitimacy of claims by the People's Republic of China (PRC) that it possesses a right to use armed force against the island.

Oddly, Taiwan's real-world success has stemmed in part from its ability to accrue, or approximate, the formal or symbolic trappings of state status. A threefold strategy has been immanent in Taiwan's accomplishments on this front for many years. The continuation and extension of this strategy hold promise in Taiwan's ongoing struggle with the difficulties and dangers posed by the U.S. "one China" policy, as well as "one China" policies more generally and Beijing's "One China Principle" (*Yige Zhongguo Yuanze*). Taiwan's tripartite approach can be summarized as:

- **Participating** in international regimes where participation does not require or entail state membership,

- **Choosing** symbolic or status-related struggles that also involve important substantive issues and consequences, and

- **Trying** to get help from U.S. laws that address matters related to Taiwan's status.

Formality Matters

The paradox that Taiwan's often-frustrated pursuit of the attributes of formal state status has helped it to preserve *de facto* state-like stature is more apparent than real. The formalities of international law and the realities of international politics here operate in a coherent if complex alignment: Although imperatives of power and preference sometimes lead states to disregard this rule, it is a relatively core principle of the international legal and political order that one state's aggression against another state is a matter of grave international concern, while a state's internal actions, including violent suppression of rebellion or secession and abuses of citizens or subjects, ordinarily are not matters of similar concern.

To put the point bluntly and starkly, such distinctions are among the factors (though certainly not the only factors) that led powers great and small to react differently to Iraq's invasion of Kuwait and Saddam Hussein's ruthless treatment of Kurds in Iraq's oil-rich north (or Shiites in its oil-rich south), or to Nazi Germany's invasion of Poland and what we would now call the severe human rights violations that the regime had already begun to commit against some of its own citizens—violations that, under principles that emerged largely in response to Hitler's genocide, now would be regarded as matters of legitimate international intervention.

This is not to say that states are punctilious about—or even much constrained by—the relevant international legal principles *per se*. Rather, and to put the point more formally and abstractly, international law reflects and reinforces a basic international political arrangement of a state-centered order in which it makes rule-consequentialist sense for leaders of states ordinarily to act in accordance with principles of nonintervention and respect for state sovereignty, even where narrowly act-consequentialist calculations might call for a contrary course. While an individual case of aggression or a particular instance of domestic atrocities may seem more or less compelling as a case for international action, other states are likely—other things being loosely comparable—to engage the former and ignore the latter because action in the first case safeguards basic norms of the system and the interests of states in the nearly sacrosanct nature of statehood, whereas action in the second case threatens those same norms, and the interests of states in the near-inviolability of states.

In a world where these are the general, if not exception-free or universally obeyed, rules of the game, it matters whether Taiwan is more like a state facing a threat from another state (China) or more like a region and group of people within a larger state of China facing coercion by that state's government—whether, in other words, Taiwan is more like Kuwait and Poland or more like the Iraqi Kurds, Marsh Arabs, and *circa* 1939 German Jews.

Beijing has understood this point in crafting its Taiwan policies and pronouncements.

- In its constitution, in its 1993 and 2000 White Papers on the Taiwan issue, in the 2005 Anti-Secession Law (all discussed at greater length in Chapter 2), and in countless other contexts, the People's Republic of China has insisted relentlessly that Taiwan already is a part of China that either has never been separated or, at least, returned to China decades ago and has not yet, and will not be allowed to, become a state separate from China.[1]

- Beijing has zealously, expensively, and effectively pursued—and has emphasized in its White Papers, exchanges with other states' governments, and elsewhere—a host of policy goals that serve this end, such as recognition of the PRC as the "sole legal government" of China; diplomatic relations with other governments to the exclusion of such governments' relations with Taipei's "Republic of China"; universal nonrecognition of Taiwan as a separate state; and widespread adoption of "one China" policies or, at least, official positions ranging from "taking note" to "acknowledgement" to "acceptance" of the PRC's position that "Taiwan is a part of China."[2]

---

[1] See, for example, Constitution of the People's Republic of China, preamble, 1982 and subsequent revisions; Information Office of the State Council, People's Republic of China, *The Taiwan Question and China's Unification*, August 31, 1993; Taiwan Affairs Office and Information Office of the State Council, People's Republic of China, *The One China Principle and the Taiwan Question*, February 21, 2000; Anti-Secession Law of the People's Republic of China, Articles 1–4, Article 8, March 14, 2005. See also Jacques deLisle, "The Chinese Puzzle of Taiwan's Status," *Orbis*, Winter 2000, pp. 38–43.

[2] Joint Communiqué on the Establishment of Diplomatic Relations Between the United States of America and the People's Republic of China, December 15, 1978 (stating that the U.S. government "acknowledges the Chinese position" that there is one China that includes Taiwan). For an overview of statements by other states incident to recognition of the PRC, see, for example, J. Bruce Jacobs, "One China, Diplomatic Isolation and a Separate Taiwan," in Edward Friedman, ed., *China's Rise, Taiwan's Dilemmas and International Peace* (London: Routledge, 2006).

- At times, official and quasi-official PRC sources even have seemed to press the archaic "constitutive theory" of recognition, which holds, contrary to the dominant view, that an entity cannot be a state until other states recognize it as such.[3]

Legal formality and political reality are, of course, intertwined here, but the PRC's Taiwan policy has been notable for the degree to which it has been highly intractable on form and relatively accommodating on substance. Examples are legion, but three from across a quarter-century suggest the point.

- Severing diplomatic relations with Taipei and derecognition of the Republic of China (ROC), as well as termination of the U.S.–ROC mutual defense treaty, were non-negotiable conditions for Beijing's 1979 normalization of U.S.–PRC relations, but China initially contented itself with a few howls of protest when Congress soon passed the Taiwan Relations Act (TRA), reinstating a good deal of the substance of the formally severed ties between Washington and Taipei.[4]

---

[3] See, for example, Convention on the Rights and Duties of States (Montevideo Convention), 49 Stat. 3907 (1933), Article 3 (rejecting the constitutive theory: "The political existence of the state is independent of recognition by the other states. Even before recognition the state has the right to defend its integrity and independence...."). See also *Restatement (Third) of the Foreign Relations Law of the United States*, Section 202(1) (Although a state is not required to recognize another state, it is required to treat as a state any entity that meets the international legal requirements for statehood). For the most formal articulations of PRC positions that stress the importance of the lack of recognition of Taiwan as a state and thereby imply an embrace of something akin to the constitutive theory, see *The Taiwan Question and China's Unification*, 1993 PRC White Paper, Section I (asserting other states' recognition/acknowledgement of the Chinese position concerning Taiwan's inclusion in China) and Section IV (rejecting "dual recognition"); see also *The One China Principle and the Taiwan Question*, 2000 PRC White Paper, Sections I and IV (similar).

[4] See, for example, Zhuang Qubing, Zhang Hongzeng, and Pan Tongwen, "On the United States' 'Taiwan Relations Act,'" *Renmin Ribao*, July 4, 1981 (excerpts from article in *Guoji Wenti Yanjiu*, July 1981); Chen Zu, "On the United States' 'Taiwan Relations Act,'" *Guangming Ribao*, May 31, 1981; *The Taiwan Question and China's Unification*, 1993 PRC White Paper, Section II. For the text of the Taiwan Relations Act, see Appendix B in this volume.

- Beijing has been at least grudgingly acquiescent in Taipei's joining many international organizations and maintaining informal relations with most governments, but it has insisted unwaveringly that Taiwan cannot participate in such institutions under the names of "Taiwan" or the "ROC," join any organization for which statehood is a criterion of membership, or enjoy formal diplomatic ties with states that maintain such relations with the PRC.[5]

- More recently, in its Anti-Secession Law, China went to great lengths to stress the principle that Taiwan is a part of China that would not be permitted to secede, not an already separated entity that needed to be reunified. There is, of course, much that is threatening to Taiwan in the Anti-Secession Law, including the provision concerning the use of force, the vagueness of key articles, and the mere fact of its enactment; but the legislation also omitted the "third if" of the 2000 White Paper, which threatened the use of force in the event of Taiwan's indefinite delay in engaging in reunification discussions, and eschewed the option of a "Reunification Law," which would have implied, from Beijing's perspective, a need to act to end Taiwan's separation.[6] The law thus reaffirmed Beijing's open-ended acquiescence in a cross-Strait *status quo* in which Taiwan has preserved and advanced, sometimes under a withering hail of criticism and threats from across the Strait, *de facto*—but not full *de jure*—status as a separate state.

Taipei too has appreciated the importance of formality. This understanding has lain behind its "dollar diplomacy" of expensive aid packages to the small number of poor and weak states whose governments maintain formal

---

[5] For overviews of these patterns, see Vincent Wei-cheng Wang, "Taiwan's Participation in International Organizations," in Freidman, ed., *China's Rise, Taiwan's Dilemmas and International Peace*, and deLisle, "The Chinese Puzzle of Taiwan's Status," pp. 37–38.

[6] Wang Te-chun, "Beijing Experts Explain the Anti-Secession Law," *Ta Kung Pao* Web site, December 18, 2004; "Chinese 'Expert' Calls Anti-Secession Law 'a Peace Law'," *Zhongguo Xinwen She*, March 14, 2005, in BBC Worldwide Monitoring (interview with Li Jiaquan); Zhu Daqiang, "Wen Jiabao Meets Local Chinese Representatives, Scholars, Students in UK," *Zhongguo Xinwen She*, May 10, 2004, in BBC Worldwide Monitoring (Wen Jiabao listening with approval to proposal by overseas Chinese for unification law).

relations with Taiwan or recognize the ROC government. The same idea surely lies behind Taiwan's quest to join a host of insignificant international organizations, as well as its clearly futile pursuit of some form of representation at the United Nations. Similar concerns impel Taiwanese leaders and diplomats to resist any embrace of Beijing's "One China Principle" by other states or any yielding to Beijing's demands that other countries adopt a "One China Policy." [7] This recognition of the importance of formalities also pervades many more focused and specific steps that Taiwan has taken, some of which are examined in greater detail below.

For Taiwan, as for China, such formalism and deadly real political interests are interwoven, but Taiwan's cross-Strait policies and related political pronouncements include a remarkable emphasis on the former simultaneously in pursuit of, and even at apparent risk to, the latter. Lee Teng-hui's "special state-to-state relations" formulation, Chen Shui-bian's "one country, each side" statement, and the many formulations by Lee, Chen, and others that offer variations on the theme that the ROC or Taiwan is an independent sovereign country that has no need to declare its independent statehood again all reflect the view that claiming as much formal, state-like status as possible, even if it might produce a cross-Strait crisis, is essential to enhancing Taiwan's security.[8]

---

[7] See, generally, T. Y. Wang, "Taiwan's Bid for UN Membership," in Friedman, ed., *China's Rise, Taiwan's Dilemmas and International Peace*; Lung-chu Chen, "Taiwan, China and the United Nations," and Linjun Wu, "Limitations and Prospects of Taiwan's Informal Diplomacy," in Jean-Marie Henckaerts, ed., *The International Status of Taiwan in the New World Order* (London and Boston: Kluwer Law International, 1996); deLisle, "The Chinese Puzzle of Taiwan's Status." For official Taiwan statements on such issues, see, for example, text of President Lee Teng-hui's interview with Deutsche Welle Radio, July 9, 1999, reprinted in *Chung-yang Jih-pao*, July 10, 1999; Ministry of Foreign Affairs, *Joining the Global Village—Taiwan's Participation in the International Community*, September 2005; Government Information Office, *The Republic of China on Taiwan and the United Nations: Questions and Answers*, April 1994; Mainland Affairs Council, *A Preliminary Analysis of Mainland China's "One China Strategy,"* February 1997; Mainland Affairs Council, *Statement on Mainland China's White Paper*, February 2000; National Unification Council, *National Unification Council's Definition of "One China,"* August 1992.

[8] Text of President Lee Teng-hui's interview with Deutsche Welle Radio; Mainland Affairs Council, *Parity, Peace and Win-Win: The Republic of China's Position on the "Special State-to-State Relationship,"* August 1, 1999; "President Chen Explains His 'One Country on Each Side' Remarks," *China Post*, August 31, 2002; "President Says Taiwan Sovereign State, No Need to Declare Independence," Central News Agency, February 19, 2004. For a fuller description of these positions, see Chapter 2 in this volume.

Washington has been less well attuned to the importance and subtleties of formal statements that have implications for Taiwan's status, and from this arguably have flowed some of the strife and snags in the triangular relationship. President Bill Clinton's "Three Noes," Secretary of State Colin Powell's statement that Taiwan "does not enjoy sovereignty as a nation," President George W. Bush's pledge that the U.S. would do "whatever it took" to help Taiwan defend itself, and numerous other examples of statements that seemed to shift U.S. positions toward—or away from—Beijing's preferred formulations concerning Taiwan, as well as the inevitable *sequelae* of corrections, counterstatements, and assurances that U.S. policy has not changed, all betoken a certain tin ear (or understandable lack of Beijing's and Taipei's focus and discipline) in dealing with the catechism of statements about Taiwan's formal status.[9] In key respects, however, and especially in the durable fundamentals of its approach to cross-Strait and Taiwan status issues, the U.S. too has understood and relied upon formalism, holding fast to the Three Communiqués and the Taiwan Relations Act, which most carefully—and, perhaps most important, lastingly—set forth U.S. positions concerning Taiwan's possession of key attributes of formal state status.

In facing this context in which the formalities of Taiwan's state or state-like status have loomed large for each of the three principal participants, albeit unequally and differently, Taiwan has followed an implicit three-pronged strategy. Embodied in numerous specific undertakings and supplementing the broader assertions of statehood or state-like status noted above, this strategy has achieved considerable success in pressing Taiwan's interests and remains promising in addressing new challenges and opportunities.

---

[9] President William J. Clinton, "Remarks in a Roundtable Discussion on Shaping China for the 21st Century in Shanghai, China," *Public Papers of the Presidents*, June 30, 1998, *Weekly Compilation of Presidential Documents*, No. 34 (1998), pp. 1267 ff.; "Clinton Reiterates 'Three Noes' Policy on Taiwan," Xinhua News Agency, July 2, 1998; Lillian Wu, "Powell's Remarks 'Harshest to Date' Says ROC Foreign Minister," Central News Agency, October 26, 2004; W. C. Lin and P. C. Tang, "U.S. Cross-Taiwan Strait Policy Remains Unchanged: State Department," Central News Agency, October 26, 2004; Brian Knowlton, "Bush Pledge: U.S. to Help If Chinese Hit Taiwan," *International Herald Tribune*, April 26, 2001, p. 1; President George W. Bush, "Remarks Following Discussions with Premier Wen Jiabao of China and an Exchange with Reporters," *Public Papers of the Presidents*, December 15, 2003.

Participating in International Regimes Without State Membership

Taiwan has pursued—and would be wise to continue to pursue—an agenda of participating in international regimes without state membership. As this somewhat ambiguous phrasing suggests, this tactic has come in at least two variants: one of trying to join organizations or regimes for which statehood is not a requirement for membership and another of seeking non–membership-based participation in institutions for which statehood is seen as a requirement of membership.

The use of the term "statehood" requires a bit of qualification. Depending on how one interprets and applies some complicated and contested international legal doctrines, Taiwan either does or does not clearly meet the criteria for being a state. With regard to its participation in international organizations, the issue is narrower and more practical: whether existing members accept Taiwan's inclusion, with those members in principle being bound to do so on the basis of whatever rules for access the institution may have. In terms of whether other members accept Taiwan, one key issue has been the vehemence and persuasiveness to an organization's gatekeepers of Beijing's opposition to Taiwan's participation; and that, in turn, has depended in part on shifting PRC policies concerning Taiwan's participation in international society generally and in part on whether the organization or regime is ostensibly "states-member-only." The U.S. "Three Noes" policy is among the many formal statements accepting the PRC's position that the latter factor—whether an organization is states-member-only—defines an important fault line.

Successes So Far. Taiwan has enjoyed growing success in joining international regimes for which statehood is not a precondition for membership. Many of these organizations are of little practical significance and little individual symbolic significance, but their sheer numbers do add up and do matter. They allow Taipei to claim levels of participation that most of the world's states do not match.[10]

Some of the organizations that Taiwan has joined as a full member matter a great deal to Taiwan and to the international or regional system and have a correspondingly greater symbolic weight. The Asia Pacific Economic Cooperation (APEC) forum, the Asian Development Bank, and the World Trade Organization (WTO) are among the key examples.

---

[10]See, generally, Michael Yahuda, "The International Standing of the Republic of China on Taiwan," *China Quarterly*, No. 148 (December 1996), pp. 1319, 1325–1330; deLisle, "The Chinese Puzzle of Taiwan's Status," pp. 37, 44–48; Wang, "Taiwan's Participation in International Organizations."

The WTO is, of course, the greatest and most recent of these major prizes grasped by Taiwan, ranking (at worst) second in prestige and importance to the U.N. among international institutions. The WTO is particularly significant as an example of a primarily states-member international treaty-based organization in which the PRC and the Hong Kong Special Administrative Region (SAR) are members alongside Taiwan. This entails a particularly important, concrete, and formal PRC acceptance of Taiwan's robust international stature—although not, of course, of any Taiwanese claim to statehood or any other status greater than that enjoyed by Hong Kong.[11]

Taiwan's pursuit of non-membership participation in international organizations has been less successful and significant, in part because Taiwan so often has been successful in its drive for full membership in many such institutions. In several organizations, observer status or other, similar forms of engagement have been a prelude to full membership. The General Agreement on Tariffs and Trade (GATT) and the successor WTO regimes are, again, a leading example. In other regimes, affiliate or observer status has been a more permanent arrangement. Examples include some of the non–East Asian regional regimes—addressing economic development, recognizing and reinforcing ties among democracies, and undertaking other forms of regional cooperation—in which full membership would be anomalous for a non-regional state.[12]

In general, because of Taiwan's ability in recent years to join fully so many East Asian regional and global regimes—including most of the major ones, particularly in economic fields—other than those for which state membership is required, or at least widely and credibly accepted as required,

---

[11]*The One China Principle and the Taiwan Question*, 2000 PRC White Paper, Section V; "Tricky Balance Between WTO and 'One China'," *United Daily News*, November 16, 2001; Su Huan-chih, "'One China' No Condition for Progress," *Taiwan News*, November 30, 2000; C. H. Lu and P. C. Tang, "ROC, PRC Hold First Bilateral Consultations Under WTO Framework," Central News Agency, December 13, 2002.

[12]See Y. F. Low, "President Hopes for Observer Status for Taiwan at OAS," Central News Agency, June 14, 2005; "Remarks by Ambassador Zhou Wenzhong, Permanent Observer of China at the Dialogue Between OAS Members and Permanent Observers," June 4, 2006, at *www.oas.org/speeches/speech.asp?sCodigo=06-0128*; "Taiwan Becomes Permanent Observer of Central American Body," Central News Agency, February 5, 2000 (concerning the Central American Integration System); Maubo Chang, "Central American Parliament Welcomes Taiwan to Join as Observer," Central News Agency, June 2, 1999; Sofia Wu, "Taiwan Hopes to Join European Group as an Observer," Central News Agency, February 18, 2005 (concerning Parliamentary Assembly of the Council of Europe); Sofia Wu, "DPP Lobbying ASEAN Observer Status for Taiwan," Central News Agency, October 16, 1998.

there has been relatively little scope for continued or expanded pursuit of observer or similar status outside of the U.N. and U.N.-affiliated organizations. Any formal role in U.N. bodies, even at the observer level, has been unattainable because of the PRC's insistence on, and others' acquiescence in, Taiwan's exclusion from any significant participation in these states-member-only organizations.

Another qualification is in order here. While it is generally accepted that the U.N. is a states-member-only organization, and while the U.N. is the focus of the U.S. policy of not supporting Taiwan's membership in states-member-only organizations, the notion that the U.N. is an exclusively states club is not beyond dispute. The principle that U.N. members must be states is not explicitly set forth in the U.N. Charter and has had to be inferred from substantive provisions and the organization's practice.

Moreover, practice has hardly been unblemished. No one seriously thought that the Byelorussian Soviet Socialist Republic and the Ukrainian S.S.R. were states distinct from the Soviet Union, but that did not preclude their membership under an arrangement that gave Moscow three votes in the General Assembly. The two Germanys and the two Koreas joined the U.N. as well, despite less than fully resolved questions about whether each pair constituted in principle two fully separate states or merely parts of a temporarily divided state, in many respects akin to what some see as the situation with Taiwan and the PRC. Additionally, during the entire 1945–1971 period of the ROC's membership in the U.N., it was an absurd—if diplomatically useful—fiction that the ROC represented the state of China as its government or even as its legitimate government in temporary exile. Functionally, although clearly not formally, the U.N. had Taiwan, which no U.N. member recognizes as a state, and not China as a member for more than two decades.

Membership aside, the U.N. and its affiliated agencies have allowed observer status and analogous arrangements for entities that have had many—but arguably not all—of the attributes of states, including the Palestine Liberation Organization, the Holy See at the Vatican, and the Knights of Malta.[13] Taiwan has sensibly pursued a strategy that evokes such precedents, albeit with little success. The most nearly successful of recent efforts was its pursuit of observer status in the World Health Organization. In the wake of the SARS (severe acute respiratory syndrome) crisis and China's secretive and bungled handling of a threat that appeared to imperil much of the world, especially Taiwan and other states with dense travel

---

[13]United Nations, *Growth in United Nations Membership, 1945–2006*, at *www.un.org/Overview/growth.htm*, and *Organizations Granted Observer Status in the General Assembly*, at *http://lib-unique.un.org/lib/unique.nsf/Link/R02020*.

links to China, Taiwan was able to secure relatively widespread support, including backing from the U.S. and Japan, for greater access and an enhanced level of participation in the key institution of the global public health order.[14]

More broadly, Taiwan's quest for some form of engagement with the U.N. has continued to emphasize primarily (though not exclusively) the issue of the representation of the 23 million people of Taiwan rather than U.N. membership for Taiwan as a state.[15] While this pursuit, like others targeting the U.N. and its affiliated agencies, has not borne fruit and arguably has provided occasions for high-profile international rejection of Taiwanese claims to state-like status, expressions of support for Taiwan from a minority of states and Taipei's success in keeping the question of Taiwan's participation and stature on the international agenda arguably outweigh the downsides on this front in the battle over forms and symbols of statehood or its near-equivalent. Focusing on U.N. representation of the people on Taiwan has many of the same virtues and some (but not all) of the risks of the secondary long-standing and recently resurgent tactic that seeks full U.N. membership for Taiwan.

Finally, Taiwan has sought a degree of participation, or even membership, in less formal regimes—those that typically do not have an "organization" or "institution" at their core. Treaty regimes are the most common and important example of this, and the ROC has joined many multilateral

---

[14]See "Bush Signs Act on Taiwan WHO Bid," *China Post*, June 16, 2004; "Taiwan in Fresh Bid to Enter WHO, Fears China," *China Post*, May 11, 2005. See also, generally, Jacques deLisle, "SARS, Greater China, and the Pathologies of Globalization and Transition," *Orbis*, Fall 2003, pp. 587 ff.

[15]See U.N. representation-related sources cited in note 7. See also Ministry of Foreign Affairs, *The Republic of China on Taiwan and the United Nations: Why the UN Resolution No. 2758 Should Be Reexamined Today*, 1996; "'Let the Cry for Justice Reach Far and Wide,' Remarks of Premier Lien Chan," reprinted in Mainland Affairs Council, *There Is No "Taiwan Question": Views on the Chinese Communists' White Paper, "The Taiwan Question and Reunification of China,"* September 16, 1993, Appendix I; Government Information Office (ROC), *The Republic of China on Taiwan and the United Nations: Questions and Answers*, April 1994; "Taiwan to Make Tenth Bid for UN Entry," *Taiwan News*, August 14, 2002; Office of the President, *President Chen Interviewed by Washington Post*, March 13, 2006; Lillian Wu, "President Urges U.N. to Heed Representation of Taiwan People," Central News Agency, August 13, 2005; "Chen Advocates Using 'Taiwan' in Bid for U.N.," *Taiwan News*, September 14, 2006; "A Dialogue with President Chen Shui-bian: Excerpts of a Transcript of a Videoconference Question and Answer Session with UN Journalists," September 14, 2006, at *www.gio.gov.tw/taiwan-website/4-oa/20060914/2006091401.html*.

treaties to which other, mostly state parties have been willing to have Taiwan accede. Like Taiwan's memberships in international organizations, such treaty regimes run the gamut from the seemingly symbolic or mundane to the vitally important.

The WTO/GATT II Agreement, although centered on a formidable formal organization, illustrates the significance of treaty regime inclusion. Concurrent membership in the WTO as an organization aside, the PRC's acceptance of Taiwan as a fellow signatory to the substantive treaty arrangements set forth in the WTO/GATT II Agreement entails or reflects Beijing's recognition of Taiwan's capacity to engage in an especially formal version of international relations typically (though not exclusively) undertaken by states. The PRC has thereby accepted that it and Taiwan bear reciprocal treaty obligations that are formally collateral to the formal institutions that are the core of the WTO-centered trade order. To be sure, Beijing's view is that Taiwan here enjoys nothing more than the Hong Kong SAR does, but there is the crucial difference that Hong Kong acceded under the sponsorship of one sovereign state (the United Kingdom) and with the endorsement of the other relevant sovereign state (China), whereas Taiwan, which joined under the later, procedurally different WTO/GATT II regime, entered on its own, not under another, higher sovereign's aegis.[16]

U.N. treaty regimes pose much the same problem for Taiwan's strategy as participation in U.N.-affiliated institutions poses. Here, Taiwan occasionally has used a clever approach of pledging that it will abide fully by a U.N. treaty, as well as the substantive rules adopted by treaty-based or treaty-implementing U.N.-affiliated organs, just as it would if it were an accepted party to the treaty or, indeed, a member of the organization. Examples of this include Taiwan's approach to the Montreal Protocol, a key U.N. environmental treaty; the principal U.N. treaty on narcotics trafficking; WHO directives and conventions, notably amid the SARS crisis but also on less transient matters such as tobacco; the nuclear nonproliferation treaty and regime, including the Non-Proliferation Treaty to which the ROC had acceded and the International Atomic Energy Agency, the U.N.-related body with which Taiwan continues to cooperate despite its ouster in conjunction with the PRC's joining; other weapons-related treaty-based regimes, including the U.N. Chemical Weapons Convention; and international air safety–related regulations associated with the U.N.-affiliated International Civil Aviation Organization (ICAO).

---

[16]See sources cited in note 11. For a relatively recent example of Taiwan's joining a multilateral convention governing a relatively obscure issue, see "Taiwan Joins Inter-American Tropical Tuna Convention," *Asia Pulse*, November 19, 2003.

Taiwan has taken steps down the same road with respect to key U.N. human rights conventions. Similarly, it has endorsed and pledged to abide by Security Council resolutions on Iraq, Yugoslavia, and counterterrorism.[17] This type of move underscores a degree of behavioral equivalence between Taiwan and the member states and thus can help to enhance Taiwan's status as a fully state-like entity.

The Road Ahead. Given Taiwan's successes in using these methods to pursue participation in international regimes without state membership, and despite the problem of diminishing returns, Taiwan's interests lie in continuing to employ this basic approach. This will require focusing on protecting the gains already made and approaching long-standing or new

---

[17]Deborah Kuo, "Taiwan Vows to Continue Supporting Montreal Protocol," Central News Agency, October 29, 1997; Ministry of Foreign Affairs, *The Republic of China on Taiwan and the United Nations*, September 1995, Section IV (Taiwan's implementation of United Nations Convention Against Illicit Traffic in Narcotic Drugs and Pyschotropic Substances); Li Li-chung, "Cracking Down on Money Laundering," *Taipei Times*, September 23, 2003 (Taiwan legislation tracking U.N. Convention); Lin Chieh-yu, "Taiwan President Argues Case for WHO Membership," *Taipei Times*, April 4, 2003; "Taiwan to Follow WHO Formula for Issuing SARS Statistics," Central News Agency, May 15, 2003; "Legislature Passes Framework Convention on Tobacco Control," Central News Agency, January 14, 2005; "IAEA to Supervise Taiwan Nuclear Activities," Xinhua News Agency, April 4, 2006; Neil Li and Sofia Wu, "ROC Has Never Violated Nuclear Agreement," Central News Agency, December 22, 1997; "ROC Not Violating Nuke Non-Proliferation Treaty: U.S. State Department," Central News Agency, March 24, 1988; "Taiwan Defense Ministry States It Does Not Develop Biological, Chemical Weapons," *Taiwan News* Web site, April 16, 2003; Maubo Chang, "Taiwan to Abide by UN Convention on Chemical Weapons," Central News Agency, February 14, 1997; "President Says Taiwan Has Improved Flight Safety," Central News Agency, October 1, 2002 (ICAO and international civil aviation rules conformity, specifically in crash investigations); Flor Wang, "Executive Yuan Approves MOFA Plan to Join U.N.-Adopted Convention," Central News Agency, July 12, 2006 (Convention on the Elimination of Discrimination Against Women); Maubo Chang, "Committee of Legislature Ratifies Two Human Rights Conventions," Central News Agency, May 30, 2002 (Covenant on Civil and Political Rights and Covenant on Economic, Social and Cultural Rights); "ROC Commended for Sharing in International Responsibility," Central News Agency, May 23, 1991 (U.S. House of Representatives committee measure praising Taiwan's abiding by U.N. resolutions concerning Iraq); "ROC Endorses U.S. Air Strikes Against Iraq," *China Post*, December 18, 1998 (supporting U.N. resolutions); "Taiwan Exclusion from UN Violates UN Charter," Central News Agency, April 4, 1994 (ROC conformity to U.N. sanctions resolutions concerning Serbia–Bosnia); Deborah Kuo, "Taiwan Part of Global Anti-Terrorism Actions," Central News Agency, November 18, 2004.

opportunities with a keen appreciation of the remaining (if limited) potential of past tactics.

In the not-states-member-only international organizations of which Taiwan is a member, defensive action is still necessary to prevent erosion of the gains in formal status that membership has offered. Here too, the WTO provides the most prominent example. Although Beijing accepted Taiwan's accession as part of the deal paving the way for its own membership, China stuck to its usual insistence that Taiwan could not join under the name "Taiwan" or "ROC." More to the point, the PRC has made sustained efforts to downgrade Taiwan's status in the WTO and undermine its claims to equality with China in the global trading body. Examples include refusing to meet with Taiwan on site, avoiding ordinary consultations with Taiwan within the WTO framework, and seeking to change the names under which Taiwan and its representative participate in the WTO.[18] China's pursuit of a Taiwan-excluding ASEAN (Association of Southeast Asian Nations)–China Free Trade Area represents another, more fundamental threat on this front, for it would take many regional trade disputes out of the immediate WTO framework, exclude Taiwan from a new major regional economic regime, and weaken Taiwan's international economic position.[19]

As the chronic tenuousness of the ROC's hold on a small and shifting cast of minor states illustrates, the diplomatic relations and government recognition side of Taiwan's participation in the formal aspects of the international order requires constant vigilance on Taipei's part. The PRC's rising wealth and power—and consequent ability to bribe or pressure Taiwan's partners—will make this an increasingly difficult task, but it is one that remains worth pursuing. The seemingly quaint institutions of recognition and diplomatic relations still matter in the formal dimension of international status, especially for Taiwan, given its relatively weak position

---

[18]"Taiwan Calls for China to Respect WTO Rules After Refusal to Consult," Central News Agency, September 3, 2002; "China Accepts Taiwan's Designation Name to WTO," Central News Agency, July 22, 2005; "Political Obstacles Prevent Taiwan Joining WTO's Procurement Agreement," Central News Agency, August 23, 2003; Jacques deLisle, "China and the WTO," in Tung-jen Cheng, Jacques deLisle, and Deborah Brown, eds., *China Under Hu Jintao: Opportunities, Dangers and Dilemmas* (World Scientific Publishing Co., 2006), pp. 287–289; Kong Qingjiang, *China and the World Trade Organization: A Legal Perspective* (World Scientific Publishing Co., 2002), Chapter 5.

[19]See Maubo Chang, "Taiwan to Suffer over Free Trade Accord Between China, ASEAN: Study," Central News Agency, February 26, 2006; Alice D. Ba, "China–ASEAN Relations: The Significance of an ASEAN–China Free Trade Area," in Cheng, deLisle, and Brown, eds., *China Under Hu Jintao*.

under any *realpolitik* calculus. More immediately relevant, however, is the fact that Taiwan's formal diplomatic partners remain vital to Taiwan's ability to maintain (through, for example, proposed General Assembly resolutions) a degree of pressure on the U.N. and other states-member-only institutions that exclude Taiwan to avoid completely evading the question of Taiwan's claim to state-like status.[20]

To the extent that Taiwan recurrently renews its campaign for some role and recognition within the U.N. system, the past contours of its approach continue to make sense. Seeking full, ordinary membership for "Taiwan" or the "ROC" will remain, at least for now, a futile frontal assault on "one China" policies of the sort adopted by the United States and many other U.N. member states. Emphasizing representation for the people of Taiwan and their interests still will be a sensible alternative to the most head-on confrontation of a "one China" policy or principle in several respects.[21] The question of representation of a discrete population does not automatically equate with the status of state membership for the political entity that the population comprises. Moreover, U.N. membership questions inevitably are channeled through procedures in which China has a veto, whereas that is not so clearly the case for the relatively unexplored question of U.N. representation for excluded people or even allowing the "ROC" to resume its former seat, but as something other than the government representing all of China.

A more hopeful avenue for Taiwan as an inroad into the U.N. system lies in seeking observer or other less than full membership status in U.N.-affiliated organizations. The WHO, again, has been the most prominent and promising example, coming in the aftermath of the potentially disastrous SARS pandemic-that-might-have-been and the PRC's dangerous mishandling of it, and as concerns over avian flu rise. Here there were two significant, if ultimately disappointing, developments. One was the support that Taiwan managed to mobilize in the post-SARS World Health Assembly (WHA) for permitting Taiwan a larger and more formal role within the organization. Another was the Chen administration's consideration of a

---

[20]See, for example, "Caricom Nations Reiterate Call for Taiwan's Full Membership in UN," in BBC Monitoring International Reports, September 25, 2005; Huang Kwang-chun, "ROC Allies Again Push U.N. to Consider Taiwan's Membership Bid," Central News Agency, August 6, 2003; "Allies Submit Proposal Calling for Taiwan Membership of UN," Central News Agency, July 21, 1996.

[21]See, generally, sources cited in note 15. See also Deborah Kuo, "Taiwan Ministry to Work 'Pragmatically' on UN Membership Bid," Central News Agency Web site, November 26, 2004.

national referendum in Taiwan on the question of whether Taiwan should participate in the WHO.[22]

Although the Referendum Law that Taiwan's Legislative Yuan passed made such a ballot question infeasible, and although its passage would have done little or nothing to change other states' positions (and would not even have had any significant binding legal effect in Taiwan), it was an ingenious idea. It did bring more international attention to the issue. Also, it forged more of a link between Taiwan's participation in the WHO and Taiwan's domestic democratization, which matters in an international legal and political order in which states and would-be states that live up to international standards of democracy, human rights, and legality enjoy a somewhat more robust status than their counterparts that fall short on those yardsticks.[23]

In addition to its attempts with the World Health Organization, Taiwan has pursued and can pursue its interests with more modest efforts (and with perhaps even more modest prospects for success) to obtain less than membership participation in other U.N.-affiliated organs such as the International Civil Aviation Organization.[24]

Formal organizations and less institutionalized regimes for which state status is not so clearly or widely accepted as a condition for membership offer additional opportunities. Possible examples include regimes focusing on economic cooperation or weapons proliferation. One example of the latter is the Australia Group, a non–U.N.-affiliated organization for the control of chemical and biological weapons and precursors of which China is not yet a member. Another example—now beyond practical reach with

---

[22]See sources cited in note 14 and Donald G. McNeil, Jr., "Taiwan Cites Epidemic in Fight at UN Agency," *International Herald Tribune*, May 21, 2003, p. 1. On the referendum issue, see Lin Chen-yu, "DPP Reiterates Pledge to Hold Referendum on 'Domestic Issues'," Global News Wire, June 24, 2003; "Chen Plays Referendum Card," *China Daily*, June 19, 2003.

[23]See sources cited in note 44. See also "Referendum Could be Based on Constitution, Chen Says," *China Post*, July 16, 2003; Lillian Wu, "Chen Shui-bian Says Referendum More Significant than Presidential Election," Central News Agency, July 15, 2003; Jacques deLisle, "Reforming/Replacing the ROC Constitution: Implications for Taiwan's State(-like) Status and U.S. Policy," Woodrow Wilson International Center for Scholars, Asia Program, *Special Report* No. 125, November 2004, pp. 12, 14–16.

[24]See, for example, "International Civil Aviation Organization Urged to Accept Taiwan as Observer," Central News Agency, April 26, 2002; Ministry of Foreign Affairs, *Joining the Global Village—Taiwan's Participation in the International Community.*

China's 2004 accession—is the Nuclear Suppliers Group. Still other related examples include the Missile Technology Control Regime (MTCR) and the Wassenaar Arrangement governing conventional weapons technology.

Possibilities of the economic sort remain as well, with the Organisation for Economic Co-operation and Development (OECD) being a notable example of an important organization with which Taiwan has made modest inroads toward observer status.[25] But some of the economic regime prospects are eroding as a result of China's growing success in engaging ASEAN and pressing an ASEAN–China Free Trade Agreement (ACFTA).

For reasons that animate the second element of Taiwan's three-pronged strategy, which are discussed more fully in the following section, the most important and promising opportunities for non-state-membership participation lie in regimes the exclusion from which threatens—or can be portrayed credibly as threatening—to have seriously adverse real-world consequences for Taiwan.

There is also much to be said for continuing and expanding the tactic of declaring that Taiwan will fulfill all obligations of particular multilateral treaties from which it remains formally excluded. The benefits go beyond the "state-like-ness" that such announced behavior implies. Many such regimes regulate areas in which Taiwan is an important player or in which it has important interests at stake. One example is the U.N. Chemical Weapons Convention, which regulates dual-use items that it is important to Taiwan to import.

The previously noted non–U.N.-centered weapons-related regimes offer similar and more promising opportunities in other fields in which Taiwan possesses or seeks relevant technology and where important international security issues are at stake. Indeed, Taiwan already has gone down this path with some of them, adopting national policies and laws that explicitly conform to the regimes' requirements.[26] So too, continuation and extension of Taiwan's recent approach to the major U.N. human rights conventions would play to an area in which Taiwan, as a leading example of a successful

---

[25]See, for example, Neil Lu and Deborah Kuo, "Taiwan to Become Observer at OECD Steel Committee," Central News Agency, August 28, 2005; C. H. Lu and P. C. Tang, "Taiwan to Attend OECD Trade Committee Meeting as 'Ad Hoc Observer'," Central News Agency, February 22, 2005.

[26]See, for example, "Taiwan Defense Ministry States That It Does Not Develop Biological Chemical Weapons," *Taiwan News* Web site, April 16, 2003 (Australia Group); "Defense Ministry Denies US Report of Possessing Nuclear Warheads," Central News Agency, May 15, 2000 (MTCR); Government Information Office, "Taiwan Premier Takes Questions at Anniversary Press Conference," in BBC Worldwide Monitoring, January 30, 2003 (Wassenaar Arrangement).

democratic transition in East Asia, has significant normative and symbolic standing. If long-stalled efforts to build a multilateral regime for international investment regain momentum, they might provide another such opportunity, given Taiwan's deep engagement with and great importance to the international economy.

Announcing a binding commitment to abide by such rules would underscore the oddity of Taiwan's exclusion from the relevant regime—a point akin to the one that Taiwan made during its long exclusion from the formal side of the international trade order. Moreover, such "unilateral declarations," when made with the requisite formality, clarity, and intent by heads of states' governments, in principle can have the same international legal obligation–creating effect as does a state's becoming a party to a treaty. For Taiwan, such an effect would again help to close the gap between its behavior and standing and those of fully accepted state parties.

As discussed more fully below, this "as if" approach to membership in U.N. and other treaty regimes and less formal international institutions could help Taiwan's chances to gain the type of help from U.S. law that could be a focus within the third strand in Taiwan's long-running strategy for securing and expanding its international space and status.

As suggested both by the Asian Development Bank and WTO examples from the past and by the Australia Group and OECD examples as possible opportunities for the future, Taiwan's quest for membership or even mere participation in regimes for which state status is not clearly required is also likely to fare better where China has not preceded Taiwan in joining.

Choosing Symbolic Struggles with Substantive Content

In trying to join or participate in international regimes, Taiwan at times has focused—and would be well advised to continue to focus—on those in which exclusion entails or portends real costs for Taiwan and, ideally, for the regime and its other members as well. The point is obvious and simple, yet fundamental and urgent: Where Taiwan picks battles that seem not to involve matters with substantial real-world consequences either for itself or for its potential partners in a regime, its efforts are more likely to be dismissed as being really about symbolism and status. Other states (principally the United States) will be less likely to support Taiwan's pursuit of participation and more likely to blame Taiwan for unreasonably and unnecessarily producing any resulting friction or crisis in relations with China. On the other hand, where Taiwan seeks to join regimes that regulate areas that are vital to its interests and in which Taiwan is a significant participant, there is likely to be a good deal more interest from other states in Taiwan's inclusion and sympathy for Taiwan's quest for entry even if it roils the waters of cross-Strait relations or U.S.–China or other bilateral relations.

Examples from the Past. Many of Taiwan's more visible and significant successes in winning membership in important international institutions have come in areas where excluding Taiwan has left a glaring and damaging hole in the regime. Taiwan's economic importance in the East Asia and Asia–Pacific regions obviously strengthened its hand in gaining or maintaining acceptance in organizations such as APEC and the Asian Development Bank. Accession to the WTO reflected Taiwan's important place in the international trading system, which Taiwanese sources relentlessly stressed with citations to Taiwan's high rank among international trading entities.[27]

Despite Taiwan's already having come into extensive conformity with WTO requirements and norms, its entry was of course held up until after a deal was reached on China's accession. Still, given the singular importance of the WTO in the international institutional order, as well as the global economic order, and the extent to which Beijing long had resisted Taiwan's full membership in major international organizations, even those not strictly requiring statehood for membership, Taiwan's WTO entry is a testament to the persuasiveness of the argument that the WTO could not be a truly "world" trade organization or, indeed, a fully effective international trade body if it excluded an entity as important as Taiwan, the world's 12th-largest trading nation (or if it continued to exclude the PRC, for that matter).

Taiwan's nearest miss at gaining a substantial participatory role in one of the core U.N.-affiliated organs reflects the same basic pattern. The SARS crisis created an opportunity. China's poor handling of the outbreak created perceptions of serious danger for the rest of the world as well as Taiwan. One of the pathways by which SARS threatened to spread internationally was through Taiwan. Excluding Taiwan from full access to rapid, real-time cooperation with the full range of foreign and international public health organs and experts, as facilitated through the WHO, could be portrayed credibly—and quite possibly accurately—as endangering vital global interests by increasing the risk that the then-mysterious illness would

---

[27]See, for example, "Paving the Way for a Sustainable Taiwan," Chen Shui-bian Presidential Inaugural Speech, May 20, 2004, reprinted in *Taipei Times*, May 21, 2004, p. 8 (noting Taiwan's 12-year struggle for WTO accession despite its high rank both as a trading nation and in international competitiveness); *Taiwan's Accession to the World Trade Organization*, January 4, 1999, at *www.taipei.org/current/un/WTO.htm*; "Taiwan's New Post-WTO Economy," *Commercial Times*, November 21, 2001.

spread more effectively to Taiwan and beyond by means of the hundreds of thousands of travelers moving between Taiwan and southern China, a perennial incubator for human influenza and other viruses.

These concerns and arguments were important in the U.S. and other countries taking up Taiwan's cause before the World Health Assembly. The PRC and others were tellingly reduced to reliance on arguments that communications among WHO member states and China (and, implicitly, the communications between Taiwan and such states, principally the U.S., that China could do nothing about and the limited cooperation of the WHO with Taiwan that China grudgingly tolerated) provided adequate substitutes for the WHO's full, ordinary direct involvement with Taiwan's public health authorities. The partial persuasiveness of this argument was reflected in WHO officials' having undertaken to assure worried publics in mid-crisis that billions of people's health was not being put at risk by China's politics of cross-Strait relations.[28]

A parallel but less internationally supported effort by Taiwan to attain some level of participation in a U.N.-affiliated organ—and the regime that it anchors—has targeted the International Civil Aviation Organization. Here too, Taiwan has stressed the costs to the international system, as well as to itself, of its exclusion. Thus, Taiwanese sources speak of the high volume of air traffic that flows through and around Taiwan's airspace and the increased danger to passengers, crew, and planes that follows from Taiwan's exclusion from the principal relevant international institution. Some statements have even invoked the ostensible sockdologer of the post-9/11 world: the argument that excluding Taiwan harms the global fight against terrorism.[29]

---

[28]For Taiwan's arguments, see Government Information Office, *The Global Health Imperative for Granting Taiwan WHO Membership*, revised March 2003, and Donald G. McNeil, Jr., "SARS Furor Heightens Taiwan–China Rift," *The New York Times*, May 19, 2003. For PRC claims of adequate alternatives, see, for example, "Another Failure for Taiwanese Separatists," *Renmin Ribao*, May 21, 2003. For WHO official's statement, see C. H. Liu and P. C. Tang, "Taiwan Not Hurt in SARS Battle by Lack of Membership: WHO Official," Central News Agency, May 16, 2003. See also L. S. Chu and Deborah Kuo, "Taiwan Maintains Smooth Communication with U.S.: Top Taiwan Envoy," Global News Wire, July 10, 2003 (citing President Chen's praise for U.S. Centers for Disease Control cooperation in SARS crisis).

[29]See sources cited in note 24. See also Wei Tiemin and Li Haiting, "Chang Hsiao-yen: Spring Festival Charter Flights Dispel Misgivings about 'Dignity and Safety,'" Xinhua News Agency, February 8, 2004, available in BBC Worldwide Monitoring. See also Lillian Wu, "Taiwan Has Taken Part in International Anti-Terrorism Efforts: Minister," Central News Agency, December 8, 2003, and Charles Snyder, "U.S. Helps Push for Taiwan's UN Body Bid," *Taipei Times*, August 28, 2004, p. 1.

These concerns have generated some understanding for Taiwan's agenda, but Taiwan's case has been hurt by the plausibility of arguments that alternative means for providing the requisite safety are available and that, because of this, there is no need for members of the organization to court Beijing's wrath by broaching the question of Taiwan's formal participation or membership. The International Maritime Organization (IMO)—another U.N. affiliate—is a case that obviously parallels the ICAO.

Another aspect of international civil aviation has produced an additional wrinkle and variation on this theme. The Warsaw Convention limits liability for accidental damage on flights originating in or traveling to the territory of a party to the treaty. The PRC, as the government of China, acceded to the treaty and, as in so many treaty-centered regimes, has stood in the way of Taiwan's separate membership, claiming explicitly in its declaration ratifying the convention that the PRC's accession extends to Taiwan.

This has given rise to litigation that has raised the issue in U.S. courts of whether Taiwan is part of the territory of China or is a separate state or near-state. Although the courts in the two most significant relevant cases did not squarely decide this question, one court emphasized that the executive branch, reinforced by the TRA, continued to deal with Taiwan separately, especially in matters of treaties, despite derecognition of the ROC and recognition of the PRC. Another court, much to the chagrin of Taiwan, which failed to seek to be heard in the case in a timely manner, went the other way, pointing to the executive branch's recognition of the PRC as the sole government of a China that includes Taiwan.

The statements of courts are a questionable source of the positions of a state's government, which is what matters for international legal and political questions, including those concerning another entity's state or state-like stature. While the independent significance of court decisions is further weakened where, as here, the courts purport to be discerning and following the will of the political branches, such judicial opinions, seemingly paradoxically, may be more politically salient provided that the courts' analyses of their coequal branches' positions are correct. However one parses them as matters of U.S. law and policy, Taiwan rightly saw these cases as sources of danger and opportunity in defining the U.S. position on the question of Taiwan's status.[30] (The context of the Warsaw Convention–related litigation oddly flipped the usual alignment of issues, however: A finding that affirms Taiwan's separate status has the effect of weakening the international regime, in this case one that is meant to create limited and predictable liability and, in turn, to facilitate international commerce.)

In most of these areas in which Taiwan has been able to argue persuasively or at least credibly that Taiwan's exclusion harms the international regime and the interests it is meant to serve, there has also been a convincing or at least plausible argument that Taiwan's exclusion harms the real, tangible interests of Taiwan and its people. Thus, Taiwanese sources have emphasized that Taiwan's exclusion from regional trade and financial regimes, including the prospective ACFTA or the WTO, harmed or threatened to harm Taiwan's economic interests, making it more vulnerable to illiberal trade policies from its trading partners, targeted sanctions or barriers from the PRC, lack of access to dispute resolution mechanisms, and lack of influence in shaping the regime's rules.[31]

Much the same can be said about the ICAO and the IMO. To the extent that international weapons and nuclear energy regimes involve dual-use or other trade-restricted and highly regulated technologies, Taiwan's being less than fully included has been criticized, quite plausibly, on the basis of economic harm to Taiwan.

Similarly, the impact of SARS in Taiwan and the specter of its wider spread or recurrence made possible vivid and compelling arguments about how exclusion from the WHO outrageously put at risk the lives and health of people in Taiwan.[32] Insofar as Taiwan's quest for representation in the U.N. has had any traction, some of that has come from a focus on the resulting harms to the people of Taiwan. Compared to a futile fight over full membership, arguments underscoring the absence of representation of the people of Taiwan better enable Taiwan to evoke the U.N. principles of universal scope and the protection of human rights of all people around the

---

[30]See *Atlantic Mutual Insurance Co. v. Northwest Airlines*, 796 F. Supp. 1188 (E.D. Wisc. 1992), 24 F.3d 958 (7th Cir. 1994) (relying on the executive branch's derecognition of the ROC and recognition of the PRC as the government of China, including Taiwan, to conclude that Taiwan is covered by the PRC's accession to the treaty), and *Mingtai Fire & Marine Insurance Co. v. United Parcel Service*, 177 F.3d 1142 (9th Cir. 1999) (deferring to the political branches' position as expressed in the TRA and executive statements to conclude that Taiwan is not covered by the PRC's accession to the treaty). See also *Atlantic Mutual Insurance Co. v. Northwest Airlines*, 829 F. Supp. 1066 (E.D. Wisc. 1993), *affirmed* 24 F.3d 958 (7th Cir. 1994), and *Coordination Council for North American Affairs v. Northwest Airlines*, 891 F. Supp. 4 (E.D. Wisc. 1995) (all concerning CCNAA's unsuccessful attempt to intervene and to have the court revisit the question of the convention's applicability to Taiwan).

[31]"Taiwan Holds High-Level Meeting with WTO," *Asia Pulse*, October 8, 2002; Lillian Wu, "Taiwan's Economy Will Benefit from WTO Accession: Economic Official," Central News Agency, November 13, 2001; *Taiwan's Accession to the World Trade Organization*. See also sources cited at note 19 above and "Trade Policies Vital for Taiwan of Avoid Marginalization," *Asia Pulse*, January 5, 2006; Fang Wen-hung, "Taiwan's Next Priority to Join Free Trade Area: Economic Official," Central News Agency, January 16, 2002.

world, including the people of Taiwan, regardless of what state—if any—is their state of nationality.[33]

Confronting the Future. It is worthwhile for Taiwan to continue to make arguments about injuries to itself, as well as arguments about threats to other states' and systemic interests, arising from Taiwan's being kept out of significant international institutions and regimes. In the hard political world of confronting or challenging the PRC over matters relating to Taiwan's status, arguments about how Taiwan's exclusion hurts other states' or broader global interests are likely indispensable, not least because altruistic efforts to protect Taiwan's interests cannot be expected to be heroic. Nonetheless, Taiwanese arguments that can be convincingly framed as seeking to safeguard important self-interests offer the best hope for rebutting suspicions that Taiwan's agenda with respect to an international regime, treaty, or organization is only ostensibly about the relevant substance and is really about the broader and more politically charged issue of Taiwan's international status.

Taiwan has good reason to continue using these tactics to address new and, in some cases, more auspicious circumstances in some of the same regimes that it already has sought to engage. Taiwan, for example, may be a principal beneficiary of WTO "mission creep."

Compared to the old GATT regime, the WTO-centered regime covers a much larger swath of international economic activity. Thus, members of the WTO are fully equal participants in the primarily states-member institution not just for trade in manufactured goods, which was the focus of the GATT system that the PRC and Taiwan sought to rejoin beginning in the 1980s, but also for trade in agricultural products, trade in many services, and important aspects of intellectual property and the regulation of international investment. Much to the dismay of zealous advocates of state sovereignty everywhere, not least in Beijing and Washington, and despite the recent setbacks over agricultural trade and other issues in the Doha Round, the scope of the WTO has grown and well may continue to grow, taking in more aspects of intellectual property rights and investment regulation and reaching out to address human rights and environmental issues that have significant (or even not so significant) effects on trade. Simply by holding on to its position as a full member in an ostensibly trade-regulating body,

---

[32]See, for example, Melody Chen, "Mystery Illness Highlights Taiwan's Health Isolation," *Taipei Times*, March 18, 2003, p. 1, and McNeil, "SARS Furor Heightens Taiwan–China Rift."

[33]See, generally, the sources cited in note 15. See also Lillian Lin and P. C. Tang, "Taiwan Cannot Operate Normally Without U.N. Membership: Envoy," Central News Agency, September 14, 2005.

Taiwan has become and can remain a more robust participant in a much wider and still-expanding range of international regimes with which the WTO-centered order increasingly overlaps. These advantages can accrue even while Taiwan remains barred from membership in the central formal organizations of some of those regimes.

East Asian regional economic regimes, organizations, and other cooperation schemes offer opportunities for Taiwan to make a still more compelling case built on the importance of the island's economy to the region's, and vice versa. Here, however, China's fast-growing economic clout and the prospective ACFTA are dark clouds looming on this otherwise promising horizon.

Although it is a rather macabre thought, the growing international fears of an avian flu pandemic or some other China-sourced scourge on global public health are strengthening the relatively powerful case that Taiwan and its supporters mustered amid the SARS crisis. Given the continued and seemingly well-founded international lack of confidence in China's competence and transparency in handling the next SARS, Taiwan can argue forcefully that the world simply got lucky with SARS and, thus, that the complacency that once made it seem acceptable to bow to China's position by continuing to exclude Taiwan from the WHO is dangerously naïve.

Taiwan's key supporter may be particularly open to such arguments. With the U.S. political establishment shaken by the fallout from the mishandling of Hurricane Katrina and chronically concerned about government preparedness for possible terrorist strikes, including those using diseases and other biological agents, there may be a more hospitable climate in Washington for Taiwanese arguments that no potentially useful form of coordination among relevant governments' public health and other agencies should be left untapped when facing the health risks emanating from China and reaching and passing through Taiwan.

On a less dramatic front, analogous opportunities may exist with respect to the ICAO and the civil aviation regime. Air traffic, of course, continues to increase rapidly, especially among major East Asian metropolises. Cross-Strait air traffic, primarily via Hong Kong and Macau, has been on an even steeper trajectory. Establishment of the "three links," which would include regular direct air travel between Taiwan and the mainland, would bring an acceleration of this trend in the particularly complicated form of flights the international, domestic, or mixed character of which has been a focus of considerable contention between Beijing and Taipei. All of this strengthens the case for including Taiwan in the regime to the extent that Taiwan can argue persuasively that there are no adequate substitutes that satisfy China's objections and the "one China" policies they have demanded.

Much the same can be said with respect to the IMO and the international maritime shipping regime. Given the importance of Taiwan as a major shipping state, the parallel arguments here may have much weight.

The implications of the Warsaw Convention–related litigation in U.S. courts also might be further explored and exploited. Although there is something of a "double or nothing" quality here, Taiwan can stress that, given a judicial determination that it is not part of the territory covered by China's accession to the treaty—or at least given the judicial creation of substantial doubt concerning the American view on the issue—there are significant economic risks to major international air carriers and their clients. A non-member entity may lack the ability to commit credibly and effectively to the liability-capping or, in some contexts, compensation-supporting provisions that the treaty imposes. While it may be possible to contract around this problem, the simpler and surer way to address it would be to allow Taiwan to become a separate party to the treaty or at least be treated in American domestic law as if it were a party. (The latter is a tactic in keeping with the third strand in Taiwan's status-enhancing strategy.)

Other issue areas and regimes offer growing opportunities for extending the basic strategy of arguing that Taiwan should be included because of the harm that exclusion causes to other members, the regime, and Taiwan. Nuclear proliferation and other weapons-related regimes provide one example. This is a promising area, given the weapons-relevant scientific prowess that Taiwan possesses, its extensive nuclear power infrastructure, recurrent worries abroad that the China threat creates temptations for Taiwan to develop weapons of mass destruction, the sharply increased international concern over weapons proliferation that flows from the North Korean and Iranian crises, exposure of Pakistani bomb-maker A.Q. Khan's black-market activities, and the prospect of Islamist terrorist organizations acquiring a nuclear, chemical, or biological device. In this issue area too, Taiwan can gain something from a climate in which no one among its potential supporters wants to take the blame for failing to take any step that might have helped to strengthen a relevant international regime or organization.

The related field of regulating trade in dual-use technology, part of which is centered on the U.N. Chemical Weapons Convention, is another example. Taiwan can argue that some of its key industries, as well as the overseas partners and foreign economies that benefit from those industries, are at risk because of restrictions on the ability to import that firms in a non-party jurisdiction face. In this case, the arguments from Taiwanese self-interest and some foreign firms' interests may be fairly strong, but the invocation of broader international interests is likely to be less persuasive because it must rely partly on diffuse interests in relatively free trade or comprehensive regulation of the relevant sector and must contend with security concerns that arguably cut primarily the other way.

Actual, or even "as if," membership in these economic, health, transportation, security, or technology regimes could contribute to Taiwan's claim to state or state-like stature that can flow from broad and extensive participation and, ideally, full membership in functionally important and primarily state-centered international organizations, agreements, and other institutions. Arguments from Taiwan that stress its willingness to conform to, and desire to join, multilateral treaties and organizations have another virtue as well: They are relatively promising fodder for helpful U.S. legislation.

Getting Help from U.S. Law

Taiwan has relied upon, and might draw additional help from, U.S. domestic legislation that accepts and enhances Taiwan's status as a state-like entity. It is an obvious point that Taiwan's leaders pay assiduous attention to formal statements of U.S. positions on matters relating to Taiwan's international stature and work to make those statements and positions as protective of Taiwan's interests as possible. It is equally clear that not all such statements are equally formal, entrenched, or protective of Taiwan's interests.

In a mixed bag that ranges from careless or reckless and hastily retracted utterances of both the strongly "pro-Taiwan" and strongly "pro-PRC" sort, through Clinton's "Three Noes" or Reagan's "Six Assurances," to the sacred texts of the three U.S.–PRC Joint Communiqués and the Taiwan Relations Act, the TRA stands as the most formal, best-entrenched, and strongly protective of Taiwan's status. These attributes stem from the TRA's content and from its formal status as federal statutory law. Taiwan would be well served by successful pursuit of additional measures that share some of these features.

The Taiwan Relations Act. As a matter of content, the TRA conspicuously includes many provisions that address, albeit sometimes only obliquely (and at times probably unintentionally), matters that relate to the accepted attributes of statehood. Key sections of the TRA mandate that the U.S. will maintain something that looks functionally very much like the diplomatic relations or relations with another state that the ROC conducted with the U.S. before the severing of diplomatic ties and the derecognition that accompanied the 1979 normalization of U.S.–PRC relations.[34]

---

[34]Taiwan Relations Act, Public Law 96-8, April 10, 1979, Sections 6–11; 22 U.S.C. Sections 3305–3310.

The TRA further provides for the continued application of treaties and international agreements to which the U.S. and the ROC were parties (except, of course, for the specifically terminated Mutual Defense Treaty) and of U.S. laws that covered Taiwan when the U.S. recognized the ROC as the government of a recognized state.[35] Such laws almost inevitably imply either continuing international relations between the U.S. and Taiwan or something very close to that. Another subsection in the same article adds a bit more, albeit a bit backhandedly, in addressing the question of Taiwan's participation in international organizations. It states that nothing in the TRA is to be construed as a basis for excluding or expelling Taiwan from any international organization of which it is already a member.

While these provisions in the TRA could not recreate fully what had been lost, they went a good distance toward affirming and supporting the continuation of Taiwan's capacity to engage in functional international relations with other states (specifically the United States), which is a key attribute of statehood under generally accepted principles of international law and in much of the practice of international relations as well.[36]

More broadly and more simply, through its mandates for continuity of treaties and application of relevant laws, the TRA also requires that Taiwan continue to be treated in U.S. law as a state or as if it were a state.[37] Although the U.S. can and does enter into treaties with non-states, most treaties are with states, and the treaties with the ROC that the TRA retained in force were signed with the ROC as the government of a state. With regard to U.S. laws, the TRA says that "[w]henever the laws of the United States refer or relate to foreign countries, nations, states, governments or similar entities, such terms shall include and such laws shall apply with respect to Taiwan."[38] This provision notably eschews formulations like "as if it were a state." Among the principal laws to which the TRA here refers is the Foreign Sovereign Immunities Act, which codifies in U.S. law an international legal

---

[35]TRA Section 4(c); 22 U.S.C. Section 3303(c).

[36]Convention on the Rights and Duties of States (Montevideo Convention), Article 1 (setting forth the traditional attributes of statehood at international law, including: "a) a permanent population; b) a defined territory; c) government; and d) capacity to enter into relations with the other states...."); *Restatement (Third) of the Foreign Relations Law of the United States*, Section 201 (defining a state as an entity that has "a defined territory and a permanent population, under the control of its own government, and that engages in, or has the capacity to engage in, formal relations with other such entities").

[37]TRA Section 4(c); 22 U.S.C. Section 3303(c).

[38]TRA Section 4(b)(1); 22 U.S.C. Section 3303(b)(1).

principle that is generally understood as recognizing and accommodating the equal dignity of sovereign states in the international system—something in which non-state actors generally do not share.[39]

In addition, the TRA famously provides that the U.S. will continue to provide "defense articles" and "defense services" to Taiwan and declares U.S. opposition to the use of any non-peaceful means to determine the future of Taiwan.[40] The compatibility of such provisions with core international legal principles and the state-centric order that those principles reflect and support would be at best problematic unless one infers or assumes that the U.S. regards Taiwan as a state or something exceedingly close to it.

Arms sales and assertions of a legitimate interest in another's freedom from coercion by a national government at least evoke, even if they might not clearly invoke, international law's limited permission to assist in another's exercise of self-defense and prohibition on using force in—or against—another state. Because only states generally enjoy a right to self-defense, it ordinarily would be unlawful for the U.S. to assist a non-state entity in its defense against another state, much less to aid a small rebel province in its attempt to secede from the larger state of China. Intervention in another state's internal conflict would be permissible if it were a matter of helping a legitimate government (the ROC) defeat a rebel challenger regime (the PRC), but that is an implausible characterization of the cross-Strait relationship and one that the U.S. had clearly abandoned on the eve of the TRA when Washington recognized the PRC as the sole legitimate government of the state of China.

Other parts of the TRA accept or assert descriptions of Taiwan that resonate positively with other established international legal criteria of statehood, such as defining "Taiwan" for the purposes of the TRA as a particular territory ("the islands of Taiwan and the Pescadores"); a particular people ("the people on those islands"); and a functioning, effective government ("the governing authorities on Taiwan recognized by the United States as the Republic of China prior to January 1, 1979, and any successor governing authorities").[41] Provisions that mandate the maintenance of something akin to the former diplomatic relations and the continuation of treaties speak directly to a fourth traditional criterion (the

---

[39]TRA Section 4(b)(1), (7); 22 U.S.C. Section 3303(b)(1), (7); Foreign Sovereign Immunities Act, 22 U.S.C. Sections 1330, 1332, 1391, 1441, 1602–1611; *The Schooner Exchange v. McFaddon*, 11 U.S. (7 Cranch) 116 (1812) (United States Supreme Court case setting forth the rationale of foreign sovereign immunity in domestic courts).

[40]TRA Sections 2(b)(4), (5), 3; 22 U.S.C. Sections 3301(b)(4)(5), 3302.

capacity to engage in relations with other states) and indirectly to the "external" face of the third criterion (that the candidate state entity's government not be subordinate or answerable to another, higher government). The conduct of foreign affairs is, of course, an area in which such subordination and accountability tend to be most clearly imposed on substate governments.

The TRA also speaks, albeit not by design and neither clearly nor forcefully, to other criteria that are relevant to state or state-like status. Its reference to "the people on those islands," when coupled with the sense of Taiwanese identity that has grown sharply in recent decades, resonates increasingly strongly with international legal principles of the self-determination of peoples. These provide that "peoples" (in the sense of distinct ethnic, cultural, or perhaps other identity groups) have rights that may—not must—include a right to their own states.[42] The TRA's articulation of a U.S. interest in human rights conditions in Taiwan, when read in light of the democratic-era human rights accomplishments on the island, implicates international legal norms that consider aspects of a political entity's internal order relevant in extending to that entity the benefits of statehood.[43]

As a matter of form and structure, even among the four sacred texts of U.S. policy concerning Taiwan, the TRA enjoys unique status as a federal statute. In the U.S. (but not the PRC) view, the Three Communiqués are not treaties or executive agreements and thus are not equal in status and dignity to domestic laws enacted by Congress and signed by the President. Under basic principles of U.S. constitutional law, the President is not free to

---

[41]TRA Section 15(2); 22 U.S.C. Section 3314(2). The standard international legal definition of statehood includes these three factors—territory (of a substantial and defined scope), population (of sufficient size and stability), and a government (that is effective and independent)—along with the capacity to engage in relations with other states (discussed above in note 37). See Convention on the Rights and Duties of States (Montevideo Convention), Article 1; *Restatement (Third) of U.S. Foreign Relations Law*, Section 201. See also TRA Section 2(b)(1); 22 U.S.C. Section 3301(b)(1) (also referring to the "people on Taiwan" with whom the U.S. is to maintain relations).

[42]On self-determination of peoples and statehood in international law, see, generally, Charter of the United Nations, Articles 1(2), 55, and Chapters XI–XIII; International Covenant on Civil and Political Rights, Article 1 (U.N. Treaty Series, No. 999, 171 (1966)); International Covenant on Economic, Social and Cultural Rights, Article 1 (U.N. Treaty Series, No. 993, 3 (1966)); and *Reference Re Secession of Quebec*, 2 S.C.R. 217 (Supreme Court of Canada, 1998), *International Legal Materials*, Vol. 37, pp. 1340 ff. With respect to Taiwan, see, generally, deLisle, "The Chinese Puzzle of Taiwan's Status," pp. 55–57.

disregard the TRA, whereas he would be free to terminate (or, on some views of presidential power, simply to breach) the Communiqués or other pledges to China even if these were binding treaties or executive agreements. The President cannot do that with the TRA, which is a law of the United States that he has sworn to execute faithfully. (At least, he cannot purport to do that absent an expansive and highly questionable claim that the TRA constitutes an impermissible congressional encroachment on the President's constitutional foreign affairs powers.)

Also, even if the Three Communiqués are assumed to be treaties or executive agreements, well-entrenched canons of construction demand that they be interpreted alongside the TRA to avoid inconsistency where possible. Established constitutional principles provide that where conflicts do exist among sources of law of equal stature, the most recent enactment wins, which would be the TRA in the case of conflicts with the first and second—although not the third—of the Communiqués. Further, the "acoustical separation" that U.S. practice and doctrine—specifically concerning the reception of international law and international legal obligations into domestic law, the self-executing (or non–self-executing) nature of particular treaties, and whether or not a treaty requires implementing legislation—create between international and internal law provide considerable insulation of the TRA from revision or supercession by subsequent international agreements.

As this analysis indicates, the TRA has served Taiwan's cause of defending and accruing attributes of formal state-like status well. Indeed, it has done so in more complicated and deep-seated ways than is often appreciated.

Other TRA-Like Legislation: The Taiwan Security Enhancement Act. Given these strengths and virtues of the TRA, there is much that Taiwan might gain from additional pieces of legislation that would have the formal or structural characteristics of the TRA and that would include content that is similarly helpful in recognizing or bolstering Taiwan's claims to the attributes of statehood.

The unenacted Taiwan Security Enhancement Act (TSEA) represented one such legislative effort, but it failed in part because it overreached politically. Considered in 1999–2000, the bill reiterated most of the TRA's

---

[43]TRA Section 2(c); 22 U.S.C. Section 3301(c). On human rights, democracy, and recognition of new states in international law, see, generally, "European Community: Guidelines on the Recognition of New States in Eastern Europe and the Soviet Union" in *International Legal Materials*, Vol. 31 (1991), pp. 1486 ff, and Thomas M. Franck, "The Emerging Right to Democratic Governance," *American Journal of International Law*, Vol. 86 (January 1992), pp. 46 ff. With respect to Taiwan, see, generally, deLisle, "The Chinese Puzzle of Taiwan's Status," pp. 57–60.

status-relevant content and particularly stressed Taiwan's separateness from the PRC. It went on to emphasize Taiwan's record on democracy, as well as its market economy, and the TRA-proclaimed interest in the now-impressively protected human rights of the people on Taiwan.[44] Again, such issues matter for state and state-like status, especially in light of post–Cold War international law and international relations precedents and practices that have sometimes linked recognition of states—and have clearly linked the relative stature of states and quasi-state entities—to their accomplishments or shortcomings on these fronts.[45] The TSEA also underscored the absence of an official U.S. position in favor of ultimate reunification of Taiwan with the mainland.

The proposed act thus endorsed the position that nothing in U.S. official policy precluded eventual U.S. support for resolutions of the Taiwan status question that might include full, conventional independent statehood for Taiwan. Given its focus on enhancing U.S. military assistance and U.S.–Taiwan defense cooperation, the TSEA centered on matters that assume that Taiwan has a state's (or a full state-like) right to self-defense against the PRC.[46]

Where the TSEA principally foundered was in the extensive and dense security cooperation and military assistance relationships that it would have mandated. Such measures went beyond what an Administration concerned with U.S.–PRC relations and many in Congress were prepared to endorse.[47] The TSEA's demise thus does not necessarily portend a similarly dismal fate for other legislation that would be similarly favorable to Taiwan's claim to state or state-like status in U.S. law but that did not suffer from these infirmities.

"As If" Legislation: Senate Confirmation of the Director of the American Institute in Taiwan. Other legislative possibilities might be called "as if" legislation—that is, bills that would provide additional ways in which

---

[44] Taiwan Security Enhancement Act, H.R. 1838, 106th Congress, 2nd Session, 2000. See Section 2 (findings concerning Taiwan's record of democracy, market principles, and separation from and contrast with China; reiterating key principles of the TRA).

[45] See sources cited in note 44.

[46] TSEA Section 2(4), 3–5 (confirming the absence of a formal U.S. position on Taiwan's ultimate status; mandating officer training, military sales, maintenance of sufficient self-defense capabilities for Taiwan and enhanced programs of operational training and exchanges, secure communications, etc.).

[47] See, for example, Robert G. Kaiser, "House Leaders Delay Taiwan Vote on Concern over China Talks," *The Washington Post*, November 2, 1999, and Associated Press, "Clinton Discusses Taiwan Bill," February 4, 2000.

Taiwan must be treated under U.S. law "as if" it were clearly a state, although, again, that particular turn of phrase is not the most helpful for Taiwan. Statutes of this type might draw on some useful ambiguities in U.S. constitutional law that are related to some of the complicated connections between international and domestic law that underlie some of the TRA's efficacy in enhancing or protecting Taiwan's status.

One example is legislation that would require that the director of the Taipei Office of the American Institute in Taiwan (AIT) must be confirmed by the U.S. Senate. The Constitution requires that all ambassadors to recognized states must be confirmed by the Senate, but there is nothing in the Constitution that prohibits Congress from requiring Senate confirmation for many other posts that the Constitution does not specify must be confirmed by the Senate.[48] Indeed, there are many posts in the U.S. government that fit this description. Making the directorship of AIT a Senate-confirmed position would make it more similar to an ambassadorship by subjecting it to the same process that applies to representatives to the recognized governments of recognized states with which the U.S. maintains diplomatic relations.

Such legislation would thus give Taiwan another small attribute of conventional statehood in U.S. law, but without committing the U.S. to any position that Taiwan is in fact a state. It also would have the greatest symbolic punch if, beyond simply saying that the post is subject to Senate confirmation, it provided that the post "shall be subject to the procedures of nomination and appointment [or confirmation] that apply to ambassadors of the United States" to "foreign states recognized by the United States and the [recognized] governments of those states."

The case for such a statute could be put in terms that are familiar from the TRA and U.S. Taiwan policy discussions more generally and that resonate with Taiwan's long-standing and still-relevant strategy of emphasizing the costs to the U.S. and other states of not including Taiwan fully in relevant international relationships. Thus, a "findings" or "policy" section could include a statement, for example, about the great importance of U.S.–Taiwan relations to U.S. interests in security, peace, and prosperity in the Asia–Pacific region and a statement that, in light of such importance, the principal U.S. representative in Taipei must be subject to the same level of Senate scrutiny as are those who represent the interests of the United States and

---

[48]Constitution of the United States, Article II, Section 2, Paragraph 2 (The President "shall nominate, and by and with the Advice and Consent of the Senate, shall appoint Ambassadors...and all other Officers of the United States...but the Congress may by law vest the Appointment of...inferior Officers" in the President alone or elsewhere and without Senate advice and consent).

conduct the international relations of the United States in foreign capitals, including those where the U.S. has far less at stake than it does in Taipei.

"As If" Legislation: International Organizations and Treaties. Finally, another type of U.S. "as if" legislation could underpin or advance Taiwan's quest for enhanced international status through participation or inclusion in international regimes. Perhaps the simplest and most promising example would be legislation to provide that the U.S. or, more specifically, the President or the relevant executive branch agencies "shall accord to Taiwan all rights, privileges and obligations under the domestic laws of the United States"—such as freedom from various export restrictions; investment restrictions; limited access to concessionary financing; limited support from the U.S. as a voting member of the World Bank, the International Monetary Fund, or other agencies; or foreign trade or other sanctions—"that are contingent on membership in an international organization or signature and ratification of an international treaty or agreement and performance of the obligations thereby imposed if Taiwan unilaterally pledges to fulfill those obligations as if it were a member of the organization or party to the treaty or agreement." Here too, the legislation could give a TRA-like boost to Taiwan's international status and echo and extend the TRA's tepid provision on international organization membership without committing the U.S. to a clearer or more assertive position on the basic question of whether Taiwan is or is not a state.

Such legislation ideally should include a qualifier along the lines of a provision that Taiwan must have been denied an opportunity to join the international organization or become a party to the treaty or agreement despite its satisfaction of the substantive criteria for membership or accession. This would address the obvious objection that Taiwan should not be given special privileges or be allowed to "shirk" or "free ride" by not fully joining regimes that are open to it. It might be advisable to include a clause providing that Taiwan would enjoy the benefits of the law if the President determines that exclusion of Taiwan from the organization or treaty is to the detriment of the interests of the United States or United States persons. It also would be sensible and ordinary to require a presidential determination that Taiwan indeed had met the regime's substantive criteria for entry. (Such a law might be more saleable politically if, rather than being limited to Taiwan, it extended to a broader category of entities.)

As the first of these possible "presidential findings" clauses suggests, the argument in favor of such a law also could parallel the venerable Taiwanese tactic of stressing the adverse impact of Taiwan's exclusion on the interests of the U.S. and other states. Here too, a "findings" or "policy" section could add language to articulate these interests and, in doing so, echo and build upon parallel sections in the TRA or the ill-fated TSEA. So too could the requisite presidential findings concerning the application of the statute's general provision to specific organizations or treaties, such as the WHO or weapons-control conventions and so on.

To be sure, any significant "as if" legislation would face an uphill battle, but so does the broader project—and so do other concrete efforts in pursuit of the project—of protecting or enhancing Taiwan's international status, whether through U.S. law or through Taiwan's efforts in international arenas.

Eroding the "One China" Policy

The three strands in Taiwan's long-standing and still-salient strategy for protecting or enhancing its claim to state or state-like status—and, especially and specifically, its claim to the vital formal dimension of such status—do not confront the "one China" policy of the United States or other relatively sympathetic states head on. Instead of attacking it, they surround and chip away at it.

Given the entrenchment of the "Three Noes," the PRC's relentless pressure on Taiwan status issues, and the unhappy fate that has befallen attempts to take on the "one China" policy more squarely or, even more clearly, to seek recognition of formal state status for Taiwan, a full frontal assault still looks quixotic. Instead, the guerrilla tactics of encircling and picking away at the enemy and ultimately outsmarting and outlasting him—embraced by no less than Chairman Mao and the heroes of the classic Chinese tales he favored—offer the more fruitful course for Taiwan.

Over time, Taiwan's enduring possession of many of the formal and substantive attributes associated with full state status and the steady expansion of Taiwan's claim to such attributes where possible can undermine the foundations of America's and other states' "one China" policy. If that happens, the "one China" policy could become so patently divorced from reality that it becomes like the new clothes–wearing emperor, its power vulnerable when someone dares to point out the truth.

The fairy tale, however, has the luxury of ending before telling us what happens next. We do not learn whether a new and presumably better ruler ascends to the throne through peaceful and regular means, whether the weakened king clings uncertainly to power despite his embarrassment, or whether the realm plunges into an anarchic struggle for power.

For Taiwan, the latter two possibilities do not suggest optimistic analogies. If a weakened "one China" policy lingers on, it might differ from the current, more robust "one China" policy only in lacking the earlier version's predictability. If the "one China" policy falls and its successor is shaped by interested parties' relative power, with less attention to legalities and formality, Taiwan and those who see a functionally independent and democratic Taiwan as an important American interest will face a more difficult challenge in securing a suitable post–"one China" policy.

6

Reason Against "Reality": A Model for a Cross-Strait Solution

Paul Monk

A PARADIGM SHIFT IS REQUIRED in order to deal with the Taiwan problem. Paradigms are ways of construing reality that are rooted in certain fundamental assumptions. A shift occurs when it is found or decided that one or more of those assumptions is at least questionable, with doubt resonating through the rest of the preconceptions that were built on those assumptions.

Most analysis of the Taiwan problem appears to proceed from a small number of largely unexamined assumptions. Chief among these is that China will never give up its claim to sovereignty over Taiwan—but also, and crucially, that China has a right to such sovereignty and would be humiliated or would suffer a loss of prestige should it fail to insist on "recovering" this sovereignty.

If the impasse in cross-Strait relations that has persisted for the past 15 years is to be resolved intelligently, these assumptions need rethinking.[1] There seems to be a very widespread assumption that rethinking them is either impossible or pointless because they are simply the unalterable realities of the case. *That* assumption, I believe, is false.

---

[1] This was the principal conclusion of the substantial four-part report on the Taiwan question that was prepared by the International Crisis Group in 2003–2004. See International Crisis Group, *What's Left of 'One China'?*, *The Risk of War*, and *The Chance of Peace*, all published on June 6, 2003, and *How an Ultimate Political Settlement Might Look*, published on February 26, 2004. The ICG did not recommend the paradigm shift that I suggest in this chapter, but it did urge that the shape of the future political settlement be seriously rethought.

In fact, I shall argue that for China to persist in its present policy of insisting on resuming sovereignty over Taiwan would be a strategic miscalculation—possibly one with very grave repercussions. While we are all aware of dramatic misjudgments in history, it is more difficult to understand precisely how they occur. They tend to be seen simply as cases of ignorance or of serious people being ambushed by the treacherous complexities of reality. It is cognitively more interesting than that.

Consider Stalin's failure in the first half of 1941 to accept that Hitler would invade the Soviet Union in June of that year. In the months before the Nazi invasion began on June 22, 1941, Stalin flatly refused to believe his generals and intelligence masters when they told him that Hitler was preparing to invade. He called them all fools, thinking himself shrewd. Hitler would never attack the U.S.S.R. before Germany had settled accounts with the British Empire, he told them; and if Soviet generals did anything to provoke the Nazi war machine, heads would roll. His assumptions were fixed even as the Wehrmacht massed along his borders; and even after they launched their staggering *blitzkrieg* into his domain, he remained in denial for hours. He believed the attacks to be the work of a few German generals who were orchestrating a provocation in order to start a war that Hitler himself did not want. "Hitler surely does not know," he told his generals and his politburo in the Kremlin.[2]

In a splendid re-examination of the May–June 1940 fall of France to Hitler's forces, Ernest May showed a similar fixed idea at work in the Allied high command. They never considered the possibility that the Germans would attack France through the Ardennes. Indeed, they were confident that Hitler would not dare to attack France at all, so powerful were its defenses. Excessively confident in their strategic assumptions, they failed to detect the plain evidence of German preparations for a massive thrust through the Ardennes, over the Meuse, and straight to the English Channel. When the German offensive began, the Allied generals refused for four days to accept the reality of what the Germans were doing. By the time they did reassess, it was too late to close the gap the Wehrmacht had opened up in the Allied defenses. France was overrun in six weeks.[3]

Abraham Rabinovich's account of the opening of the Yom Kippur War in 1973 begins with the observation that "a military satellite beaming images of the Middle East to Earth late on the afternoon of 5 October 1973 would

---

[2] See Gabriel Gorodetsky, *Grand Delusion: Stalin and the German Invasion of Russia* (New Haven and London: Yale University Press, 1999), esp. Chapters 13 and 14. The quotes are from pp. 299 and 311.

[3] See Ernest R. May, *Strange Victory: Hitler's Conquest of France* (New York: Hill and Wang, 2000), esp. Chapters 17–18, 24 –25.

have confronted analysts with a perplexing picture." Egypt had amassed 100,000 troops, 1,350 tanks, and 2,000 artillery pieces and heavy mortars along the west bank of the Suez Canal. On the other side, the Israelis had only 450 soldiers and 44 artillery pieces and only 290 tanks in the whole of Sinai. Along the Golan Heights, where there was no canal to protect Israeli positions, 100,000 Syrian troops confronted only token Israeli forces, enjoying an advantage of eight-to-one in tanks and even more in artillery. Yet the Israeli intelligence and military high command did not raise an alarm. They were convinced the Arabs would not attack. The stage was set for near catastrophe for Israel.[4]

Reexamining Old Assumptions

In all three cases, unexamined assumptions and overconfidence generated gross military error and disabled strategic planning. This is something that should be reflected on within the specific context of Taiwan. The thinking that frames the Taiwan question, both in China and elsewhere around the world, needs to be brought out into the open and examined unsparingly. Otherwise, there is reason to fear that it could trap China itself and the other states of the region in a confrontation—perhaps even a war—that would serve no-one's interests.

Three assumptions seem to govern such thinking:

- *First*, that Taiwan is, as a matter of historical and international legal reality, an inalienable part of China;
- *Second*, that China will not under any circumstances accept the independence of Taiwan; and
- *Third*, that China is a rising strategic competitor of the United States in Eurasia.

All three of these ideas need to be reexamined if the matter is to be handled intelligently, justly, and constructively. The key assumption is the first: that Taiwan is an inalienable part of China. The chief grounds for this claim are that it was part of the Qing empire until ceded to Japan in 1895 and that Japan's army surrendered the island to the Republic of China in 1945, so that the legitimate government of China must necessarily be

---

[4] For further discussion of this fascinating "intelligence failure," see Abraham Rabinovich, *The Yom Kippur War: The Epic Encounter that Transformed the Middle East* (New York: Schocken Books, 2004). The quote is from the Prologue, p. 3.

deemed the legitimate government of Taiwan—and the legitimate government of China now is the regime in Beijing.

Because these grounds are repeated endlessly, the inferences from them come to seem not only reasonable, but to many people, especially in China itself, also compelling. Yet the claims themselves are more tenuous than repetition contrives to make them appear. Taiwan had a Chinese governor for only 10 years before it was ceded to Japan in 1895 and was never a significant part of the Manchu Empire.

Indeed, the island of Taiwan was never part of the Chinese empire before the Manchus established the Qing dynasty in the mid-17th century, and this was an alien dynasty imposed on China itself from outside its classical borders.[5] When the island was ceded to Japan, admittedly as the result of one of the clearest instances of a "war of aggression" as had been seen in that century, it was ceded "in perpetuity," giving Japan every bit as good a claim to the island now as the Beijing regime has.

---

[5] The earliest ethnographic analyses of Taiwan's early 17th century population are from the Dutch and describe an Austronesian society. The predominant populations on Taiwan were "eight" indigenous aboriginal tribes who governed themselves in autonomous villages through "a nominal council, consisting of twelve men of good repute." Also on the island were small populations of Chinese and Japanese. As of 1622, there were on the island about 25,000 "fighting men" among a Chinese community "driven from their country by war." That population remained stable until Koxinga's invasion in 1664, 20 years after the defeat of the Ming by the "Tartar" Manchu invasion when it was still described as 25,000 able-bodied men. Those early Dutch reports cite a memorandum from the Viceroy in Xiamen [Totok of Amoy] to the Dutch in 1624 offering to permit Chinese trade from Taiwan to the mainland once the Dutch had dismantled their fortress at "Pehoe" on the Pescadores [*Penghu*] islands. The Dutch company collected duties from the Chinese farmers (rice and sugar). There also appears to have been a substantial Japanese community on Formosa that objected strenuously to Dutch customs taxes "on the plea that they were there six years before the agents of the company arrived." The Dutch granted export duty exemptions to the Japanese but justified their right to collect them under terms of the Xiamen memorandum. The Dutch, however, continued to levy other taxes on the Japanese, a practice that the Dutch ambassador in Japan noted "caused great dissatisfaction" in the Japanese court at Edo. At one point, Japanese residents of Taiwan took a deputation of aboriginal Taiwanese Austronesians to Japan "and through them…offered the sovereignty of Formosa to the Emperor." See William Campbell, *Formosa Under the Dutch, Described from Contemporary Records* (London: Kegan Paul Trench Trubner & Co. Ltd, 1903; reprinted Taipei: Ch'eng Wen Publishing, 1972), pp. 34–61, and Inez de Bouclaire, *Neglected Formosa*, San Francisco, Chinese Materials and Research Center, Occasional Series No. 21, p. 14. *Neglected Formosa* is a heavily annotated translation from the Dutch of Frederic Coyett, *'t Verwaerloosde Formosa* (Amsterdam, 1675).

Unlike the Manchu emperors, who neglected Taiwan completely, even after they sent a provincial governor there in 1885, the Japanese vigorously developed the island during the half-century they ruled it. In 1945, pursuant to Japanese Imperial General Headquarters General Order No. 1, issued at the direction of the Supreme Commander for the Allied Powers, General Douglas MacArthur, Japanese commanders on Taiwan surrendered to Generalissimo Chiang Kai-shek "acting on behalf of the United States, the Republic of China, the United Kingdom and the British Empire, and the Union of Soviet Socialist Republics."[6]

Japan renounced "all right, title, and claim to Formosa and the Pescadores" both in the instrument of surrender and in Article 2(b) of the San Francisco Treaty of Peace of 1951. But Japan never designated a state to assume sovereignty over the island, and neither the people of Taiwan nor the governments that administered them subsequent to 1945 have ever accepted rule by the Communist regime in Beijing. Finally, the people of Taiwan resented and resisted the imposition of undemocratic rule by the "Republic of China" in 1947[7] and, over the past two decades since 1988, have managed to win back their freedom and their identity.

Even if these many considerations were judged to be outweighed by an argument that Taiwan truly was part of the Republic of China from 1945 and that the Republic of China is, in some sense or other, part of China, there is an overarching consideration that needs to be brought into play: Empires and nation states do, in fact, change both their boundaries and the nature of their sovereignty over time. There is, therefore, no self-evident reason why China, whether or not it is governed by the Communist Party, should insist that it must reestablish formal sovereignty over Taiwan. Such a claim can stand only for as long as Beijing insists on it and demands—under threat of war—that everyone else agree. Therefore, it is neither necessary to accept as true the proposition that Taiwan is an inalienable part of China nor sufficient to argue against it. What is needed, rather, is to work from

---

[6] Quoted in memorandum from the Office of the Legal Advisor, "The Legal Status of Taiwan," reprinted in John J. Tkacik, Jr., ed., *Rethinking "One China"* (Washington, D.C.: The Heritage Foundation, 2004), p. 182.

[7] On January 10, 1947, Taiwan's martial law governor Chen Yi announced that the democratic rights accorded under the new Constitution of the Republic of China would not apply to Formosa when it went into effect on the mainland on December 25, 1947. The mainland Chinese, he said, were advanced enough to enjoy the privileges of constitutional government, but because of long years of despotic Japanese rule, the Formosans were politically retarded and were not capable of carrying on self-government in an intelligent manner. See George H. Kerr, *Formosa Betrayed* (Boston: Houghton Mifflin, 1965), p. 240.

inside the mind-set of those (chiefly in China) who hold to this proposition and see whether it is possible to induce a shift in that mind-set.

Only when we come at the assumption of China's sovereign right to Taiwan from this angle can we reach a point where the second assumption—that China will not under any circumstances accept the independence of Taiwan—can also be flipped around. While the assumption that Taiwan is a part of China remains entrenched, the alienation of Taiwan will naturally be seen as an offense, a loss of face, a threat to China's territorial integrity, or a key part of American and Japanese containment strategy directed at keeping China weak—and not only by Chinese of a nationalist mind-set. China's revitalized nationalism in recent years feeds the emotional sense of many Chinese that their dignity is at stake in this matter.[8] Such emotion tends to prevent an effort to rethink the question critically.

This is a crucial point, because both the first and second fixed assumptions are fatefully linked to the third. Taiwan is seen as a crucial front-line pawn in the chess game that has opened between strategic "realists" in both China and the United States. For that reason, and through those sets of lenses, everything that each side does to buttress its position will be viewed with suspicion by the other: in China, as clear evidence that the U.S. intends to contain it and even weaken it; in the U.S., as evidence that China is indeed an aspiring strategic competitor. The three assumptions, therefore, form a sort of vicious circle that could become a downward spiral to war.

Yet these assumptions constitute the conventional wisdom, the dominant paradigm, in terms of which the future of Taiwan is most commonly understood. The standard approaches to trying to "manage" the matter tend to entail obeisance to the first two assumptions and tacit acknowledgment that the third is the looming danger. They have floundered thus far because they depend on papering over the real problem: that the claim to sovereignty by the People's Republic of China, especially given that it remains a one-party dictatorship, is rejected by almost the entire people of Taiwan.

Reunification vs. Independence

This problem cannot be papered over in the end. It is the root cause of the tension that has been building up in cross-Strait relations for over a decade. Although war is not a metaphysical certainty, it is a clear possibility, but it is

---

[8] For a thoughtful reflection on the rise of such an emotional sense in China in the past decade, see Peter Hays Gries, *China's New Nationalism: Pride, Politics and Diplomacy* (Berkeley: University of California Press, 2004).

a possibility only because of China's threats to use force in pursuit of its sovereignty claim. No one else will start a war over the matter. Moreover, even if war does not come, the above three assumptions and the paradigmatic vicious circle they form stand in the way of the constructive evolution of Asia–Pacific affairs.

There are those who believe that the whole problem will be resolved peacefully so long as the people of Taiwan are given no encouragement to believe that they can ever have their *de facto* independence legitimized *de jure*. They believe that over time China will simply absorb Taiwan economically and the U.S. will gradually recede from the picture, as Britain has receded from Hong Kong. While this is certainly one possibility, there are reasons to be skeptical of this scenario.

There are clearly many people in Taiwan—arguably a majority—who do not desire unification with China, or at least not on the terms that the current regime on the mainland is disposed to offer. The results of the legislative elections in Taiwan in December 2004 or the National Assembly elections of May 2005 were not conclusive as regards the desire for a move to independence, but only because no serious political candidate campaigned for reunification and Taiwan was already, for practical purposes, independent: that is to say, wholly self-governing.

Specifically, the Taiwan Solidarity Union (TSU), the most outspoken pro-independence party, failed to gain the extra legislative seats predicted in pre-election polls. The TSU was, nonetheless, the third largest vote getter in the National Assembly election during which Taiwan's relations with China were the primary campaign issue. The Democratic Progressive Party, campaigning on a strong Taiwanese identity platform, gained two extra seats in the legislative elections. It was also the largest vote-getter in both the Legislative Yuan and National Assembly balloting. Even more significantly, the Kuomintang (KMT) and the People First Party avoided campaigning on a pro-unification policy.

Meanwhile, there are senior American figures who question whether it would be in America's national interest to see Taiwan unified with China, even if such unification was voluntary.[9] The United States has sought to restrain Taiwan's behavior but also has urged it to buy more arms, established a *de facto* embassy in Taipei in 1979, and upgraded its military advisory presence on the island state in 2004. Japan has also begun quietly to strengthen itself and, under Prime Minister Junichiro Koizumi, began to show signs of growing resistance to what it perceives as China's hegemonic

---

[9] For a good discussion of this issue, see Nancy Bernkopf Tucker, "If Taiwan Chooses Unification, Should the United States Care?" *The Washington Quarterly*, Summer 2002, pp. 15–28.

ambitions in East Asia and the Western Pacific. When former Taiwanese President Lee Teng-hui requested a visa to visit Japan in late 2004, the Japanese government granted the visa over China's strenuous objections. The heated exchanges between Beijing and Tokyo in early 2005 served to underscore the simmering tensions between the two East Asian giants.

Then there is the question of where China itself is heading, both economically and politically. In both respects, it faces major challenges in the next decade or two. It is by no means self-evident that reabsorbing Taiwan politically, especially if force and conflict were involved, would help it to deal with those challenges. To the contrary, a case could be made that it would be better served by avoiding the reabsorption of Taiwan, even if it could readily do so, for the foreseeable future—if only for the slyly pragmatic reason that the issue provides the barely legitimate regime in Beijing with a means to bolster its nationalistic credentials. In any case, it cannot readily do so, which complicates the matter considerably, both for its own declaratory policy and for the strategic calculations of other states.

Paradoxically, the mounting nationalist fervor in China, which the Communist Party leadership has promoted aggressively in recent years, could carry its leaders into a confrontational stance from which they would find it difficult to back down. Under present circumstances, China has a great deal to lose if it resorts to force; but it is afraid to renounce its use, lest this make it seem weak and lead to a straightforward Taiwanese declaration of independence.

Equally, Taiwan is afraid to declare formal independence, lest China resort to force. Taiwan is actually independent in every respect, except that this is a reality that neither China nor the majority of the nations of the world acknowledge, preferring instead to humor, if not recognize formally, the legal fiction that Taiwan is part of the People's Republic of China.

For its part, the U.S. continues to insist not only that it has "our 'one China' policy," but also that it will defend Taiwan with "whatever it takes" if China uses force to try to turn a legal fiction into a political reality.[10] This puts the U.S. in a highly conflicted position, since it officially does not recognize the "Republic of China" on Taiwan as a state and is therefore technically interfering in the internal affairs of the People's Republic of China, just as Beijing claims.[11] Meanwhile, Taiwan's President Chen Shui-bian has

---

[10]In an interview with ABC News on April 25, 2001, President Bush was asked, "if Taiwan were attacked by China, do we have an obligation to defend the Taiwanese?" He responded, "Yes, we do…and the Chinese must understand that," adding that the United States would do "whatever it takes to help Taiwan defend herself." See a report of President Bush's remarks at *http://archives.cnn.com/2001/ALLPOLITICS/04/25/bush.taiwan.03/*.

openly indicated that Taiwan will declare independence if China uses force against it.[12] Thus, all three circle around and around in a deadlock, which could break down into a disastrous conflict for all concerned.

A Way Out: *De Jure* Independence

A counterintuitive insight may offer the basis for a solution. Such insight must begin with the observation that empires have no irrevocable claim to their provinces or territories. If they did, China would have a basis for claiming territorial sovereignty over Mongolia, while the British Empire would have had no basis for ceding Hong Kong Island to China after China ceded it to the British "in perpetuity." Nor would the Republic of Ireland have had any claim to independence from the British crown in the 1920s, having been ruled from London for longer than Taiwan was ever part of the Chinese Empire.

Such examples could very easily be multiplied. The northern part of Vietnam, for example, might be deemed part of China on the basis that it was occupied by the Chinese for 1,000 years, as could northern Korea, which was a "Chinese kingdom" for 700 years during the first millennium—again, periods of time incomparably longer than that during which Taiwan was, in any sense at all, part of the Chinese Empire.

The above observation collides with the notion that China will not accept the independence of Taiwan under any circumstances. This is the main shibboleth inhibiting clear and critical thinking about the issue. Doubtless there are many who sincerely and firmly believe this proposition. It is based, however, on at least one largely unexamined assumption: that China's national interest and dignity as a nation-state would be harmed if it was to accept the independence of Taiwan. The case that this is so remains

---

[11]Nancy Bernkopf Tucker, in "Strategic Ambiguity or Strategic Clarity?"—the final chapter in the book she edited on the Taiwan question, *Dangerous Strait: The U.S.–Taiwan–China Crisis* (New York: Columbia University Press, 2005)—explored and defended the studied strategic ambiguity inherent in U.S. policy. "In fact," she wrote on p. 187, "the roots of Washington's approach to the Taiwan Strait problem are firmly planted in the policy of ambiguity and the overpowering reasons for that original choice have neither disappeared nor been significantly altered. Moreover, any expectation that clarity can predict behaviour exaggerates what can be known about the future."

[12]Or at least he came close to it. He said that "as long as the CCP regime has no intention to use military force against Taiwan, I pledge that during my term in office, I will not declare independence." See President Chen Shui-bian's inauguration speech, "Taiwan Stands Up," Office of the President, Republic of China, May 20, 2000.

plausible only so long as one does not cross-examine it. Arguably, China's national interest and dignity could be better served by coming to terms with the fact that Taiwan has been juridically separate from the Chinese mainland for at least 100 of the past 110 years, as well as with the fact of Taiwan's current *de facto* independence, and by developing a new, non-sovereign relationship with it. This ought to be relatively easy, for the simple reason that China already has a more or less viable non-sovereign relationship with Taiwan.

China's advantage could, in fact, lie in doing *precisely the opposite* of what the Chinese government currently declares, in law, as its sacred duty: that is, retaking Taiwan by force if necessary, regardless of the cost in blood and treasure. In this case, the most rational answer to the question of Taiwan's future is a Chinese offer of *de jure* independence to Taiwan. Leave aside for the moment the consideration that this seems improbable and that many Chinese tempers flare when the mere idea is raised. The argument is that, if such an offer could be arranged, it would turn out to be to China's benefit. Whether it would be to the Communist Party's benefit is not quite so clear. What would shift the whole question onto another plane, however, would be a declaration from Beijing that the civil war is over and that Chinese civilization—rather than one political regime or ideology—has won.

Within "one China" understood as Chinese civilization or a broad Chinese commonwealth, there would be no need for Taiwan to bow to Beijing's sovereignty. Rather, it would be embraced warmly as a little brother and offshoot state and praised for its extraordinary achievements. A new relationship would then become possible. In such a relationship, cross-Strait trade could thrive, unfettered by political fears or historical animosities. China could benefit from Taiwan's freedom instead of seeking to stifle it. The revitalization and modernization of Chinese civilization and the rejuvenation of its worn and despoiled natural environment could then become the joint project of the mainland state together with its truly liberated scion.

Let me emphasize that I am not here making a *prediction* that this is about to happen or arguing that it would be easy to bring about. I am simply spelling out the possibility of an alternative and peaceful resolution to the present impasse and arguing that it need not be harmful to China's national interests or dignity.

The common, intuitive response to this proposal is likely to be similar to Edward Friedman's observation, made to me in Taipei in 2002, that this is a nice idea but will never happen.[13] He was right, up to a point. It is entirely

---

[13]Edward Friedman is Hawkins Chair Professor of Political Science at the University of Wisconsin—Madison.

possible that it will not come to fruition; but given that neither threats of force nor economic integration has shown much promise of achieving China's goal, and bearing in mind that resort to force would be enormously destructive, there is a need to put such a proposal on the table. Friedman and most others doubt that China could be induced to make this kind of offer to Taiwan because of a combination of pessimism about China and a deeply ingrained assumption that it would not be in China's interests.

This is an attitude of mind redolent of Bill Jenner's *The Tyranny of History.*[14] To gain a different perspective, we need to turn that basic assumption around, which entails making a sound case that Taiwanese independence is perfectly consistent with China's national dignity and that avoiding hostilities over the matter is vitally important to China's enduring national interests.

Advantages to China

There are four major *advantages* that China would gain from offering Taiwan *de jure* independence:

- Taiwan could be converted from an enemy (or, at best, a wary neighbor) into a friend;
- A serious cause of tension and misunderstanding with the United States could be removed;
- All over Asia, other countries would feel significantly less apprehensive about the rise and territorial ambitions of China and be impressed by its vision and self-confidence; and
- A constructive dialogue could begin with Taiwan about how to move carefully to bring about political reform in China.

To the first of these, it is possible to retort that the Communist Party or a post-Communist military dictatorship in China might find it useful to have Taiwan as an enemy and the United States wrong-footed, much as Mao Zedong calculated in regard to Quemoy and Matsu in the 1950s. With respect to the second point, tension with the United States might play well with a restive domestic population in need of a diversion from their own discontents and anxieties.

---

[14]W. J. F. Jenner, *The Tyranny of History: The Roots of China's Crisis* (London: Allen Lane, 1992).

The third point might fetch the retort that the Communist Party believes it is making quite an impression all over Asia as it is and that a "firm" line on Taiwan is all to the good in this respect. The likely rejoinder to the fourth point is that the last thing the Communist Party seeks is dialogue with its democratic nemesis about political reform in China.

All of these objections, however, surely entail the corollary that the Communist Party's ulterior motives and hidden agenda, not China's best interests as a nation, are what stand in the way of a constructive, imaginative, and truly liberating solution to the Taiwan question. Moreover, even the Communist Party is likely to be more or less aware of certain *disadvantages* that China would suffer should it use force in an attempt to compel Taiwan to kowtow:

- It might suffer a humiliating military rebuff, with serious political consequences;

- It could find itself at war with the United States—at a point when the U.S. is its biggest market—over Taiwan, which is its biggest foreign investor;

- It would cause very serious alarm in Japan, Vietnam, and the Philippines, probably precipitating Japanese rearmament and leading the smaller states to seek closer security relations with the U.S.; and

- Even if Taiwan was defeated and the U.S. retreated, the resentment and anger in Taiwan and the economic damage done would be both grave and long-lasting.

Of course, the Communist Party's preferred strategy is not to use force, but to prevail through a combination of coercive diplomacy and economic inducements. This is likely, at least in part, because the architects of Chinese strategic policy are rational enough to perceive the negative side of the equation just drawn. The creative task at hand is to make clear the positive side and to develop the case for a vital Chinese commonwealth in the 21st century, which includes a prospering and gradually democratizing republic in China alongside a dynamic island democracy on Taiwan that is motivated by affinity with the mainland, not fear of it.

If this state of affairs could be brought into being, the third paradigmatic assumption—that China is a rising strategic competitor of the United States—might also be challenged more convincingly. The debate over this proposition in the United States is increasingly strenuous and analytically very interesting. America's leading regional allies, Japan and Australia, have a very great stake in how it turns out. It is often remarked that regional states in general, and Australia in particular, would prefer on practical grounds not to have to choose sides between the two great powers should they collide in conflict. What is less seldom observed is that it would not be in China's interests to force such choices on the countries around it; on the contrary, just to the extent that it would prefer not to have its neighbors look to the United States for protection against its rising power, it would do well not to give them cause to fear that power.

The "Singapore Gambit"

The scenario of China's freely and generously acknowledging the existing independence of Taiwan might be dubbed "the Singapore gambit" in order to distinguish it from "the Hong Kong gambit," which would entail someone "handing back" Taiwan to China, just as the British handed back Hong Kong in 1997. A number of facts make the Hong Kong gambit deeply problematic in the case of Taiwan.

- *First,* Taiwan is not a colony of the United States, whereas Hong Kong was a colony of Great Britain.

- *Second,* the United States has no treaty with China comparable to the 1898 treaty under which Britain took a 99-year lease on the New Territories in Hong Kong, so there is no preset deadline against which negotiations might be initiated.

- *Third,* Taiwan, unlike Hong Kong, is eminently defensible in purely military terms, is quite well armed, and has a substantial population long accustomed to self-government who hold indelible historical memories of massacre and oppression by mainland Chinese (albeit not Communist Chinese) forces.

The Singapore gambit, while superficially less plausible, holds a promise of being vastly more practical and more easily achieved—if the authorities in Beijing could be induced to attempt it. It is modeled on the manner in which Singapore was separated from Malaysia 40 years ago in order to minimize communal strife within the unitary Malaysian state.[15] The probable beneficial consequences of the Singapore gambit might be dubbed

---

[15]Lee Kwan Yew, *From Third World to First: The Singapore Story, 1965–2000* (New York: HarperCollins, 2000), p. xiv.

"the Australian outcome." By offering Taiwan its *de jure* independence with goodwill, China could achieve a future relationship with it comparable to the one that has existed between Britain and Australia for just over 100 years, ever since Britain offered the Australian colonies full self-government. One might be skeptical of Chinese willingness to attempt such a future, but once contemplated, it must surely exert a certain attraction.

The immense changes that have come about in China since 1900—and even more since Deng Xiaoping repudiated Maoism and began to open China up to market reform and foreign trade—demonstrate beyond rational dispute the possibility of a conceptual breakthrough along these lines. That there are other possibilities is not in dispute, but the Singapore gambit is the *best* possibility because it springs from the most generous assessment of the Chinese future. Instead of the parties to this complex matter succumbing to fatality by drifting into conflict, it would have them transform the situation to their mutual benefit.

Those who think that the only future is one that is rooted in the fixed ideas previously mentioned will insist that some version of the Hong Kong gambit is the only way to avert a Sino–American war. This is more a fatalist than a rationalist position, however, and adopting it would suggest a refusal to learn from the numerous unanticipated breakthroughs in world affairs that we have seen in recent decades—especially since 1989, the year of the Tiananmen Square repression in China. The future is not foreordained; it is waiting to be created.

7

Conceptual Underpinnings for New Policies Toward China and Taiwan

J. Bruce Jacobs[1]

AMERICAN AND AUSTRALIAN POLICIES TOWARD CHINA AND TAIWAN have great similarity. Both countries emphasize the importance of maintaining peace and stability in the region. Both emphasize the importance of maintaining the "*status quo*." Both have a "one China" policy. Both have major embassies in Beijing and very substantial, "officially unofficial" offices in Taipei, which in fact operate as embassies under the U.S. Department of State and the Australian Department of Foreign Affairs and Trade, respectively. Both give Taiwan's representatives in the United States and Australia such diplomatic privileges as diplomatic bags and tax concessions.

This chapter argues that some of the arrangements initiated by the United States and Australia when the Chinese "colonial regime"[2] of Chiang Kai-shek and Chiang Ching-kuo controlled Taiwan have become dangerously outdated for several reasons.

- *First* and foremost, the term "*status quo*" has become meaningless;

---

[1] This chapter is part of a larger project on "Democratizing Taiwan" funded by a Discovery Grant from the Australian Research Council.

[2] In recent years, the description of the Kuomintang regime of Chiang Kai-shek and Chiang Ching-kuo as a "colonial regime" has become much more frequent. An early use of this term comes from Parris Chang in Harvey J. Feldman, ed., *Constitutional Reform and the Future of the Republic of China* (Armonk, N.Y., and London: M. E. Sharpe, 1991), p. 45.

- *Second,* Taiwan has democratized;

- *Third,* as Taiwan has democratized, the forced imposition of a "Chinese" identity on the island has faded and more and more people in Taiwan identify as Taiwanese rather than as Chinese; and

- *Fourth,* our understanding of Chinese history and Taiwan's role in that history has grown substantially in recent years. This history too raises doubts about whether Taiwan is Chinese.

Naturally, there are some differences between the American and Australian approaches to China and Taiwan. When recognizing the People's Republic of China in December 1972, Australia "acknowledged" (rendered by the Chinese as "*chengren*") "the position of the Chinese government that Taiwan is a province of the People's Republic of China."[3] Although Henry Kissinger and Richard Nixon may have said similar things privately during their 1971 and 1972 visits, the United States has never stated publicly that Taiwan is a part of the People's Republic of China.

The United States passed the Taiwan Relations Act (TRA) in 1979 to give a legal basis to its ties with Taiwan.[4] Australia has never passed such an act. The TRA had three important provisions.

- It made "clear that the United States decision to establish diplomatic relations with the People's Republic of China rests upon *the expectation that the future of Taiwan will be determined by peaceful means.*"[5]

---

[3] "Quarterly Chronicle and Documentation," *The China Quarterly*, No. 53 (January/March 1973), p. 200. For works on Australia's establishing relations with the People's Republic and breaking relations with Taiwan, see Gary Klintworth, *Australia's Taiwan Policy 1942–1992* (Canberra: Australian National University, Research School of Pacific Studies, Department of International Relations, Australian Foreign Policy Publications Programme, 1993), and J. Bruce Jacobs, "Australia's Relationship with the Republic of China on Taiwan," in Nicholas Thomas, ed., *Re-Orienting China–Australia Relations: 1972 to the Present* (Aldershot, England; Brookfield, U.S.A.; Singapore; and Sydney: Ashgate, 2004), pp. 35–50.

[4] For the text of the Taiwan Relations Act, see Appendix B in this volume.

[5] Taiwan Relations Act, Section 2(b)(3). Emphasis added.

- It declared the U.S. government's intention "to provide Taiwan with arms of a defensive character."[6]

- It declared that Taiwan would be treated as equivalent to a nation-state:

> The absence of diplomatic relations or recognition shall not affect the application of the laws of the United States with respect to Taiwan, and the laws of the United States shall apply with respect to Taiwan in the manner that the laws of the United States applied with respect to Taiwan prior to January 1, 1979.... Whenever the laws of the United States refer or relate to foreign countries, nations, states, governments, or similar entities, such terms shall include and such laws shall apply with respect to Taiwan.[7]

In addition, except for the "Mutual Defense Treaty,"[8] which ceased operation one year *after* the United States began diplomatic relations with Beijing, all treaties and agreements with Taiwan continued in force:

> For all purposes, including actions in any court in the United States, the Congress approves the continuation in force of all treaties and other international agreements, including multilateral conventions, entered into by the United States and the governing authorities on Taiwan recognized by the United States as the Republic of China prior to January 1, 1979, and in force between them on December 31, 1978, unless and until terminated in accordance with law.[9]

Taiwan's Historical Status

Most of our understanding of Taiwan as a Chinese territory comes from the authoritarian Kuomintang regime of President Chiang Kai-shek and his son, President Chiang Ching-kuo. During the latter years of Taiwan's subjugation as a Japanese colony (1895–1945), the Kuomintang under

---

[6] TRA, Section 2(b)(5).

[7] TRA, Sections 4(a) and 4(b)(1).

[8] See Chapter 3.

[9] TRA, Section 4(c).

Chiang Kai-shek took the lead in declaring Taiwan "Chinese."[10] Ironically, during this period, on July 16, 1936, Mao Zedong told Edgar Snow that Taiwan was not Chinese. It is worth citing this passage of Snow's book at length:

> Question: "Is it the immediate task of the Chinese people to regain all the territories lost to Japanese imperialism, or only to drive Japan from North China, and all Chinese territory above the Great Wall?"
>
> Answer: "It is the immediate task of China to regain all our lost territories, not merely to defend our sovereignty below the Great Wall. This means that Manchuria must be regained. We do not, however, include Korea, formerly a Chinese colony, but when we have re-established the independence of the lost territories of China, and if the Koreans wish to break away from the chains of Japanese imperialism, we will extend them our enthusiastic help in their struggle for *independence. The same thing applies for Formosa.* As for Inner Mongolia…"[11]

We know that Mao Zedong and the Chinese Communist Party very carefully examined the text of *Red Star Over China* before it was published. This statement clearly reflected the views of Mao Zedong and the Chinese Communist Party at the time.

Although most Taiwanese welcomed the Kuomintang to Taiwan in the months after Japan's surrender in 1945, relations between the Chinese and the native Taiwanese quickly deteriorated. Many Chinese viewed Taiwanese as the enemy because Taiwanese conscripts had fought in the Japanese armies in China and some Taiwanese had worked for the Japanese puppet government in Nanjing during World War II. Thus, many Chinese perceived Taiwan as captured enemy territory and were ready both to exploit the wealth of "Treasure Island" *(baodao)* and to exclude Taiwanese from working in the Kuomintang government. This systematic prejudice against Taiwanese led to the explosion called the "February 28 [1947] Incident" or "February 28 [1947] Uprising." As a result, a huge gulf

---

[10] See, for example, J. Bruce Jacobs, "Taiwanese and the Chinese Nationalists, 1937–1945: The Origins of Taiwan's 'Half-Mountain People' (Banshan ren)," *Modern China*, Vol. 16, No. 1 (January 1990), pp. 84–118.

[11] Edgar Snow, *Red Star Over China* (New York: Grove Press, 1961), p. 96. Emphasis added. This paperback edition is a reprint of the original 1938 edition.

separated the recent Chinese arrivals from the mainland and the ethnic Taiwanese on the island.[12]

Following their defeat on the Chinese mainland and retreat to Taiwan in late 1949, the Kuomintang had a major "Party Reform" (1950–1952) that substantially reduced corruption,[13] but they also established their Chinese "colonial regime," which systematically excluded Taiwanese from high posts. Thus, although mainlanders accounted for less than 15 percent of Taiwan's population after 1949, they always accounted for at least a majority of both the Central Standing Committee of the Kuomintang and the Executive Yuan of the Republic of China (the governmental cabinet) in the four decades from 1949 until the death of President Chiang Ching-kuo in 1988. Only with Lee Teng-hui's succession to the presidency following Chiang Ching-kuo's death did Taiwanese account for a majority of these two bodies.[14] Furthermore, a Taiwanese did not become foreign minister until 1988 or premier until 1993.[15]

The Kuomintang, in a key point of their party ideology, asserted that Taiwan had always been Chinese. In recent years, since the presidency of Lee Teng-hui, both democracy and a new Taiwanese nationalism have enabled considerably more research on Taiwan and its history,[16] which

---

[12]The classic discussion of the February 28 Uprising is George H. Kerr, *Formosa Betrayed* (Boston: Houghton Mifflin, 1965). A more recent work, written during the early days of Taiwan's democratization, is Lai Tse-han, Ramon H. Myers, and Wei Wou, *A Tragic Beginning: The Taiwan Uprising of February 28, 1947* (Stanford: Stanford University Press, 1991). Also very useful is Steven E. Phillips, *Between Assimilation and Independence: The Taiwanese Encounter Nationalist China, 1945–1950* (Stanford: Stanford University Press, 2003).

[13]On the Party Reform, see Bruce J. Dickson, "The Lessons of Defeat: The Reorganization of the Kuomintang on Taiwan, 1950–52," *China Quarterly*, No. 133 (March 1993), pp. 56–84.

[14]Jaushieh Joseph Wu, *Taiwan's Democratization: Forces Behind the New Momentum* (Hong Kong, Oxford, New York: Oxford University Press, 1995), pp. 44, 103.

[15]In both cases, the person was Lien Chan, who had a Taiwanese father but was born in China. Later, Lien began to be perceived more as a Chinese than as a Taiwanese on the island. Taiwan's first Taiwan-born premier was Vincent Siew, who was appointed to the post on September 1, 1997.

[16]For the vast increase in publications about Taiwan since the late 1980s and in the 1990s, see Fu-chang Wang, "Why Bother About School Textbooks? An Analysis of the Origin of the Disputes over *Renshi Taiwan* Textbooks in 1997," in John Makeham and A-chin Hsiau, eds., *Cultural, Ethnic, and Political Nationalism in Contemporary Taiwan: Bentuhua* (New York: Palgrave Macmillan, 2005), pp. 70–71.

together with more Western research raises many questions about Taiwan's earlier status as a "Chinese territory."

Until the Dutch founded their colony in southern Taiwan in 1624, Taiwan's population consisted primarily of Austronesian indigenous peoples who belonged to several tribes. They never unified and never founded an island-wide organization or state.[17] Furthermore, Taiwan remained "quite isolated" prior to the 16th century.[18] According to Ming Dynasty records, "early settlers…were predominately [Chinese] fishermen," but it appears that many of these fisherman came from Fujian Province and usually stayed in Taiwan only for short periods while fishing.[19] Since it lacked a sovereign government, Taiwan became a type of "free port" and was visited by merchants from China, Japan and Okinawa. The Ming Dynasty's "ban on sea trade" led to an increase in piracy.[20] An important earlier Western history reinforces these points:

> Taiwan is rarely mentioned in early Chinese historical records, and archaeological and ethnographic data confirm that these trade routes largely bypassed Taiwan.… The key to Taiwan's historical isolation appears to lie…in its lack of attractions.… The hostility of Taiwan's head-hunting inhabitants toward intruders further inhibited the development of trade.[21]

In the early 17th century, the Dutch were well established in what is now Indonesia, while the Spanish controlled the Philippines. The Dutch, in their attempt to trade with China, tried to establish a base in Penghu, west of Taiwan, but were forced by the Ming government to build in Taiwan. The Dutch established their base in southern Taiwan in 1624, and the Spanish then built a base in northern Taiwan in 1626 in order to compete with the Dutch. These European powers "first established formal political power on

---

[17]Huang Fu-san, *A Brief History of Taiwan—A Sparrow Transformed into a Phoenix* (Taipei: Government Information Office, 2005), esp. Introduction, p. 2, and Chapter 1, p. 1, at *www.gio.gov.tw/taiwan-website/5-gp/history/tw01.html*. Huang Fu-san is one of the leading historians now re-examining Taiwan's history.

[18]*Ibid.*, Chapter 2, p. 1.

[19]*Ibid.*, Chapter 2, p. 2.

[20]*Ibid.*, Chapter 2, p. 3.

[21]John Robert Shepherd, *Statecraft and Political Economy on the Taiwan Frontier 1600–1800* (Taipei: SMC Publishing, 1995; reprinted Stanford: Stanford University Press, 1993), pp. 6, 7.

Taiwan."[22] The Dutch defeated the Spanish in 1642 and became the sole rulers of Taiwan until 1662. During their rule, the "Dutch formulated policies while the Chinese implemented them." Yet the Dutch and Chinese also proved "competitive" and "even confrontational."[23]

Dutch rule in Taiwan lasted from 1624 until 1662. During this phase of Western colonial rule in Taiwan, China underwent substantial dynastic change as the Manchu Qing Dynasty replaced the Chinese Ming Dynasty in 1644. Yet Taiwan remained under the control of the Dutch. The man who overthrew the Dutch 18 years later, Zheng Chenggong, has a reputation as a Ming loyalist who, some argue, hoped to restore the Ming Dynasty, but Huang Fu-san raises questions about this. He believes that Zheng, who died soon after his capture of Taiwan, established an independent "administration [that] exercised full authority over Taiwan and dealt with foreign countries as a sovereign nation."[24]

The Manchus conquered Taiwan in 1683 as part of their suppression of the Rebellion of the Three Feudatories *(sanfan zhi luan)* in southern China. Zheng Chenggong's son, Zheng Jing, had intervened in the war on the side opposing the Manchus. Originally, the Qing "court had never intended to send forces overseas but, in the aftermath of the rebellion, the Manchu rulers began devising a plan to eliminate" Zheng Jing.[25] In 1683, the powerful Manchu Kangxi emperor himself declared that Taiwan had never belonged to either the Manchus or China: "Taiwan is a small pellet of land. There is nothing to be gained by taking it, and no losses in not taking it."[26] His son, the Yongzheng Emperor, stated in 1723: "From ancient times, Taiwan has not been part of China. My holy and invincible father brought it into the territory."[27]

Most Chinese who assert that Taiwan is "Chinese" focus on the two centuries of Manchu control from 1683–1895. The Manchu empire was

---

[22]Huang Fu-san, *A Brief History of Taiwan—A Sparrow Transformed into a Phoenix*, Chapter 3, p. 1.

[23]*Ibid.*

[24]*Ibid.*, Chapter 4, p. 1.

[25]*Ibid.*, p. 3.

[26]Xue Huayuan, Dai Baocun, and Zhou Meili, *Taiwan, bushi Zhongguo de: Taiwan guomin de lishi* [*Taiwan Is Not Chinese: A History of the Taiwanese People*] (Danshui: Quncehui, 2005), p. 59. For an English translation, see Hsueh Hua-yuan, Tai Pao-tsun, and Chow Mei-li, *Is Taiwan Chinese? A History of Taiwanese Nationality* (Tamsui: Taiwan Advocates, 2005), p. 56.

[27]Xue *et al.*, *Taiwan, bushi Zhongguo de: Taiwan guomin de lishi*, p. 135; Hsueh *et al.*, *Is Taiwan Chinese? A History of Taiwanese Nationality*, p. 132.

very complex, both administratively and ideologically. Its rulers were all Manchus, as were many of its high officials. Manchus, for example, dominated the Grand Council.[28] As Han Chinese accounted for over 90 percent of the empire's population, many high officials were naturally Chinese, but the ultimate sources of power rested with the Manchus, not with Chinese. The following passage from a study by Justin Tighe indicates the empire's vastness and complexity:

> At the end of the eighteenth century the Qing empire encompassed an area twice the size of Ming China.... The court handled this expansion in a range of fashions without any one model of incorporation and administration. Differentiation and heterogeneity came to be the keys to the division of space within the empire. As a conquest dynasty, Qing political culture and institutions derived as much from the traditions of Inner Asia as they did from traditional Confucian political theory.[29]

Qing attitudes toward Taiwan remained ambivalent over their two centuries of rule. According to John Robert Shepherd, "even after paying a high price to defeat the rebel Cheng [Zheng] regime, the court still had to be convinced that the strategic importance of Taiwan justified retaining the revenue-poor island within the empire."[30] In Taiwan, "the state was saved the expense of initial pacification of the natives...because it inherited the system of taxation and control created by the Dutch and continued by the Chengs."[31] This substantially reduced the costs of administering Taiwan, yet in its first century of rule, Qing administration remained limited to the western plains of Taiwan.[32]

The situation did change in the 19th century. In the early 19th century, Han migration into the isolated Yilan plain in Taiwan's northeast "began

---

[28]Pamela Kyle Crossley, *A Translucent Mirror: History and Identity in Qing Imperial Ideology* (Berkeley, Los Angeles, London: University of California Press, 1999), p. 14, note 24.

[29]Justin Tighe, *Constructing Suiyuan: The Politics of Northwestern Territory and Development in Early Twentieth-Century China* (Leiden and Boston: Brill, 2005), p. 21.

[30]Shepherd, *Statecraft and Political Economy on the Taiwan Frontier 1600–1800*, p. 408.

[31]*Ibid.*, p. 409.

[32]*Ibid.*, pp. 178–214, esp. Maps 7.1, 7.2, and 7.3, pp. 188, 192–193, 196–197.

suddenly and on a large scale." Qing government administration arrived in 1810 after Han Chinese colonization of the Yilan plain was well underway.[33] Yet it appears that the Qing government still did not claim the "uncivilized" parts of Taiwan. This became clearest when the Qing government refused responsibility for protecting foreign seamen whose ships were wrecked in aboriginal areas of Taiwan.

In 1867, an American ship ran aground off Pingtung in southern Taiwan, and aborigines killed most of the surviving crew. The American consul at Xiamen, General Charles William Le Gendre, signed a treaty with the aboriginal Chief Tauketok rather than with the Qing government.[34]

In late 1871, matters became even more serious when Taiwan aborigines killed 54 shipwrecked Ryukyuan sailors. When China said that "it could not be held responsible for the behavior of [Taiwan] aborigines, because it always allowed them large measures of freedom and never interfered in their internal affairs," Japan responded that "sovereignty over a territory was evidence[d] by effective control; since China did not control the Formosan aborigines, they were clearly beyond its jurisdiction."[35] Clearly, different people in the Qing government had different perspectives. Li Hongzhang wanted to accept responsibility for the actions of the Taiwan aborigines, but in July 1873, another group of Qing leaders informed the Japanese foreign minister "that China claimed no control over the savage tribes in the mountainous eastern half of Formosa...."[36]

In summary, the record of Qing rule on Taiwan beginning in the 18th century "was one of corrupt but minimal government, punctuated by periodic suppression of uprisings. The shelling of Keelung by British ships during the Opium War and the opening of Tamsui and Ta-kao (the present Kaohsiung) as treaty ports in the early 1860s barely began to awaken Peking to the importance of the island."[37] The ensuing Japanese invasion of 1874–1875, however, as well as the later French attacks on Taiwan during the Sino–French war of 1884–1885, "did...convince a few statesmen of the urgent need to strengthen [Taiwan's] defences."[38] The Qing established

---

[33]*Ibid.*, pp. 358–359.

[34]Huang Fu-san, *A Brief History of Taiwan—A Sparrow Transformed into a Phoenix*, Chapter 5, p. 6. For Le Gendre's first-person account of this expedition, see James W. Davidson, *The Island of Formosa: Past and Present* (London: Macmillan & Co., 1903), pp. 117–122.

[35]Immanuel C. Y. Hsü, *The Rise of Modern China,* 3rd ed. (Hong Kong: Oxford University Press, 1983), p. 316.

[36]Hosea Ballou Morse, *The International Relations of the Chinese Empire*, Vol. II (London, New York, Bombay: Longmans, Green, 1918), p. 271.

new administrative units in 1875 and 1887[39] and made Taiwan a province in 1885.[40]

Yet, despite this apparent last-minute appreciation of Taiwan by at least some Qing officials, such a view was apparently not unanimous. In the words of Taiwan's President Lee Teng-hui, at the end of the Sino–Japanese War in 1895, the first thing the Qing Dynasty negotiators gave the Japanese was Taiwan. According to Lee Teng-hui, Li Hongzhang, the Qing Dynasty lead negotiator, "implied he did not want Taiwan as it was land beyond civilization (*huawai zhi di*)!"[41] A Japanese source confirms that Li Hongzhang "surrendered nothing which he was not prepared and glad to get rid of, except the indemnity. He always considered Formosa [Taiwan] a curse to China and was exceedingly pleased to hand it over to Japan, and he shrewdly guessed that Japan would find it a great deal more trouble than it was worth."[42] It should be noted, however, that Hosea Ballou Morse suggests Li Hongzhang did not give up Taiwan quite so easily.[43]

This analysis raises three aspects of Qing control of Taiwan.

- *First*, Qing control was—at best—loose, "minimal," and partial. Substantial parts of Taiwan remained outside of Qing control throughout whole period of Qing rule in Taiwan (1683-1895).

---

[37]Kwang-Ching Liu and Richard J. Smith, "The Military Challenge: The Northwest and the Coast," in John K. Fairbank and Kwang-Ching Liu, eds., *The Cambridge History of China*, Vol. 11 (Cambridge: Cambridge University Press, 1980), p. 260.

[38]*Ibid.*

[39]Shepherd, *Statecraft and Political Economy on the Taiwan Frontier 1600–1800*, p. 360.

[40]Yang Bichuan, ed., *Taiwan lishi cidian* [*Taiwan Historical Dictionary*] (Taipei: Qianwei, 1997), p. 259.

[41]Lee Teng-hui made this statement in his famous interview with Shiba Ryotaro, which took place in Japanese. See Shiba Ryotaro, *Taiwan kiko* [*A Taiwan Journey*] (Tokyo: Asahi Shinbun, 1994), p. 489. Two different Chinese translations follow the Chinese text closely: Shiba Ryotaro, *Taiwan jixing* [*A Taiwan Journey*], translated into Chinese by Li Jinsong (Taipei: Taiwan Dongfan, 1996), p. 525, and Lee Teng-hui, *Jingying da Taiwan* [*Managing a Great Taiwan*] (Taipei: Yuanliu, 1995), p. 472. This latter version, translated by Luo Yi-wen, appeared originally in the Taiwan magazine *Heibai xinwen zhoukan* [*Black and White Newsweekly*], No. 34 (29 May–4 June 1994).

- *Second,* even this partial Qing control was not Chinese, but Manchu.

- *Third,* Chinese need to confront their history accurately. Rather than claiming that the Chinese assimilate foreign rulers such as Mongols and Manchus, they need to realize that these peoples have in the past dominated China as colonial rulers of domains that included extensive territories beyond China Proper.

Thus, historically, Chinese cannot use the Qing period to claim sovereignty over Taiwan. In their struggle with the Manchu Qing dynasty, the Kuomintang, a key Han Chinese political organization involved in the overthrow of the Manchus in late 1911, invoked racial hatred against the Manchu rulers. Ironically, in the 1930s and 1940s in China and during the 1950s through the 1980s on Taiwan, the Kuomintang used the existence of the Manchu Qing dynasty's "control" of Taiwan to "prove" that the island was "Chinese."

The Japanese takeover of Taiwan in 1895 marks a seminal stage in the complete separation of Taiwan from China. Soon after the Chinese signed the Treaty of Shimonoseki with Japan, Chinese officials in Taiwan attempted to forestall the Japanese occupation by establishing a "Republic of Taiwan" (*Taiwan minzhu guo*). Although this entity is sometimes termed Asia's first republic, and despite valiant gestures of its government in producing a flag, currency, and stamps, the Republic of Taiwan was short-lived.[44]

The 50 years of Japanese colonial rule from 1895 to 1945 provided Taiwan with a culture quite different from that in China. Although people

---

[42]Hayashi Tadasu, *The Secret Memoirs of Count Tadasu Hayashi*, A. M. Pooley, ed. (New York: G. P. Putnam's Sons, 1915), p. 57, as quoted in S. C. M. Paine, *The Sino–Japanese War of 1894–1895: Perceptions, Power, and Primacy* (Cambridge: Cambridge University Press, 2003), pp. 291–292.

[43]See Morse, *The International Relations of the Chinese Empire*, Vol. III, pp. 43–56.

[44]In English, see the early work of Harry Lamley, including Harry Lamley, "The 1895 Taiwan Republic: A Significant Episode in Modern Chinese History," *Journal of Asian Studies*, Vol. 27, No. 4 (August 1968), pp. 739–762, and Harry Lamley, "A Short-lived Republic and War, 1895: Taiwan's Resistance Against Japan," in Paul K. T. Sih, ed., *Taiwan in Modern Times* (New York: St. John's University Press, 1973), pp. 241–316. In Chinese, see Li Xiaofeng, *Taiwan Shi 100 Jian Dashi* [*100 Important Events in Taiwan History*], Vol. I (Taipei: Yushan she, 1999), pp. 97–102.

continued to speak their native Hokkien, Hakka, and indigenous languages, the Japanese educated significant numbers of Taiwanese who became both literate and conversant in the Japanese language.[45] Within this context, the Taiwanese people created and joined a wide variety of political and cultural organizations and movements that advocated ideas ranging from support for China to Taiwan independence to assimilation within the Japanese Empire. With World War II, the Japanese pushed assimilationist policies much more strongly.[46]

Most reports suggest that the Taiwanese welcomed the Kuomintang after World War II. As noted earlier, China's exploitation of Taiwan and the arrogant attitude of the Chinese toward the Taiwanese quickly led to division between the Taiwanese and Chinese and to the "February 28 [1947] Uprising." Interestingly, the period of the Chinese Civil War (1945–1949) is the only period since 1895 when the same government ruled both China and Taiwan, and it is perhaps the saddest period in Taiwan's history.

Following the "February 28 [1947] Uprising," the Kuomintang implemented its White Terror against those who advocated Taiwanese independence as well as those who advocated Communism.[47] The Kuomintang colonial regime deliberately excluded native Taiwanese from senior political positions in Taiwan. Chiang Ching-kuo, when he became premier in 1972, increased the numbers of Taiwanese at local levels, but

---

[45]The percentage of school-age Taiwanese that were educated by the Japanese grew significantly during Japanese rule. In 1917, the Japanese educated 13.1 percent of the school-age children (21.4 percent of the males and 3.7 percent of the females). These proportions increased steadily to 71.9 percent of the school-age population in 1943 (80.9 percent of the males and 60.9 percent of the females). Even if these numbers overstate the numbers of Taiwanese educated, they were several times greater than the numbers of those educated in China. The statistics appear in *Taiwan sheng wushiyi nian lai tongji tiyao* [*Statistical Abstract of Taiwan Province for the Past Fifty-One Years*] (Taipei: Statistical Office of the Taiwan Provincial Administration Agency, February 1946; photo-reprinted Taipei: Guting Shuwu, 1969), p. 1241.

[46]An especially good survey of this period is Phillips, *Between Assimilation and Independence: The Taiwanese Encounter Nationalist China, 1945–1950*, pp. 17–39. See also Harry J. Lamley, "Taiwan Under Japanese Rule, 1985–1945: The Vicissitudes of Colonialism," in Murray A. Rubinstein, ed., *Taiwan: A New History* (Armonk, N.Y., and London: M. E. Sharpe, 1999), pp. 201–260.

[47]For a useful perspective on the White Terror in English, see Tehpen Tsai, *Elegy of Sweet Potatoes: Stories of Taiwan's White Terror*, trans. Grace Hatch (Taipei: Taiwan Publishing Co., 2002). This book, which tells the story of one Taiwanese who was arrested as part of the White Terror, was originally written in Japanese. It has also been translated into Chinese.

significant Taiwanese representation in the central levels of the government or the KMT party apparatus occurred only after Chiang Ching-kuo's death and his succession by Lee Teng-hui, a native Taiwanese, in 1988.[48]

Lee Teng-hui, working explicitly and tacitly with liberal elements in the Kuomintang as well as with the Democratic Progressive Party, implemented democracy in Taiwan. This led to Lee's overwhelming victory as the first popularly elected president of Taiwan in March 1996 and to the election of the then-opposition Democratic Progressive Party candidate, Chen Shui-bian, as president in March 2000 and to Chen's re-election in March 2004.

The Taiwanization of Taiwan

The political and constitutional processes of democratization in Taiwan under Presidents Lee Teng-hui and Chen Shui-bian have been discussed elsewhere.[49] The "Taiwanization" of Taiwan that accompanied this democratization has resulted in a rapid, steady, and significant change in the self-identification of Taiwan's population.

In 1992, the Election Study Center at National Chengchi University in Taiwan began to examine identity in Taiwan semiannually. The surveys asked respondents to identify themselves in one of three categories: "both Taiwanese and Chinese," "Taiwanese," and "Chinese." Over time, with blips in the data, the proportion of respondents replying that they are "Chinese" has shown a consistent downward trend from more than one-quarter to less than one-sixteenth of those surveyed. In other words, in just over 12 years, the number identifying as "Chinese only" is less than one-fourth the number of the earliest surveys. On the other hand, the number replying that they are "Taiwanese" has increased some 2.5 times, from about one-sixth to over two-fifths of the respondents. The percentage of those claiming to be both Taiwanese and Chinese has remained in the low forties. The halving of the non-response rate from 11 percent to less than 5 percent also demonstrates that these issues have been widely discussed in Taiwan and that people are not afraid to respond to surveys.[50]

Two scholars from National Chengchi University, Szu-yin Ho and I-chou Liu, have analyzed these data in greater detail.[51] They show that these

---

[48]Taiwanese had held several deputy positions such as vice-president and vice-premier. According to Lee Teng-hui, even though Chiang Ching-kuo had appointed him vice-president in 1984, Chiang never indicated that he had Lee Teng-hui in mind as a successor.

[49]See, for example, J. Bruce Jacobs, "'Taiwanization' in Taiwan's Politics," in Makeham and Hsiau, eds., *Cultural, Ethnic, and Political Nationalism in Contemporary Taiwan: Bentuhua*, pp. 17–54.

trends have occurred among all ethnic groups in Taiwan, though ethnic Taiwanese Hokkien (or Minnan) and Hakka have higher rates of "Taiwanese" identification, while respondents born on the mainland or their children have higher rates of "Chinese" identification. From 1994 to 2000, the numbers of mainlanders identifying as "Chinese" declined from 55.6 percent to 29.9 percent.[52]

Ho and Liu are conservative in attributing reasons for these significant trends, but the popular influence of both Lee Teng-hui and the Democratic Progressive Party has clearly had a powerful impact on self-identification. In addition, self-identification has had an impact on "national consciousness" (*guojia rentong*) in Taiwan. The perceived hostility of the Chinese regime toward Taiwan has also increased this sense of Taiwan identity and helped to cause the loss of Chinese identity on the island.

The Problematic *Status Quo*

The policies of both the United States and Australia toward China and Taiwan stress maintenance of the *status quo*. The term "*status quo*" means "the existing state or condition." In terms of American and Australian China policy, "*status quo*" means the state of China and Taiwan in the early 1970s. At that time, China was under the leadership of Chairman Mao Zedong, while Taiwan was led by the Chinese "colonial regime" of Chiang Kai-shek.

Both China and Taiwan have changed greatly since the 1970s. The political system in Taiwan has evolved peacefully from a colonial, authoritarian Chinese regime with little participation from the native-Taiwanese majority into a democratic Taiwanese government. This democratization deserves praise from Western democracies, but it also means that Taiwanese—who now finally have achieved their own voice—do not want to be part of China.

This is a significant cultural and psychological transformation that resonates, for example, to a similar alteration in Australian culture. Thirty

---

[50]The whole range of survey results through December 2005 may be found at *http://esc.nccu.edu.tw/eng/data/data03-2.htm*. The December 2005 results show that 46.5 percent identify as Taiwanese, 42.0 percent identify as both Taiwanese and Chinese, and 7.3 percent identify as Chinese. The non-response rate was 4.1 percent.

[51]Szu-yin Ho and I-chou Liu, "The Taiwanese/Chinese Identity of the Taiwan People in the 1990s," in Wei-chin Lee and T. Y. Wang, eds., *Sayonara to the Lee Teng-hui Era: Politics in Taiwan, 1988–2000* (Lanham, Md.: University Press of America, 2003), pp. 149–183.

[52]*Ibid.*, p. 155, Table 6.2.

or 40 years ago, many Australians referred to "going home"—meaning Britain—even if they had never been there. Now no one says such things. Similarly, many Taiwanese once saw China as the "homeland." Now very few Taiwanese hold that view. These cultural changes in Australia and Taiwan have been relatively quiet and peaceful, but they are very significant nonetheless.

China too has undergone significant change. Its policies of "reform" *(gaige)* and "opening to the outside" *(kaifang)* have vastly increased both the size of China's economy and the living standards of its people. At the same time, however, the Chinese regime has also become vastly more aggressive toward Taiwan. China's military, for example, has steadily increased the numbers of short-range ballistic missiles aimed at Taiwan—a number that reached 784 in early 2006. Many new fighter and bomber aircraft squadrons are now stationed in Fujian Province opposite Taiwan, only seven minutes flying time from the island. China's building of a blue-water navy also threatens Taiwan. The missile buildup, the purchase and construction of many other advanced weapons systems, and bellicose rhetoric amply demonstrate that the *status quo* in the Taiwan Strait has morphed dramatically from the 1970s paradigm.

On March 14, 2005, China passed its Anti-Secession Law *(fan fenlie guojia fa)*, which made it illegal for people to advocate Taiwan's independence. Thus, China, a large authoritarian state with a seat on the Security Council of the United Nations but with no freedom of the press or speech at home, declared unilaterally that Taiwan belongs to it despite Taiwan's never having been a part of the People's Republic of China. As noted, China and Taiwan have been ruled by the same government only during four very unhappy years of the Chinese Civil War and as parts of the foreign Manchu empire from 1683 to 1895.

If China wished to maintain the *status quo*, it would be happy to retain the name "Republic of China" for Taiwan. In fact, China has resolutely rebuffed all efforts by Taiwan to use the term "Republic of China" internationally or in cross-Strait situations. Thus, when using the term, China always puts it in quotation marks. The 2000 Chinese White Paper on Taiwan makes this crystal clear:

> Since the KMT ruling clique retreated to Taiwan, although its regime has continued to use the designations "Republic of China" and "government of the Republic of China," it has long since completely forfeited its right to exercise state sovereignty on behalf of China and, in reality, has always remained only a local authority in Chinese territory.[53]

During the so-called friendly visits of Kuomintang Chairman Lien Chan and PFP Chairman James Soong to Beijing in late April and early May 2005, the Chinese refused to allow both visitors to use the term "Republic of China" in their public speeches. [54] In this way too, China has changed the *status quo*.

Closely linked to the *status quo* issue is the issue of "one China." Again, this difficulty arises from the period of Mao Zedong and Chiang Kai-shek, when both agreed that Taiwan was a part of China and that there was only "one China." Of course, as stated earlier, the people of Taiwan had no say in the matter, and more recent and objective historical research casts considerable doubt on the "one China" analysis.[55]

The acceptance of "one China" by the United States, Australia, and many other countries means that Taiwan finds it difficult to establish formal diplomatic relations with most of the world's nations and makes it impossible for Taiwan to participate in most international organizations (though, as noted earlier, Taiwan does have substantial "officially unofficial" ties with both the United States and Australia as well as with many other countries). The question remains: Should agreements made in the years when the Chinese colonial regime ruled Taiwan and Taiwan's people had no say in the matter be used to repress the people of Taiwan today?

Some Alternative Policies

Clearly, China's claims to Taiwan have no historical basis. Evidence shows that China's claims from the Qing period are false. Furthermore, during the Japanese period, Chairman Mao Zedong clearly stated that Taiwan should be independent. All of China's current claims for Taiwan can only date from the assertions of Chiang Kai-shek, who, as we have noted,

---

[53]Taiwan Affairs Office and Information Office of the State Council, People's Republic of China, *The One China Principle and the Taiwan Question*, February 21, 2000, February 21, 2000, at *http://english.people.com.cn/features/taiwanpaper/taiwanb.html*.

[54]Jason Dean, "China Cedes Little in Talks with Soong: Taiwan Opposition Leader Gets Small Concession on 'One China' Definition," *The Wall Street Journal*, May 13, 2005, at *http://online.wsj.com/article/0,,SB111593132420632092,00.html*.

[55]For the development of Taiwan's "One China" policy under Chiang Kai-shek, see J. Bruce Jacobs, "One China, Diplomatic Isolation and a Separate Taiwan," in Edward Friedman, ed., *China's Rise, Taiwan's Dilemmas and International Peace* (London and New York: Routledge, 2006), pp. 84–109. For modern research on Taiwan's historical status, see this chapter and the sources cited in the footnotes.

implemented a dictatorial "colonial regime" in Taiwan. To break the current logjam, we therefore need to think in new ways.

First, "one China" is fine as long as it is clear that Taiwan does not belong to China unless the 23 million people of Taiwan freely and willingly choose to join with China. In the present circumstances, there seems little likelihood that such unification would occur. Only 2 percent of Taiwan's population want unification now, and ultimate unification is favored by fewer than one in six persons.[56]

Second, we should understand that the term "*status quo*" has lost its meaning to define cross-Strait relations. Too much has changed in both Taiwan and China since 1972. Unless "*status quo*" is defined simply to mean "a state of peace," the term has little relevance today.

Third, we need to recognize change in the international system. A case with important parallels is East Timor. In 1975, Indonesia invaded and occupied East Timor. Australia and, to the best of my knowledge, the United States collaborated with Indonesian President Haji Mohammad Soeharto and acquiesced in Indonesia's military invasion and occupation of the former Portuguese colony. Only after Soeharto fell did Australian Prime Minister John Howard suggest to Soeharto's successor, Jusuf Habibie, that the East Timorese people vote on East Timor's future.

Of course, the East Timorese people voted overwhelmingly for independence on August 20, 1999, and without a trace of irony, the People's Republic of China was the very first nation to recognize independent East Timor on May 20, 2002. If China can accept East Timor's independence after 24 years of Indonesian occupation, why cannot it use the same logic to agree that Taiwan too may be independent, especially when the People's Republic of China has *never* occupied Taiwan?

Fourth, there are several moves that the United States and Australia can make now. Taiwan has good formal diplomatic relations with several Pacific island nations, including the Solomon Islands, the Marshall Islands, Tuvalu, Palau, Nauru, and Kiribati. In the Pacific, many of these nations face the status of "failed states" as they lack resources, industries, and educated leaders. Thus, both Australia and the United States are concerned with good governance on these islands. Although the democratic government of President Chen Shui-bian needs to try to retain diplomatic relations, it has decided to reduce spending and create true aid programs. Certainly in such locations as the Solomon Islands where several nations, including Australia, the United States, and Japan, cooperate in multilateral aid programs, Taiwan should be included. This will help to regularize Taiwan's diplomatic efforts

---

[56]Jacobs, "'Taiwanization' in Taiwan's Politics," p. 46.

and create opportunities for formal international cooperation between Taiwan and other nations.

The United States and Australia could welcome Taiwan to other groups. The Australia Group, founded in 1984, seeks to assure that the industries of the member countries do not assist states that seek to acquire chemical and biological weapons. China is not one of the 38 Australia Group members despite being invited in late May 1997.[57] Rather, according to the official Web site of the Foreign Ministry of China, "China strongly opposes the actions by the member states of the Australia Group in obstructing the normal chemical trade between States Parties to the convention under the pretext of non-proliferation."[58] Taiwan has the world's 11th largest chemical industry.[59] Why not invite it to become a member?

Taiwan is clearly an independent sovereign state. It meets all of the conditions of Article 1 of the Convention on the Rights and Duties of States that was signed in Montevideo, Uruguay, on December 26, 1933: "The state as a person of international law should possess the following qualifications: (a) a permanent population; (b) a defined territory; (c) government; and (d) capacity to enter into relations with the other states."[60] In addition, Taiwan's government is chosen by the people of Taiwan.

In view of all these factors, it makes eminent policy sense to invite Taiwan to participate more fully in international cooperative regimes, especially those where it has a significant role to play. To be sure, Taiwan's participation in the United Nations will be blocked by China's veto on the Security Council, but there is nothing to prevent Taiwan's fellow democracies from asking China why it believes that Taiwan's participation would impede the possibility of eventual reunification. Both East and West Germany had separate U.N. memberships, but they ultimately decided to unite into one nation.[61]

---

[57]On the Australia Group, see U.S. Department of State, fact sheet, "The Australia Group," August 10, 2004, at *www.state.gov/t/isn/rls/fs/35052.htm*, and Nuclear Threat Initiative, "Australia Group (AG)," undated, at *www.nti.org/db/china/agorg.htm*.

[58]*Ibid.* The relevant page on the Web site of the Chinese Foreign Ministry has been deleted.

[59]Richard T. Cupitt with Morgan Flo, "Export Controls in Taiwan (ROC)," at *www.uga.edu/cits/documents/html/nat_eval_taiwan.htm*.

[60]See Convention on the Rights and Duties of States (Montevideo Convention), 49 Stat. 3907 (1933), at *www.yale.edu/lawweb/avalon/intdip/interam/intam03.htm#art3*.

Other organizations should also open membership to Taiwan. Health threats and diseases, for example, do not confine themselves within national boundaries. China has said repeatedly that it will involve Taiwan in World Health Organization matters, but it often forgets (or ignores) Taiwan. In the few cases where China has tried to involve Taiwan, Beijing has simply used the occasion for its own political purposes. Several Taiwan citizens died of SARS, but the WHO had difficulty helping Taiwan (though it ultimately did provide some assistance). Similarly, China has not helped Taiwan in monitoring the transmission vectors of avian flu. Taiwan is clearly an independent health entity and deserves at least participation in WHO disease control efforts, if not its own WHO membership.

Such names for Taiwan as "Chinese Taipei" at the Asia–Pacific Economic Cooperation (APEC) forum or in the Olympics are meaningless. Taiwan is not part of China. Furthermore, Taiwan is much more than Taipei. No other country is treated in this way.

A substantial Gallup Organization survey of ordinary citizens as well as opinion leaders in five major democratic countries suggests that these policy suggestions would have wide popular support among Western democratic nations. The Gallup Organization surveyed 1,500 ordinary citizens and 200 leaders in the United States, Japan, the United Kingdom, France, and Germany, for a total of 8,500 persons. Over 60 percent of the respondents in the five countries see Taiwan and China as two separate countries. Among the opinion leaders, 89 percent of the Americans and 92 percent from the U.K. said that Taiwan should belong to the WHO.[62]

At the same time, both the United States and Australia have stated that nurturing and spreading democracy is an important strategic goal. Both have sent troops to Iraq and Afghanistan in efforts to support democracy in those countries. Taiwan is already a democracy. Clearly, the United States and Australia cannot let a large dictatorship invade this vibrant democracy any more than they could allow Saddam Hussein to invade and occupy Kuwait, which he once claimed as Iraq's "nineteenth province."

China is an important country just as the Soviet Union was important during the Cold War. It is clearly desirable to have cooperation with China

---

[61]The Chinese argument that China and Taiwan are different from East and West Germany and different from North and South Korea because China and Taiwan are still in a state of civil war while the German and Korean cases were ended by international agreements is legally suspect. In fact, there is no pragmatic difference among the three cases.

[62]See Government Information Office, Republic of China (Taiwan), "Multinational Survey on Image of Taiwan," November 24, 2005, at *www.gio.gov.tw/taiwan-website/4-oa/20051124/2005112401.html.*

in many aspects of international politics. But the survival and success of freedom and democracy in such places as Taiwan must not be sacrificed to the demands of an ever more powerful dictatorship that views its place in the modern world in terms of past empires.[63]

---

[63]See, for example, Ross Terrill, *The New Chinese Empire and What It Means for the United States* (Sydney: University of New South Wales Press, 2003).

The Etiology and Immunology of America's "One China" Policy

RICHARD C. KAGAN

WHY DO I USE THE WORD "ETIOLOGY" IN MY TITLE? The word in Greek referred to legendary or mythological explanations of the causes of particular phenomena. It was borrowed in Catholic theology to describe explicit scriptural explanations for the origins of a particular doctrine or moral law. In medicine, it refers to the cause of pathologies, and in literary criticism, it refers to an unreasonable explanation for the way things are.

By "etiology of 'one China,'" I want to go beyond the usual, and correct, description of how the unfortunate policy evolved. John Tkacik and others have ably charted the case for its specific origins in *Rethinking "One China,"* the companion volume to this book that was published in 2004.[1] Rather than narrating the content of the documents that have laid out this policy and its consequences, I hope to illuminate how a pernicious fixation on "one China" puts not only Taiwan, but also China and the Chinese in a dangerous and self-destructive situation.

To begin, we must divide the analyses into two linguistic parts: "China" and "One."

The term "*Zhongguo*" or "Middle Kingdom" or "Central Kingdom" was not generally used to describe China until the 1902 writings of Liang Qichao. Liang was very disturbed that the Han people (known now as the Han Chinese) had no territorial name.

---

[1] See John J. Tkacik, Jr., ed., *Rethinking "One China"* (Washington, D.C.: The Heritage Foundation, 2004).

Liang and his nationalistic colleagues were well read in the writings of Leopold von Ranke, a German historian who had developed and transmitted the idea of historicism to his fellow Germans and to Europe and Japan. The idea was that there was a history of a people that was constant, ahistorical, and racially essentialist. The German tribes were not just an amalgam of peoples who had various experiences through time. The German people all shared certain values and psychic mindsets. They were inspired by a Divine Will that gave them a common identity and was never-changing. One of von Ranke's students traveled to Japan in the 1880s and had his mentor's works translated into Japanese. They were eventually translated into Chinese, resulting in their complete publication in China during the 1920s.

Liang and other Chinese who had studied in Japan or who had been exposed to the Japanese or Chinese translations were attracted to von Ranke's romantic and idealistic nationalism. Thus inspired, they became frustrated that there was no term for the historical China. The earlier terms were the name of the ruling dynasty, or a specific geographical area such as the Nine Regions, or a metaphor such as "*Zhonghua*" or "The Flourishing Center."

In the 1920s, Liang's ideas became more popular. The immediate reason was the discovery of the archaic characters "*Zhongguo*" ("Middle Kingdom") on oracle bones (or "dragon bones"—*jiaguwen*) dating from the second millennium B.C. The term seemed to date from prehistoric times and corroborated the thinking that China was an old, essentialist civilization. It did not matter that the original term was used in a very specific way to denote the central kingdoms surrounded by barbarian rulers. Nor did it matter that the term was not used again until the 20th century. The concept of a continuous "Chinese" polity had not really existed because it was never true, and the Chinese knew it. So-called barbarians had ruled the geographical area of China for perhaps half of China's five millennia of historical experience. Nationalistic Chinese historians—and Harvard's dean of Sinology, John King Fairbank—popularized the idea of a "Middle Kingdom" that had Sinicized the rest of the world with its admittedly magnificent culture. One reason for this conclusion is that neither the Harvard school of Sinology nor the Beijing scholars were familiar with the literature and history of the barbarians. But another reason was that the concept of "China" was fundamental to the belief in racial superiority and consciousness and unbroken history cultivated in modern times by the Chinese leadership.

With regard to Taiwan, this nationalistic and false irredentist surge occurred late in World War II. Until then, neither the Communists nor the Nationalists laid claim to Taiwan. The idea first seems to have appeared in

June 1942 when the Chinese press in Chungking (*Chongqing*) published several editorials about "the return of Formosa and the Liu Chius [Ryukyu Islands]" after the war. As one U.S. embassy officer reported, a Chungking Foreign Ministry official confided that "Regarding Formosa...its return seemed fitting to the Chinese because the greater part of the population was Chinese and had continued to maintain close ties with China." On the other hand:

> [R]egarding the Liu Chius...it was unfortunately inevitable during wartime that there should be exaggerated statements by private individuals concerning war aims; that the truth of the matter was that the people of the Liu Chius were not Chinese...and that the islands, which had only been a tributary to China, had been entirely separated from it for almost eighty years.[2]

This did not deter Chiang Kai-shek's brother-in-law, T. V. Soong, from stating in his first press conference as foreign minister in November 1942 that "China will recover Manchuria and Formosa and the Ryukyu Islands after the war and Korea will be independent."[3] On December 23, 1942, a letter to Chiang Kai-shek was prepared for the signature of President Franklin Roosevelt's emissary, Owen Lattimore, that contained the sentence, "The President is much impressed by your clear view that only bases in the two key areas of Liaotung and Formosa can effectively coordinate land, sea and air power for the long term prevention of renewed aggression." It was the only sentence deleted from the three-page letter by President Roosevelt himself.[4]

It was evident that the Chinese Nationalists in Chungking were making it up as they went along. "One China" wasn't part of their lexicon, merely territorial aggrandizement in a post war environment. It was also clear that President Roosevelt, at least, was not interested that early on in encouraging Chiang's expansionist instincts.

The Chinese Communists, on the other hand, were actually anti-national, pro-international at the time. They organized themselves on class and social organization, not national institutions. In the 1920s, both Chen Duxiu, a founder of the Chinese Communist Party, and Mao Zedong argued, for

---

[2] *Foreign Relations of the United States Diplomatic Papers: 1942 China* (Washington, D.C.: U.S. Government Printing Office, 1956), pp. 732–733.

[3] *Ibid.*, pp. 174–175.

[4] *Ibid.*, p. 186.

different reasons, for the breakup of China. Chen actually thought that China would be better off as a colony than under the rule of the warlords who represented traditional feudal values. Chen had popularized the idea that "Mr. Science" and "Mr. Democracy" should replace the feudal and militaristic values of a backward China.[5]

In any event, Roosevelt eventually acquiesced to Chiang's demand for Taiwan and, under the terms of the Cairo Declaration of 1943, agreed that "all the territories that Japan has stolen from the Chinese, such as…Formosa and the Pescadores, shall be restored to the Republic of China."[6] The defeat of Japan and the subsequent misrule and corruption of Chiang Kai-shek's occupying administration highlighted the fragile identity and legitimacy of Taiwan. Once Chiang's armies had accepted the surrender of Japanese forces on the island, they prepared for eventual international approval in the form of a peace treaty that would formally deed the island over to the "Republic of China."

The Nationalist Chinese claim on Taiwan was even more urgent when, by the end of the Chinese Civil War in 1949, the retreating Kuomintang (KMT) had no place else to go. The KMT government had outlawed the use of the Japanese language in Taiwan and began a half-century of indoctrinating Taiwanese with a Chinese education. In the exams, the Taiwanese had to learn not only the macro history of China, but also bus routes and train schedules of cities on the China mainland.

During the KMT's rule of Taiwan, there were efforts among the elite and the intellectuals in Taiwan to change the *status quo*. The most remarkable was the proposal by Chiang Kai-shek's deputy foreign minister, Yang Hsi-kun, for an independent "Chinese Republic of Taiwan" and the wholly new constitution such a new state would require. Deputy Foreign Minister Yang believed that "a new image needed to be created with the government freed of the outworn trappings, encumbrances and shibboleths of the party and the establishment."[7]

While this sentiment was rare among mainlanders in the Taipei elite, they were the rule among Taiwanese intellectuals—academics, Christian ministers, and overseas Taiwanese—who advocated an independent and democratic Taiwan. Almost always, these figures were jailed, blacklisted, and punished for their beliefs whenever they came to the attention of the

---

[5] For an accessible description of Chen's political thought, see Jonathan Spence, *The Search for Modern China* (New York: W. W. Norton & Co., 1990), pp. 315–332.

[6] *A Decade of American Foreign Policy: Basic Documents, 1941–1949* (Washington, D.C.: U.S. Government Printing Office, 1950), p. 22.

[7] See Chapter 1.

notorious Taiwan Garrison Command. Nonetheless, they remained a strong moral and political force in criticizing the idea of "one China."

The Myth of Chinese "Essentialism"

The pathology of Chinese "essentialism" is that it creates and enforces rigid boundaries of thought. Any deviation from orthodoxy labels one as a deviant who is a threat to the order, the society, and the ruling class. In Taiwan, the reified construction of "China" was a major impediment to political freedom, cultural creativity, and psychological independence. It is not widely appreciated in the United States how an American policy of "one China," an essentialist "China," limits the freedom of people in Taiwan (and elsewhere, for that matter) to envision their future.

For diplomacy and diplomats, the idea of "China" as an unbroken entity with claims on territory in East Asia and its littoral islands is in essence anti-democratic. If it is indeed U.S. government policy to promote democracy in China, abetting the rather recently created myth of "one China" constrains freedom of thought and discourse. It conspires with Chinese nationalism against dissent or creativity in political debate. China's von Rankeism is not all that dissimilar to great totalitarian myths of the 20th century: Apartheid's white supremacy, Germany's Aryanism, Japan's "Greater East Asia Co-prosperity Sphere," and the pan-Arabist Baathism that calls for a united Islamic Caliphate. As long as the Western democracies acquiesce in this Chinese essentialist myth, they impede an open, democratic, historically based society from developing either in Taiwan or, truth be told, in China. The anti-Apartheid movement in South Africa was a counter ideology to racism. In the same way, Western democracies should reject the nationalist ideology of "China" in favor of an environment of free thought, expression, assembly, and tolerance.

This ahistorical myth, which demands an orthodoxy of national unification, not only infects China, but is also an obstacle to intercommunal conciliation in Indonesia, Vietnam, Cambodia, the two Koreas, Burma, and other political agglomerations that have risen in Asia over the past half-century. On October 24, 2003, President Hu Jintao addressed the Australian Parliament. Hu began his speech with an historical record that connected China with Australia:

> Though located in different hemispheres and separated by high seas, the people of China and Australia enjoy a friendly exchange that dates back centuries. The Chinese people have all along cherished amicable feelings about the Australian people. Back in the 1420s, the expeditionary

> fleets of China's Ming dynasty reached Australian shores. For centuries, the Chinese sailed across vast seas and settled down in what was called "the southern land," or today's Australia. They brought Chinese culture here and lived harmoniously with the local people, contributing their proud share to Australia's economy, society and thriving pluralistic culture.[8]

The problem with this historical record is that it is based on the faulty and fictional writings of Mr. Gavin Menzies' account of the voyages of a Ming dynasty eunuch in the early 15th century.[9] There is no evidence for this extravagant view of so-called China's outreach into the South Pacific.

The egregiousness of official China's misrepresentation of historical cartography has managed to sour even its relations with South Korea, one of China's few neighbors that had not previously been suspicious of Chinese territorial claims on its territory. *The Korea Herald* for November 15, 2005, describes Seoul's attempts to correct China's views of Korean history: "China laid claim to Goguryeo [Koguryo], an ancient kingdom of Korea (37 bce–668 ce), whose territory partly lied around the border area between itself and North Korea."[10] The Korean government has campaigned to correct China's claims to Korean territory by, among other things, producing unofficial stamps featuring Koguryo and encouraging on-line protests.

China's claims to Tibet and other minorities' territories have resulted in further distortions of history and the repression of advocates for self-determination and independence. Without firm pushback from the world's democracies, China's rhetoric about the inviolability of its ancient territorial integrity becomes more histrionic and no doubt, without some furrowed brows and raised hands urging "steady on, old chap," will become even more heated. For example, in his October 2003 speech to the assembled worthies of Australia's Federal Parliament, President Hu warned:

---

[8] See Hu Jintao, "Building a Better Future Together for the China–Australia Relationship of All-round Cooperation," Address to the Federal Parliament of the Commonwealth of Australia, October 24, 2003, at *www.smh.com.au/cgi-bin/common/popupPrintArticle.pl?path=/articles/2003/10/24/1066631618612.html*.

[9] Gavin Menzies, *1421: The Year China Discovered America* (New York: HarperCollins, 2002). The book so offended eminent scholars of Asian history that a group set up an entire Web site devoted to debunking its contents. See *www.1421exposed.com/html/about.html*.

[10] See *www.koreaherald.co.kr/SITE/data/html_dir/2005/11/16/200511160019.asp*.

> Taiwan is an inalienable part of Chinese territory. The complete reunification of China at an early date is the common aspiration and firm resolve of the entire Chinese people.... The greatest threat to peace in the Taiwan Straits is the splittist activities by Taiwan independence forces. We are firmly opposed to Taiwan independence.[11]

The "one" in "one China" is even more susceptible to being exposed as an act of political power-grabbing. It is not unlike Kim Il-sung's *juche*. The identity of the country is to be preserved despite any sacrifice. The sense of "oneness" is a sign of trying to subordinate all citizens to the sacrificial will of the ruler and the ruler's fortress ideology.

Why is the above analysis important? It is important primarily because it defies the mistaken belief that if we just manipulate the notion of "one China," we can move away from the current hostile relationships. It is of little use to declare, no matter how correctly, that China's idea of a "One China Principle" is different from the American idea of "our 'one China' policy."[12] These words, "one China," are a magnification of an invocation of a sacred will to preserve a mythical past and impose it on the future.

We must think in short-term and long-term strategies about how totally to neutralize this assumption. It is part of an historical movement that will not be nullified in one or two diplomatic moves, but it must begin to dawn on the Chinese leadership in Beijing that the United States has not accepted and will not accept the etiology of this policy. In other words, America sees "one China" as a myth that incorporates an irredentist fantasy that aims at the destruction of democracy on Taiwan through the advocacy of war. This propaganda thread is readily discernible, for example, in Chinese films by directors sympathetic to China's mythical creations. Movies like *The Emperor and the Assassin* promote the idea of a single, naturally ordained "China under Heaven" (*Tian xia*) and a sense that China's unification is the will of destiny.[13]

Saying that America is committed to the "*status quo*" of the 1972 Shanghai Communiqué is to retreat to the defensive. The *status quo* reflects a mindset that derives from an essentialist, non-changing perspective. It is itself part of the problem. We are placed in the position of waiting for someone else to

---

[11]Hu Jintao, "Building a Better Future Together."

[12]See Chapter 2.

[13]Sony Pictures Classics, Shin Corporation, Le Studio Canal, New Wave Co., and Beijing Film Studio, directed by Chen Kaige, 1999. For a description of the film, see *www.sonypictures.com/homevideo/catalog/catalogDetail_DVD043396050457.html.*

take some step that alters the *status quo* and then remonstrating without thought as to what the *status quo* really encompasses. To some, this undefined policy provides us with the great flexibility of ambiguity: We can choose when and where to complain. For me, however, the policy undercuts our ability to develop and create new policies to accommodate the ever-evolving *status quo*, which might make clear to both sides that what we are actively protecting and supporting is not the *status quo*, but democracy in East Asia. We need to be proactive and not just reactive.

The additional problem of a "one China" policy is that we have tied our hands about "interfering" in Taiwan–China relations. In fact, we are an integral third part of the relationship. We "interfere" when we try to act as an umpire by criticizing equally China for developing missiles and Taiwan for initiating a referendum to protest those missiles.[14] By focusing on preserving a long-gone *status quo*, we undermine the legitimacy of our national security goal of promoting freedom, democracy, and, in the end, peace.

Operationalizing Ronald Reagan's "Free Choice"

The United States supports the Taiwanese people's right to determine their own future. At least that was the stated policy of Presidents Ronald Reagan and Bill Clinton. President Reagan's statement accompanying the announcement of the August 17, 1982, Communiqué was explicit. Although Reagan, somewhat hamstrung by a policy he did not want, grudgingly repeated that "the Taiwan question is a matter for the Chinese people, on both sides of the Taiwan Strait, to resolve," he was emphatic that "we will not interfere in this matter or prejudice the free choice of, or put pressure on, the people of Taiwan in this matter."[15] In February 2000, when China threatened Taiwan with armed invasion if it were to elect a pro-independence president, President Clinton averred that the United States "will also continue to make absolutely clear that the issues between Beijing and Taiwan must be resolved peacefully *and with the assent of the people of Taiwan*."[16]

---

[14]Taiwan announced the referendum text on January 16, 2004. The relevant portion read: "1. The People of Taiwan demand that the Taiwan Strait issue be resolved through peaceful means. Should Mainland China refuse to withdraw the missiles it has targeted at Taiwan and to openly renounce the use of force against us, would you agree that the Government should acquire more advanced anti-missile weapons to strengthen Taiwan's self-defense capabilities?"

[15]See Presidential Statement on Issuance of Communiqué, August 17, 1982, in hearing, *China–Taiwan: United States Policy*, Committee on Foreign Affairs, U.S. House of Representatives, 97th Cong., 2nd Sess., August 18, 1982, p. 33.

But what are we doing to assure that their "free choice" is truly free? When the KMT ruled Taiwan, it actively indoctrinated Taiwanese in the dogma that they are "Chinese" and that their island is a part of "one China." Many, though by no means most, Taiwanese have internalized this notion, and it persists in them even today, in part because they are swayed by the economic profits to be made in China, are afraid of war, are fatigued by the political debates over the issue, or—most of all—feel isolated internationally because of "one China" policies adhered to by the United States and much of the rest of the world's democracies. Would their "free choice" be to be rid of the China threat? Do they want a nation juridically separate from China? It would seem so.

My point here is not to divine the "free choice of the people of Taiwan," but rather to stress that as long as the United States reinforces Beijing's notion of "one China," it perpetuates a psychological repression among Taiwanese regarding their island's identity. Is that a good thing? Perhaps, one might answer, doing so helps in the short term to avoid a war; but American policymakers have to imagine what the Asia–Pacific region would look like with a Taiwan that, contrary to its "free choice," was so baldly pressured by the United States and its regional allies into accepting Beijing's sovereignty solely because Beijing threatens war and not because a Platonic ideal of "one China" is a good thing for mankind. As pointed out in an earlier chapter, a senior State Department official, frustrated with the Taiwan government's resistance to a dialog with China predicated on Taiwan's submission to "one China," warned that "we expect Taiwan will not interpret our support as a blank check to resist such dialogue."[17] It is not a pretty image. It reminds one of Henry Kissinger's warning to the Thieu government in Saigon not to resist the U.S.-negotiated cease-fire with North Vietnam in 1972.

What Should Be Done

Recommendation #1: Return to the Reagan ideal. There is compelling reason for the United States to resist the temptation to give into China's insistent demands that America belittle its Taiwanese partners. It is discouraged by U.S. law, and as Beijing sees that it is able to browbeat

---

[16]William J. Clinton, "Remarks by the President to the Business Council," Washington, D.C., February 24, 2000. Emphasis added.

[17]See "House International Relations Committee Hearing on Taiwan: Statement of Assistant Secretary of State James Kelly," April 21, 2004, at *http://wwwa.house.gov/international_relations/108/Kel042104.htm.*

Washington into ignoring parts of the Taiwan Relations Act, it looks for additional ways to whittle away at the TRA's policy authority. President Ronald Reagan clearly understood this imperative. Prior to his first visit to Beijing in April 1984, he authorized his emissary in Taipei, James R. Lilley, to tell Taiwan's foreign minister that "President Reagan is going to Beijing…but, by God, he will protect your interests."[18] Reagan did protect Taiwan's interests, and Taiwan's leaders were comfortable with the progress of U.S. relations during the Reagan Administration.

Recommendation #2: Make a deal with Taiwan's leaders. One clear reason that Taiwan's leaders have insisted so vehemently that their country exists is because the United States keeps undermining the legitimacy of their existence. If the United States would be a bit more supportive of Taiwan's "free choice," Taiwan's leaders would be a bit more self-assured and a bit less terrified that the *status quo*—as the Americans define it—is being methodically dismantled by the Chinese. An explicit understanding on this issue between Washington and Taiwan, accompanied by a much-enhanced but still confidential senior dialogue between the U.S. and Taiwanese Presidents, would certainly ease tensions across the Strait and enable Washington to maintain control of these tensions.

Of course, this would strain U.S. political relations with China; but the fact is that China itself has been straining relations with the U.S. on matters like North Korea, Iran, proliferation, military expansion, Japan, piracy of intellectual property rights, and exchange rate manipulation, not to mention its own human rights behavior and concomitant support for dictatorships around the world. In this environment, the time is past due for Washington to demonstrate that China's bad behavior has consequences. Indeed, Taiwan could be an effective diplomatic lever with China so long as Washington understood that backtracking on Taiwan was not an option. Put another way, China's failure to comply on critical strategic issues could lead the U.S. to improve relations with Taiwan; but even Chinese compliance on critical strategic issues would not result in our downgrading relations with Taiwan. Rather, it would result only in a slower rate of improvement.

Recommendation #3: Support Taiwan's international identity. This tactic seemed to work well during the 1980s. The Reagan Administration was fairly faithful to its obligations under the Taiwan Relations Act. And one

---

[18]James R. Lilley and Jeff Lilley, *China Hands: Nine Decades of Adventure, Espionage, and Diplomacy in Asia* (New York: PublicAffairs Books, 2004), p. 253.

clear intent of the U.S. Congress in 1979 when it passed the TRA was to enhance Taiwan's international footprint. The text of Section 3301(b) of the TRA is explicit:

> It is the policy of the United States to preserve and promote *extensive, close, and friendly commercial, cultural, and other relations between* the people of the United States and the people on Taiwan, as well as the people on the China mainland and *all other peoples of the Western Pacific area.*[19]

The way the Reagan State Department approached this responsibility was to play a leadership role in getting international organizations to open their doors to Taiwan's participation. Unfortunately, the Reagan enthusiasm for Taiwan was undercut by later policy gaffes.

The Asian Development Bank (ADB). One example was Taiwan's membership in the Asian Development Bank. In the mid-1980s, the United States wanted to get China into the ADB, where it would qualify for massive, concessionary development financing. China stubbornly insisted that it could not live with ADB money so long as Taiwan was a member. After long wrangling over nomenclature, the State Department persuaded Beijing in 1986 that Taiwan's continued ADB membership under the designation "Taipei, China" was consonant with Beijing's "One China Principle." After additional wrangling with Taiwan, the KMT accepted the name "Taipei,China"[20] (note the curious lack of a space after the comma, which no doubt holds some arcane diplomatic significance) to retain its membership in the Asian Development Bank.

The key to this "breakthrough" came with a bribe to Taiwan: The U.S. would approve technology transfers to enable Taiwan to manufacture an indigenously developed advanced fighter aircraft.[21] However, the designation, accepted against Taiwan's better judgment, falsely signaled that Taiwan indeed believed that "Taipei" was subordinate to "China," which had accepted membership under its own designation of "China." Moreover, Taiwan was a founding member of the ADB dating from 1966, with an overall contribution of over $500 million to the Bank, all of which would have to have been returned should Taipei have been obliged to leave. Thus, ADB membership was neither a hard call nor a striking

---

[19]Emphasis added. For the text of the Taiwan Relations Act, see Appendix B in this volume.

[20]See the "Taipei,China" ADB page at *www.adb.org/TaipeiChina/default.asp.*

[21]Lilley and Lilley, *China Hands*, p. 254.

instance of the U.S. "protecting" Taiwan's interests. Nonetheless, it showed that a "deal" could be made with Taiwan's leaders so long as the U.S. was willing to demonstrate a firm commitment to Taiwan's security.

The Asia–Pacific Economic Cooperation Forum (APEC). Another example of a well-intentioned but poorly executed American initiative to integrate Taiwan further into the international community was APEC. In 1991, not quite two years after the notorious Tiananmen Massacre, the George H. W. Bush Administration persuaded APEC to admit China, Taiwan, and Hong Kong as equal "member economies." But when it came time for the United States to host the first APEC "CEOs Summit" in Seattle in November 1993, the Clinton Administration pointedly refused to permit Taiwan's "CEO," President Lee Teng-hui, to attend. The Clinton Administration also persuaded Hong Kong Governor Chris Patton to avoid the Seattle Summit because of China's biting resentment of Patton's support for democratization of Hong Kong.

Taiwan and Hong Kong were the only APEC members so singled out for such scorn from the U.S. State Department—at China's insistence. It was a shameful act, and in *Beyond Tiananmen*, the otherwise encyclopedic history of Clinton's foreign policy by Robert L. Suettinger, Clinton's top China aide in the National Security Council, the incident is ignored.[22] It was purely within President Bill Clinton's power to invite Taiwan's leader; and if China's leader boycotted, it would have been his loss. Nor was there a need to be overly solicitous of China. They had violated for the umpteenth time their pledges not to transfer missile technology to Pakistan, their human rights behavior had been labeled abominable, and President Clinton had linked human rights improvements to China's continued most favored nation trade status. At bottom, snubbing Taiwan at the Seattle summit was rewarding China for very, very bad behavior.

I, for one, do not condone cynical foreign policies that subordinate human rights and political freedoms to some greater national interest, but I can understand them. What I cannot understand is diplomatic stupidity of the type that bends to China's demands for obeisance at the altar of "one China" as a reward for China's pernicious human rights abuses, not to mention its violation of its nonproliferation commitments.

Yet this is a posture that the State Department routinely takes on Taiwan. The statutory policy requiring that the United States "promote extensive, close…relations between…the people on Taiwan…and all other peoples of the Western Pacific area" obliges the State Department

---

[22]Robert L. Suettinger, *Beyond Tiananmen: The Politics of U.S.–China Relations 1989–2000* (Washington, D.C.: Brookings Institution, 2003), pp. 181–183.

to exert at least minimal efforts to ensure that Taiwan is able to participate in those international organizations to which it has contributed substantial sums of money. Taiwan's ADB membership was in service to a U.S. policy to strengthen China's economy as a bulwark against Soviet expansion. It was not a hard call.

The World Trade Organization (WTO). Nor was promoting Taiwan's membership in the World Trade Organization a hard call, considering that Taiwan is the world's 12th largest trading nation. The U.S. worked to get Taiwan accepted into the WTO under the formal title of Separate Customs Territory of Taipei, Penghu, Kinmen and Matsu (TPKM).[23] Then, without any particular U.S. pressure to the contrary, the WTO refrained from allowing Taiwan to join until such time as China could join, and Taiwan's membership application languished for 12 years while the WTO fretted about how China, a state-mercantilist economy if there ever was one, could possibly qualify.

Taiwan's Bilateral Ties with Third Countries. Other than these three rather half-hearted efforts to preserve Taiwan's international personality, the burden of this responsibility has been placed on the Taiwanese government. Taiwan's "unofficial" offices in Japan, South Korea, the Philippines, Vietnam, Australia, and other countries have not, to my knowledge, received mutual or commensurate support from their U.S. counterparts. Washington, in the broad scheme of things, should give at least *sub rosa* support to Taiwan's continued diplomatic ties with third countries. In 2001, Taiwan was prepared to extend several hundreds of millions of dollars in development assistance to the newly independent Balkan nation of Macedonia but was eventually forced to break its diplomatic ties with the country because of United Nations pressure—and without a finger in Washington being lifted to consider Macedonia's humanitarian needs.[24]

The United States, for whatever reason, went along with China's 2004 proposal to send "law enforcement" teams to Haiti as part of a United Nations peacekeeping force. There was considerable concern at the Pentagon about the contingent of 180 Chinese peacekeepers who arrived in Haiti in mid-September "to teach anti-riot techniques," on which they were no doubt experts, but it was soon apparent that the U.S. mission to the U.N. gave the U.N.'s acceptance of China's offer a free pass without consulting the Western Hemisphere Bureau at the State Department or

---

[23]See World Trade Organization Web site at *www.wto.org*.

[24]Monique Chu, "Taiwan Severs Ties with Skopje," *Taipei Times*, June 19, 2001, p. 1, at *www.taipeitimes.com/News/front/archives/2001/06/19/90603*.

letting anyone at the Defense Department know. The Pentagon was not concerned about Taiwan; it was alarmed that Chinese police had showed up in their backyard virtually unannounced.[25]

As pointed out in an earlier chapter, some American officials hint that the U.S. really has tried to sustain Taiwan's last diplomatic bridgeheads in Central America.[26] If so, they are to be applauded. I suspect there is less there than even the microscopic bit that meets the eye.

Recommendation #4: Address poor interagency communication on China–Taiwan policy. To remedy this situation, I recommend that the Administration recognize its TRA obligations to "preserve and promote" Taiwan's participation in the international community and articulate a policy to do so, in a classified manner, if need be. One way to do this would be for the White House to direct all executive branch agencies to designate an office that would keep track of China issues and report them rapidly to the Department of State.

Additionally, because the State Department itself seems to have trouble keeping track of China issues, I would also recommend that the State Department establish "focal point officers" in each bureau—functional and geographic, and especially at the U.S. missions in the various United Nations agencies as well as in New York—who would be responsible for keeping the Department's deputy assistant secretary for China and the China and Taiwan desks up-to-date on China-related developments in their area on a real-time basis.

It would also be a good idea to expand language training to include formal instruction in the Taiwanese-Minnan dialect for U.S. foreign service, intelligence, and military officers assigned to Taiwan. It is a truism that not knowing the everyday language of the majority of the people narrows our interpretation and understanding of the policies, expressions, and needs of the society. In Taiwan, our representatives end up speaking to Chinese who know English or who feel free to speak in Mandarin. This limits their understanding of the society as a whole. I

---

[25]See Reed Lindsay, "Chinese Presence on Island Viewed with Concern," *The Washington Times*, December 9, 2004, p. 15, at *www.washingtontimes.com/world/20041208-095901-3064r.htm*. See also Joseph Guyler Delva, "Chinese Arrive in Haiti to Help Restore Order," Reuters, October 17, 2004, and Bill Gertz, "China Will Send Troops to Haiti," *The Washington Times*, September 6, 2004, p. 13, at *www.washingtontimes.com/national/20040906-123723-3774r.htm*.

[26]See "Michael Green Interview—The Gambit Behind the NUC's Removal," *The Taipei Times*, February 24, 2006, p.4, at *www.taipeitimes.com/News/taiwan/archives/2006/02/24/2003294388*.

have sat through many, many conversations with Chen Shui-bian and Lee Teng-hui and others unable to understand their Taiwanese, yet realizing that the Chinese transcripts were not always accurate.

Facing Up to the Ever-Changing "*Status Quo*"

Rather than being reactive to changes in the *status quo*, America needs a proactive policy that preempts the changes or sanctions them when the changes become too extreme. This is most important in the case of Chinese attacks on the "*status quo*." It might be a useful exercise for the National Security Council to actually define "the *status quo* as we define it,"[27] again, in a classified document if that is really needed. What follows are some specific pre-emptive countermeasures that would signal our increasing pressure on China and Taiwan.

America should state clearly that the 700-plus missiles facing Taiwan are provocative. Imagine that these missiles were arrayed by Iraq against Kuwait or Israel. We must not allow ourselves to be hostages to these weapons. If Washington cannot convince China to dismantle these missiles, which have changed the *status quo* and are not of a defensive nature, then the Administration should consider adopting Ronald Reagan's "Zero Option" response to the Soviet "intermediate nuclear force" in Europe. Reagan and British Prime Minister Margaret Thatcher gained support for the deployment of Pershing II missiles in West Germany as a strategic response to Soviet deployments of SS-20 missiles in Eastern Europe.[28] This would mean supporting Taiwan's development of short-range ballistic missiles capable of hitting Chinese targets in an effort to augment the diminutive deterrent value of Taiwan's anti-ballistic missile defense systems.

Inasmuch as an American (or Australian, Japanese, or European) "one China policy" creates a teleological expectation in Taiwan and abroad that the ultimate solution to the Taiwan Strait friction is to reunite democratic Taiwan with Communist China despite the consequences, the Western democracies have to counteract that expectation. This need not be done by junking the "one China" policy immediately, but simply by including Reagan's reassurance that "we will not interfere...or prejudice the free choice of, or put pressure on, the people of Taiwan in this matter." (I will

---

[27]See Chapter 2 and "House International Relations Committee Hearing on Taiwan: Statement of Assistant Secretary of State James Kelly," April 21, 2004, at *wwwa.house.gov/international_relations/108/Kel042104.htm*.

[28]For further information, see "Intermediate-Range Nuclear Forces [INF] Chronology," Federation of American Scientists Web site, at *www.fas.org/nuke/control/inf/inf-chron.htm*.

admit, however, that the exigencies of diplomacy may require that China be eased into the realization that the West's "one China" does not necessarily mean that Taiwan is part of it.)

In sum, the "one China" policy is in itself an anti-democratic weapon. It limits the imagination; it places the U.S. in a defensive position; and it fails to give support to citizens in Taiwan—or China for that matter—whose free choice is prejudiced by a political process in Beijing that is predicated on evocations of a mythical past and threats of war to resurrect that past. China undermines the values of the world's democracies by enforcing its view of this policy.

By adopting Beijing's idiosyncratic view of "one China," we are in fact endorsing it. Understanding the etiology of "one China," however, makes the nature of the cure clear.

Appendix A

P 301130Z NOV 71 — 7 4 79 Q
FM AMEMBASSY TAIPEI
To SecState WashDC Priority 4272 — 30 NOVEMBER 8 28 AM
BT
S E C R E T Section 1 of 2 Taipei 5869 — - CORRECTED COPY

NODIS

EYES ONLY FOR THE SECRETARY
AND ASSISTANT SECRETARY GREEN

SUBJ: Conversation of Vice Foreign Minister Yang Hsi-kun with Ambassador

1. Following is an account of an important presentation which Foreign Vice Minister Yang Hsi-kun made to me end of last week at a tete-a-tete luncheon. Its extremely sensitive nature will be self-evident. I feel any additional distribution should be severely restricted but undoubtedly White House should be aware of it. I hope that Green will be in a position to discuss it with me preliminarily when I see him in Honolulu next week.

2. H. K. Yang launched almost immediately into discussion of critical situation facing GRC following October 25 expulsion from UN. He recalled he had told President Chiang last winter that withdrawal from UN would mean "eventual political suicide" for GRC. Expulsion amounted to about the same thing as withdrawal, and he feared that the increasing isolation that the Chinese Communists can force on the GRC from their improved position within the UN will mean the rapidly increasing besiegement and eventual strangulation of the GRC unless drastic change is undertaken immediately.

3. Yang continued that he has spoken very privately and frankly to President Chiang since his recent return after the UN debacle. Yang had found President Chiang impressively open-minded and willing to listen. Yang said he had spelled out the full depth of his misgivings and had indicated in a general way the sweeping nature of the changes which he felt

would be mandatory if not only the GRC but the future of the people on Taiwan is to be preserved. He characterized the President as not necessarily concurring in any proposed changes but as showing a profound awareness of the existing realities and dangers and a willingness to examine the case for far-reaching changes in the existing structure.

4. Yang said he had told the President that it is of paramount importance to issue in the near future a formal declaration to the world that the government on Taiwan is entirely separate and apart from the government on the mainland and that henceforth the government here "will have nothing to do with the mainland." The declaration should prescribe a new designation for the government here, namely "the Chinese Republic of Taiwan." It would be stipulated that the term Chinese did not have any political connotation but was used merely as a generic term stemming from the Chinese ethnic origin of the populace on Taiwan. It would be used in a away similar to the manner in which the various Arab countries use "Arab" in their official governmental titles.

5. Yang said that most of the President's top advisers around the President [*sic*] see the need for some sort of sweeping move to counter the ChiCom drive to isolate the GRC internationally and force general recognition of ChiCom right to take over Taiwan as an integral part of China. It does not mean they necessarily endorse his formula but they are showing some resilience in the face of the crisis and are open to persuasion.

6. He said that the principal negative, stand-pat influence was exerted by Mme. Chiang who seems determined not to budge an inch from the old claims, pretensions and "return to the mainland" slogans. He believes she still wields considerable influence on the President. He said she in turn is greatly influenced by her nephew, K. L. Kung, the son of Mme. Chiang's elder sister and her deceased husband H. H. Kung. He said K. L. Kung from the security of his New York residence is waging a reactionary campaign for the GRC to stand absolutely rigid. He termed K. L. Kung's influence extremely malign. He said that K. L. Kung is very vocal in various influential quarters. Yang said that he had refused to see K. L. Kung on his trips to New York in recent years despite various requests from Kung. Yang spoke contemptuously of the Soong-Kung family group as fanatically advocating a die-hard line, although he said most of them were among the first to retreat to safety when the Communists moved.

7. Yang said that when Chang Chun was in Japan last summer, he had a very significant talk with Prime Minister [Eisaku] Sato and ex-Prime

Minister [Nobusuke] Kishi. After that talk Sato and Kishi transmitted a closely-guarded message to President Chiang through Chang Shun to the effect that the only hope for the future of the Republic of China was to adopt a course of separation, giving up all mainland claims and pretensions. The message strongly urged President Chiang to adopt such a course. He felt sure that CCK knew of the message but he believed that neither Vice President C. K. Yen nor Foreign Minister S. K. Chow knew about it.

P 301130Z NOV 71 7496 Q
FM AMEMBASSY Taipei
To SecState WashDC Priority 4273 30 NOVEMBER 9 11 AM
BT
S E C R E T Section 2 of 2 Taipei 5869

NODIS

8. Yang said that in his view the President in making the sort of declaration described should concurrently, or very soon thereafter, use his emergency powers to set aside the constitution and dissolve all of the parliamentary type bodies. He should then set up a new unicameral provisional representative body to be composed of two-thirds Taiwanese and one-third mainlanders. A new Cabinet should be formed with some Taiwanese and some younger men included. He said a new image needed to be created with the government freed of the outworn trappings, encumbrances and shibboleths of the party and the establishment. He said the emergency decree of the President should provide for an island-wide referendum with universal suffrage to determine the future status of Taiwan and provide for a constituent body. Yang indicated further that he felt that the President might do well to make these fundamental moves next spring just before the end of his current term, and then move up to an emeritus position as head of the reformed party and revered elder statesman (somewhat parallel to Mao's position), with C. K. Yen taking over as Chief of State and Chiang Ching-kuo as Premier.

9. Yang identified George Yeh and Y. S. Tsiang as associated with his thinking. He identified as top officials who are concerned, realistic and open-minded, but not yet committed: Vice President C. K. Yen, Presidential Secretary General Chang Chun, Director of the National Security Council Huang Shao-ku, and secretary of the KMT Chang Pao-shu.

10. Yang said no member of the current Cabinet is informed of his thinking and none of them are involved or likely to take a position. He spoke rather deprecatingly of Foreign Minister S. K. Chow as not inclined to become exposed and he said K. T. Li and Y. S. Sun were nonpolitical in the sense he was talking about. He added that former Foreign Minister Wei Tao-ming was entirely out of the picture, also.

11. Yang said that although President Chiang is incresingly [*sic*] convinced of the imperative requirement for some early and radical action, he is not likely to move without the application of a powerful persuasive effort by the

US government. He felt that Vice President [Spiro T.] Agnew would be the right man to present the US position and make the major effort, supported of course by myself. He felt that Agnew even with direct message and mandate from President [Richard M.] Nixon would need the help of an advance group of private American citizens who are old and close friends of President Chiang and completely trusted by him. (Presumably he has in mind such personages as Dr. [Walter H.] Judd, Admiral [Arthur W.] Radford, ex-Senator [William F.] Knowland and General [Albert C.] Wedemeyer.) He said even Americans who know China can hardly visualize how difficult it will be for the President to fly in the face of all the deepest traditions and articles of faith by which he, his government and his people have lived since departure from the mainland. Such a reversal of the course would be traumatic in the extreme, but he felt that the President is showing incredible adaptability and flexibility for a man of such advanced age. He had not yet given in to the urgings of his wife and he is keeping his options open.

12. Yang indicated that he had shared some but not all of what he had just said with Ambassador Christopher Phillips at USUN Headquarters. I gather that Phillips is the only other American representative who has been even partially clued in. Yang said he knew he did not need to urge on me the extreme sensitivity of the subject and the absolutely overriding need of total security. Any leak should be disastrous and he hoped the number of persons informed could be kept to the absolute minimum of those who had to know in order to support the handful of senior officials who should be involved on the US side.

13. Comment: I have reported this conversation at length because it seems so pertinent to the kind of study you have requested regarding the prospect if US-Taiwan relations. I should emphasize, however, that although H. K. Yang is an important and highly responsible official, his views reflect the outer dimension of tolerable concepts and undoubtedly go beyond the point where practical considerations are likely to lead the government in the near future. Yang himself is imaginative and broad-gauged. He is also bold and seems to feel adequately protected to pursue his proposals. However, he tends to underrate the practical complications that inescapably concern the principal ROC leaders, or he rather casually seeks to enlist external intervention to help overcome resistance from his fellow countrymen. For example, there is not much real prospect that President Chiang would sweep away institutions and commitments of the past and establish a legislature composed of two-thirds Taiwanese and one third mainlanders.

Similarly Yang probably underestimates the domestic and foreign consequences of chaining the ROC's international identity.

14. Nevertheless, Yang's views strike me as highly important, both as indications of the direction in which some responsible officials are thinking and as a symbol of the considerable ferment developing on Taiwan concerning the future. In brief, the evolution of US China policy and the UN defeat have precipitated some of the thinking that many would not have expected at least until President Chiang departed the scene.

GP-1

MCCONAUGHY

Appendix B

Taiwan Relations Act

United States Code, Title 22, Chapter 48, Sections 3301–3316
Enacted April 10, 1979

[*Editor's Note: Several revisions were made in Public Law 96–8 when it was codified. Sections 1, 12(d), and 18 were omitted. In addition, the United States Code contains a section not included in the original Act: Section 3310a. The United States Code version is the authoritative version.*]

§ 3301. Congressional findings and declaration of policy.
- (a) Findings.
- (b) Policy.
- (c) Human rights.

§ 3302. Implementation of United States policy with regard to Taiwan.
- (a) Defense articles and services.
- (b) Determination of Taiwan's defense needs.
- (c) United States response to threats to Taiwan or dangers to United States interests.

§ 3303. Application to Taiwan of laws and international agreements.
- (a) Application of United States laws generally.
- (b) Application of United States laws in specific and enumerated areas.
- (c) Treaties and other international agreements.
- (d) Membership in international financial institutions and other international organizations.

§ 3304. Overseas Private Investment Corporation.
- (a) Removal of per capita income restriction on Corporation activities with respect to investment projects on Taiwan.
- (b) Application by Corporation of other criteria.

§ 3305. The American Institute in Taiwan.
(a) Conduct of programs, transactions, or other relations with respect to Taiwan.
(b) Agreements or transactions relative to Taiwan entered into, performed, and enforced.
(c) Preemption of laws, rules, regulations, or ordinances of District of Columbia, States, or political subdivisions of States.

§ 3306. Services to United States citizens on Taiwan.
(a) Authorized services.
(b) Acts by authorized employees.

§ 3307. Exemption from taxation.
(a) United States, State, or local taxes.
(b) Charitable contributions; transfers for public, charitable, and religious uses; charitable and similar gifts.

§ 3308. Activities of United States Government agencies.
(a) Sale, loans, or lease of property; administrative and technical support functions and services.
(b) Acquisition and acceptance of services.
(c) Institute books and records; access; audit.

§ 3309. Taiwan instrumentality.
(a) Establishment of instrumentality; Presidential determination of necessary authority.
(b) Offices and personnel.
(c) Privileges and immunities.

§ 3310. Employment of United States Government agency personnel.
(a) Separation from Government service; reemployment or reinstatement upon termination of Institute employment; benefits.
(b) Employment of aliens on Taiwan.
(c) Institute employees not deemed United States employees.
(d) Tax treatment of amounts paid Institute employees.

§ 3310a. Commercial personnel at American Institute of Taiwan.

§ 3311. Reporting requirements.
(a) Texts of agreements to be transmitted to Congress; secret agreements to be transmitted to Senate Foreign Relations Committee and House Foreign Affairs Committee.
(b) Agreements.
(c) Congressional notification, review, and approval requirements and procedures.

§ 3312. Rules and regulations.

United States Code

Title 22—Foreign Relations and Intercourse
Chapter 48—Taiwan Relations

Sec. 3301. Congressional findings and declaration of policy

(a) Findings

The President having terminated governmental relations between the United States and the governing authorities on Taiwan recognized by the United States as the Republic of China prior to January 1, 1979, the Congress finds that the enactment of this chapter is necessary—

(1) to help maintain peace, security, and stability in the Western Pacific; and

(2) to promote the foreign policy of the United States by authorizing the continuation of commercial, cultural, and other relations between the people of the United States and the people on Taiwan.

(b) Policy

It is the policy of the United States—

(1) to preserve and promote extensive, close, and friendly commercial, cultural, and other relations between the people of the United States and the people on Taiwan, as well as the people on the China mainland and all other peoples of the Western Pacific area;

(2) to declare that peace and stability in the area are in the political, security, and economic interests of the United States, and are matters of international concern;

(3) to make clear that the United States decision to establish diplomatic relations with the People's Republic of China rests upon the expectation that the future of Taiwan will be determined by peaceful means;

(4) to consider any effort to determine the future of Taiwan by other than peaceful means, including by boycotts or embargoes, a threat to the peace and security of the Western Pacific area and of grave concern to the United States;

(5) to provide Taiwan with arms of a defensive character; and

(6) to maintain the capacity of the United States to resist any resort to force or other forms of coercion that would jeopardize the security, or the social or economic system, of the people on Taiwan.

(c) Human rights

Nothing contained in this chapter shall contravene the interest of the United States in human rights, especially with respect to the human rights of all the approximately eighteen million inhabitants of Taiwan. The preservation and enhancement of the human rights of all the people on Taiwan are hereby reaffirmed as objectives of the United States.

Sec. 3302. Implementation of United States policy with regard to Taiwan

(a) Defense articles and services

In furtherance of the policy set forth in section 3301 of this title, the United States will make available to Taiwan such defense articles and defense services in such quantity as may be necessary to enable Taiwan to maintain a sufficient self-defense capability.

(b) Determination of Taiwan's defense needs

The President and the Congress shall determine the nature and quantity of such defense articles and services based solely upon their judgment of the needs of Taiwan, in accordance with procedures established by law. Such determination of Taiwan's defense needs shall include review by United States military authorities in connection with recommendations to the President and the Congress.

(c) United States response to threats to Taiwan or dangers to United States interests

The President is directed to inform the Congress promptly of any threat to the security or the social or economic system of the people on Taiwan and any danger to the interests of the United States arising therefrom. The President and the Congress shall determine, in accordance with constitutional processes, appropriate action by the United States in response to any such danger.

Sec. 3303. Application to Taiwan of laws and international agreements

(a) Application of United States laws generally

The absence of diplomatic relations or recognition shall not affect the application of the laws of the United States with respect to Taiwan, and the laws of the United States shall apply with respect to Taiwan in the manner that the laws of the United States applied with respect to Taiwan prior to January 1, 1979.

(b) Application of United States laws in specific and enumerated areas

The application of subsection (a) of this section shall include, but shall not be limited to, the following:

> (1) Whenever the laws of the United States refer or relate to foreign countries, nations, states, governments, or similar entities, such terms shall include and such laws shall apply with respect to Taiwan.
>
> (2) Whenever authorized by or pursuant to the laws of the United States to conduct or carry out programs, transactions, or other relations with respect to foreign countries, nations, states, governments, or similar entities, the President or any agency of the United States Government is authorized to conduct and carry out, in accordance with section 3305 of this title, such programs, transactions, and other relations with respect to Taiwan (including, but not limited to, the performance of services for the United States through contracts with commercial entities on Taiwan), in accordance with the applicable laws of the United States.
>
> (3A) The absence of diplomatic relations and recognition with respect to Taiwan shall not abrogate, infringe, modify, deny, or otherwise affect in any way any rights or obligations (including but not limited to those involving contracts, debts, or property interests of any kind) under the laws of the United States heretofore or hereafter acquired by or with respect to Taiwan.
>
> (3B) For all purposes under the laws of the United States, including actions in any court in the United States, recognition of the People's Republic of China shall not affect in any way the ownership of or other rights or interests in properties, tangible and intangible, and other things of value, owned or held on or prior to December 31, 1978, or thereafter acquired or earned by the governing authorities on Taiwan.
>
> (4) Whenever the application of the laws of the United States depends upon the law that is or was applicable on Taiwan or compliance therewith, the law applied by the people on Taiwan shall be considered the applicable law for that purpose.
>
> (5) Nothing in this chapter, nor the facts of the President's action in extending diplomatic recognition to the People's Republic of China, the absence of diplomatic relations between the people on Taiwan and the United States, or the lack of recognition by the United States, and attendant circumstances thereto, shall be construed in any administrative or judicial proceeding as a basis for any United

States Government agency, commission, or department to make a finding of fact or determination of law, under the Atomic Energy Act of 1954 (42 U.S.C. 2011 et seq.) and the Nuclear Non-Proliferation Act of 1978 (22 U.S.C. 3201 et seq.), to deny an export license application or to revoke an existing export license for nuclear exports to Taiwan.

(6) For purposes of the Immigration and Nationality Act (8 U.S.C. 1101 et seq.), Taiwan may be treated in the manner specified in the first sentence of section 202(b) of that Act (8 U.S.C. 1152(b)).

(7) The capacity of Taiwan to sue and be sued in courts in the United States, in accordance with the laws of the United States, shall not be abrogated, infringed, modified, denied, or otherwise affected in any way by the absence of diplomatic relations or recognition.

(8) No requirement, whether expressed or implied, under the laws of the United States with respect to maintenance of diplomatic relations or recognition shall be applicable with respect to Taiwan.

(c) Treaties and other international agreements

For all purposes, including actions in any court in the United States, the Congress approves the continuation in force of all treaties and other international agreements, including multilateral conventions, entered into by the United States and the governing authorities on Taiwan recognized by the United States as the Republic of China prior to January 1, 1979, and in force between them on December 31, 1978, unless and until terminated in accordance with law.

(d) Membership in international financial institutions and other international organizations

Nothing in this chapter may be construed as a basis for supporting the exclusion or expulsion of Taiwan from continued membership in any international financial institution or any other international organization.

Sec. 3304. Overseas Private Investment Corporation

(a) Removal of per capita income restriction on Corporation activities with respect to investment projects on Taiwan

During the three-year period beginning on April 10, 1979, the $1,000 per capita income restriction in clause (2) of the second undesignated paragraph of section 2191 of this title shall not restrict the activities of the Overseas Private Investment Corporation in determining whether to provide any insurance, reinsurance, loans, or guaranties with respect to investment projects on Taiwan.

(b) Application by Corporation of other criteria

Except as provided in subsection (a) of this section, in issuing insurance, reinsurance, loans, or guaranties with respect to investment projects on Taiwan, the Overseas Private [Investment] Corporation shall apply the same criteria as those applicable in other parts of the world.

Sec. 3305. The American Institute in Taiwan

(a) Conduct of programs, transactions, or other relations with respect to Taiwan

Programs, transactions, and other relations conducted or carried out by the President or any agency of the United States Government with respect to Taiwan shall, in the manner and to the extent directed by the President, be conducted and carried out by or through–

(1) The American Institute in Taiwan, a nonprofit corporation incorporated under the laws of the District of Columbia, or

(2) such comparable successor nongovernmental entity as the President may designate, (hereafter in this chapter referred to as the "Institute").

(b) Agreements or transactions relative to Taiwan entered into, performed, and enforced

Whenever the President or any agency of the United States Government is authorized or required by or pursuant to the laws of the United States to enter into, perform, enforce, or have in force an agreement or transaction relative to Taiwan, such agreement or transaction shall be entered into, performed, and enforced, in the manner and to the extent directed by the President, by or through the Institute.

(c) Preemption of laws, rules, regulations, or ordinances of District of Columbia, States, or political subdivisions of States

To the extent that any law, rule, regulation, or ordinance of the District of Columbia, or of any State or political subdivision thereof in which the Institute is incorporated or doing business, impedes or otherwise interferes with the performance of the functions of the Institute pursuant to this chapter, such law, rule, regulation, or ordinance shall be deemed to be preempted by this chapter.

Sec. 3306. Services to United States citizens on Taiwan

(a) Authorized services

The Institute may authorize any of its employees on Taiwan—

(1) to administer to or take from any person an oath, affirmation, affidavit, or deposition, and to perform any notarial act which any notary public is required or authorized by law to perform within the United States;

(2) [t]o act as provisional conservator of the personal estates of deceased United States citizens; and

(3) to assist and protect the interests of United States persons by performing other acts such as are authorized to be performed outside the United States for consular purposes by such laws of the United States as the President may specify.

(b) Acts by authorized employees

Acts performed by authorized employees of the Institute under this section shall be valid, and of like force and effect within the United States, as if performed by any other person authorized under the laws of the United States to perform such acts.

Sec. 3307. Exemption from taxation

(a) United States, State, or local taxes

The Institute, its property, and its income are exempt from all taxation now or hereafter imposed by the United States (except to the extent that section 3310(a)(3) of this title requires the imposition of taxes imposed under chapter 21of title 26, relating to the Federal Insurance Contributions Act) or by any State or local taxing authority of the United States.

(b) Charitable contributions; transfers for public, charitable, and religious uses; charitable and similar gifts

For purposes of title 26, the Institute shall be treated as an organization described in sections 170(b)(1)(A), 170(c),2055 (a), 2106(a)(2)(A), 2522(a), and 2522(b) of title 26.

Sec. 3308. Activities of United States Government agencies

(a) Sale, loans, or lease of property; administrative and technical support functions and services

Any agency of the United States Government is authorized to sell, loan, or lease property (including interests therein) to, and to perform administrative and technical support functions and services for the operations of, the Institute upon such terms and conditions as the President may direct. Reimbursements to agencies under this subsection shall be credited to the current applicable appropriation of the agency concerned.

(b) Acquisition and acceptance of services

Any agency of the United States Government is authorized to acquire and accept services from the Institute upon such terms and conditions as the President may direct. Whenever the President determines it to be in furtherance of the purposes of this chapter, the procurement of services by such agencies from the Institute may be effected without regard to such laws of the United States normally applicable to the acquisition of services by such agencies as the President may specify by Executive order.

(c) Institute books and records; access; audit

Any agency of the United States Government making funds available to the Institute in accordance with this chapter shall make arrangements with the Institute for the Comptroller General of the United States to have access to the books and records of the Institute and the opportunity to audit the operations of the Institute.

Sec. 3309. Taiwan instrumentality

(a) Establishment of instrumentality; Presidential determination of necessary authority

Whenever the President or any agency of the United States Government is authorized or required by or pursuant to the laws of the United States to render or provide to or to receive or accept from Taiwan, any performance, communication, assurance, undertaking, or other action, such action shall, in the manner and to the extent directed by the President, be rendered or provided to, or received or accepted from, an instrumentality established by Taiwan which the President determines has the necessary authority under the laws applied by the people on Taiwan to provide assurances and take other actions on behalf of Taiwan in accordance with this chapter.

(b) Offices and personnel

The President is requested to extend to the instrumentality established by Taiwan the same number of offices and complement of personnel as were previously operated in the United States by the governing authorities on Taiwan recognized as the Republic of China prior to January 1, 1979.

(c) Privileges and immunities

Upon the granting by Taiwan of comparable privileges and immunities with respect to the Institute and its appropriate personnel, the President is authorized to extend with respect to the Taiwan instrumentality and its appropriate personnel, such privileges and immunities (subject to appropriate conditions and obligations) as may be necessary for the effective performance of their functions.

Sec. 3310. Employment of United States Government agency personnel

(a) Separation from Government service; reemployment or reinstatement upon termination of Institute employment; benefits

(1) Under such terms and conditions as the President may direct, any agency of the United States Government may separate from Government service for a specified period any officer or employee of that agency who accepts employment with the Institute.

(2) An officer or employee separated by an agency under paragraph (1) of this subsection for employment with the Institute shall be entitled upon termination of such employment to reemployment or reinstatement with such agency (or a successor agency) in an appropriate position with the attendant rights, privileges, and benefits [which] the officer or employee would have had or acquired had he or she not been so separated, subject to such time period and other conditions as the President may prescribe.

(3) An officer or employee entitled to reemployment or reinstatement rights under paragraph (2) of this subsection shall, while continuously employed by the Institute with no break in continuity of service, continue to participate in any benefit program in which such officer or employee was participating prior to employment by the Institute, including programs for compensation for job-related death, injury, or illness; programs for health and life insurance; programs for annual, sick, and other statutory leave; and programs for retirement under any system established by the laws of the United States; except that employment with the Institute shall be the basis for participation in such programs only to the extent that employee deductions and employer contributions, as required, in payment for such participation for the period of employment with the Institute, are currently deposited in the program's or system's fund or depository. Death or retirement of any such officer or employee during approved service with the Institute and prior to reemployment or reinstatement shall be considered a death in or retirement from Government service for purposes of any employee or survivor benefits acquired by reason of service with an agency of the United States Government.

(4) Any officer or employee of an agency of the United States Government who entered into service with the Institute on approved leave of absence without pay prior to April 10, 1979, shall receive the benefits of this section for the period of such service.

(b) Employment of aliens on Taiwan

Any agency of the United States Government employing alien personnel on Taiwan may transfer such personnel, with accrued allowances, benefits, and rights, to the Institute without a break in service for purposes of retirement and other benefits, including continued participation in any system established by the laws of the United States for the retirement of employees in which the alien was participating prior to the transfer to the Institute, except that employment with the Institute shall be creditable for retirement purposes only to the extent that employee deductions and employer contributions, as required, in payment for such participation for the period of employment with the Institute, are currently deposited in the system's fund or depository.

(c) Institute employees not deemed United States employees

Employees of the Institute shall not be employees of the United States and, in representing the Institute, shall be exempt from section of title 18.

(d) Tax treatment of amounts paid Institute employees

(1) For purposes of sections and 913 of title 26, amounts paid by the Institute to its employees shall not be treated as earned income. Amounts received by employees of the Institute shall not be included in gross income, and shall be exempt from taxation, to the extent that they are equivalent to amounts received by civilian officers and employees of the Government of the United States as allowances and benefits which are exempt from taxation under section 912 of title 26.

(2) Except to the extent required by subsection (a)(3) of this section, service performed in the employ of the Institute shall not constitute employment for purposes of chapter 21 of title 26 and title II of the Social Security Act (42 U.S.C. 401 et seq.).

Sec. 3310a. Commercial personnel at American Institute of Taiwan

The American Institute of Taiwan shall employ personnel to perform duties similar to those performed by personnel of the United States and Foreign Commercial Service. The number of individuals employed shall be commensurate with the number of United States personnel of the Commercial Service who are permanently assigned to the United States diplomatic mission to South Korea.

Sec. 3311. Reporting requirements

(a) Texts of agreements to be transmitted to Congress; secret agreements to be transmitted to Senate Foreign Relations Committee and House Foreign Affairs Committee

The Secretary of State shall transmit to the Congress the text of any agreement to which the Institute is a party. However, any such agreement the immediate public disclosure of which would, in the opinion of the President, be prejudicial to the national security of the United States shall not be so transmitted to the Congress but shall be transmitted to the Committee on Foreign Relations of the Senate and the Committee on Foreign Affairs of the House of Representatives under an appropriate injunction of secrecy to be removed only upon due notice from the President.

(b) Agreements

For purposes of subsection (a) of this section, the term "agreement" includes–

> (1) any agreement entered into between the Institute and the governing authorities on Taiwan or the instrumentality established by Taiwan; and
>
> (2) any agreement entered into between the Institute and an agency of the United States Government.

(c) Congressional notification, review, and approval requirements and procedures

Agreements and transactions made or to be made by or through the Institute shall be subject to the same congressional notification, review, and approval requirements and procedures as if such agreements and transactions were made by or through the agency of the United States Government on behalf of which the Institute is acting.

Sec. 3312. Rules and regulations

The President is authorized to prescribe such rules and regulations as he may deem appropriate to carry out the purposes of this chapter. During the three-year period beginning on January 1, 1979, such rules and regulations shall be transmitted promptly to the Speaker of the House of Representatives and to the Committee on Foreign Relations of the Senate. Such action shall not, however, relieve the Institute of the responsibilities placed upon it by this chapter.

Sec. 3313. Congressional oversight

(a) Monitoring activities of Senate Foreign Relations Committee, House Foreign Affairs Committee, and other Congressional committees

The Committee on Foreign Affairs of the House of Representatives, the Committee on Foreign Relations of the Senate, and other appropriate committees of the Congress shall monitor—

(1) the implementation of the provisions of this chapter;

(2) the operation and procedures of the Institute;

(3) the legal and technical aspects of the continuing relationship between the United States and Taiwan; and

(4) the implementation of the policies of the United States concerning security and cooperation in East Asia.

(b) Committee reports to their respective Houses

Such committees shall report, as appropriate, to their respective Houses on the results of their monitoring.

Sec. 3314. Definitions

For purposes of this chapter—

(1) the term "laws of the United States" includes any statute, rule, regulation, ordinance, order, or judicial rule of decision of the United States or any political subdivision thereof; and

(2) the term "Taiwan" includes, as the context may require, the islands of Taiwan and the Pescadores, the people on those islands, corporations and other entities and associations created or organized under the laws applied on those islands, and the governing authorities on Taiwan recognized by the United States as the Republic of China prior to January 1, 1979, and any successor governing authorities (including political subdivisions, agencies, and instrumentalities thereof).

Sec. 3315. Authorization of appropriations

In addition to funds otherwise available to carry out the provisions of this chapter, there are authorized to be appropriated to the Secretary of State for the fiscal year 1980 such funds as may be necessary to carry out such provisions. Such funds are authorized to remain available until expended.

Sec. 3316. Severability

If any provision of this chapter or the application thereof to any person or circumstance is held invalid, the remainder of the chapter and the application of such provision to any other person or circumstance shall not be affected thereby.

Contributors

James E. Auer is director of the Center for U.S.–Japan Studies and Cooperation at the Vanderbilt Institute for Public Policy Studies, which, among other things, conducts the annual U.S.–Japan (Defense–Dual Use) Technology Forum for American and Japanese businessmen in Nashville, Tennessee, and the annual U.S.–Japan Critical Infrastructure Protection Forum in Washington, D.C. Dr. Auer teaches U.S.–Japan relations and the history of sea power to Vanderbilt University graduate and undergraduate students and has served as adjunct professor of management at Vanderbilt's Owen Graduate School of Management and research professor of the management of technology at the Vanderbilt University School of Engineering. He served in the U.S. Navy from 1963 to 1983, largely in Japan, where he was a visiting student at the Japan Maritime Self-Defense Force Staff College in Tokyo, and as commanding officer of a guided missile frigate home-ported in Yokosuka. From April 1979 until September 1988, he served as special assistant for Japan in the Office of the Secretary of Defense. His doctorate is from the Fletcher School of Law and Diplomacy, Tufts University. He is the author of *The Postwar Rearmament of Japanese Maritime Forces 1945–1971*, published in English by Praeger Publishers and in Japanese translation.

Daniel Blumenthal is a resident fellow in Asian studies at the American Enterprise Institute for Public Policy Research and president of Strategic Education and Research International, Inc. In January 2006, he was appointed a member of the U.S.–China Security and Economic Review Commission by Senate Majority Leader Bill Frist (R–TN) for a two-year term. Mr. Blumenthal was senior director for China, Taiwan, and Mongolia in the Office of the Secretary of Defense for International Security Affairs from March 2004–November 2004 during the first George W. Bush Administration. Before his service at the Department of Defense, he was an associate attorney, Corporate and Asia Practice Groups, at Kelley Drye & Warren L.L.P. Earlier, he was an editorial and research assistant at the Washington Institute for Near East Policy. Mr. Blumenthal received a Master of Arts in International Relations and International Economics from the Johns Hopkins University School of Advanced International Studies and a J.D. from the Duke University School of Law in 2000.

JACQUES DELISLE is the Stephen Cozen Professor of Law at the University of Pennsylvania, a member of the faculty of the university's Center for East Asian Studies, and director of the Asia Program at the Foreign Policy Research Institute. His writings, which have appeared in foreign affairs journals, law reviews, edited volumes, and other media, focus on the international status of Taiwan and cross-Strait relations; legal, economic, and political reform in China; legal and political issues in Hong Kong's reversion to China and post-reversion Hong Kong; China's engagement with the international legal and institutional order (including the World Trade Organization); U.S. efforts to promote reform in the post-Communist world; and uses of U.S. law to address human rights in China. He received a J.D. degree from Harvard, graduate education in political science at Harvard, and an A.B. from Princeton. He also clerked for Stephen Breyer (then chief judge of the First Circuit Court of Appeals) and served as attorney-adviser in the Office of Legal Counsel, U.S. Department of Justice, where his work focused on separation of powers and foreign affairs law.

RUPERT J. HAMMOND-CHAMBERS is president of the U.S.–Taiwan Business Council. Born and raised in Scotland, he emigrated to the United States in 1987. He worked at the Center for Security Policy in Washington, D.C., as an associate for development in 1993 and joined the U.S.–Taiwan Business Council in 1994. He was promoted to vice president of the council in 1998 and was elected president in November 2000. Mr. Hammond-Chambers sits on the advisory boards of Redwood Partners International, The Sabatier Group, and the Pacific Star Fund; is a trustee of Fettes College; and is a member of both the National Committee on United States–China Relations and the Council on Foreign Relations. He is a 1991 graduate of Denison University in Ohio, having completed undergraduate studies begun at Fettes College in Scotland.

J. BRUCE JACOBS is professor of Asian languages and studies at Monash University in Melbourne, Australia. He first went to Taiwan as a postgraduate student at National Taiwan University in 1965–1966 and later conducted his doctoral field research in Taiwan during 1971–1973 and received his Ph.D. from Columbia University in 1975. From 1976 until 1980, he visited Taiwan annually, but in 1980 he was blacklisted from visiting the island and was unable to return for 12 years. He then visited China frequently. Dr. Jacobs has published widely on both Taiwan and China and in recent years has concentrated on cross-Strait relations, Taiwan's democratic development, and the growth of Taiwan identity on the island.

RICHARD C. KAGAN is professor emeritus in history at Hamline University in St. Paul, Minnesota. From 1965–1967, he studied in Taiwan at the Stanford Center in National Taiwan University, where he became friends with many Chinese and Taiwanese political and literary dissidents including Peng Ming-min, Yin Hai-kuang, Yang Ching-chu, and Lee Ao. After obtaining his Ph.D. from the University of Pennsylvania in 1969, he made several trips to Taiwan in the 1970s. He became active in Taiwan human rights issues and testified twice before committees of the U.S. Congress regarding the 1979 "Kaohsiung Incident" and abuses of martial law in Taiwan. In 1981, he was blacklisted until 1994. He returned to Taiwan to write a biography of then-Taipei Mayor Chen Shui-bian that was published in 1998. In 2002, he received a human rights award in Taiwan. Dr. Kagan has recently completed a book manuscript entitled *Taiwan's Democrat: Lee Teng-hui*.

PAUL MONK is managing director of Austhink Consulting, a firm in Melbourne, New South Wales, that offers training in strategic analysis. He received his doctorate in international relations from Australia National University in 1989 and taught Chinese politics at La Trobe University until 1999. He also served in the Australian Defense Intelligence Office from 1990 to 1995 as East Asia intelligence analyst and head of China analysis. Dr. Monk is the author of *Thunder from the Silent Zone: Rethinking China* (Scribe, 2005), which was short-listed for the Gleebooks Prize (NSW) and The Age Book of the Year (Victoria) in 2006, and has published over 100 essays on subjects ranging from opera to sports, from religion to climate change, and from ancient history to geopolitics.

RANDALL GRAHAM SCHRIVER is one of five founding partners of Armitage International LLC and a senior associate at the Center for Strategic and International Studies. From 2003 to 2005, he was Deputy Assistant Secretary of State for East Asian and Pacific Affairs responsible for China, Taiwan, Mongolia, Australia, New Zealand, and the Pacific Islands. Before that, he was chief of staff and senior policy adviser to Deputy Secretary of State Richard Armitage. Mr. Schriver served for four years in the Office of the Secretary of Defense, including as senior country director for the People's Republic of China, Taiwan, and Mongolia during 1997–1998. He also served as an active duty Navy Intelligence Officer from 1989–1991, including a deployment in theater for service in Operation Desert Shield/ Desert Storm, and has experience as an attaché at the U.S. embassy in Beijing and the U.S. embassy in Ulaanbaatar, Mongolia. He holds a master's degree from Harvard University and is a graduate of Williams College.

JOHN J. TKACIK, JR., is senior fellow in Asian studies at The Heritage Foundation. He is a retired Foreign Service officer with over 20 years in Chinese language postings, including five years in the People's Republic of China, six years in Taiwan affairs, and three years in Hong Kong, and from 1992–1994 was chief of China analysis in the Department of State's Bureau of Intelligence and Research. After retiring in 1994, he was Asia–Pacific vice president for external affairs at R.J. Reynolds Tobacco International and subsequently launched a consulting firm, China Business Intelligence, which published a weekly newsletter on Taiwan politics and economics from 1998 to 2001. He has written extensively on China and edited *Rethinking One China*, published by The Heritage Foundation in 2004. He holds a master's degree from Harvard University and a bachelor's degree from Georgetown University and is a proud member of the Class of 1989 at the National War College, Ft. McNair, Washington, D.C.

Acknowledgments

A BOOK LIKE THIS IS NEVER THE MERE PRODUCT of the chapter authors and the editor. Certainly, the initial "Reshaping the Taiwan Strait" conference would not have been possible without funding, for which I must thank The Heritage Foundation's Director of Development at the time, Ann Fitzgerald, who found the financial resources. The book also benefited greatly from the wholehearted support of Asian Studies Center Director Michael Needham and Vice President for Communications and Marketing Rebecca Hagelin.

Thanks also to my scholarly colleagues, Jim Auer, Dan Blumenthal, Jacques deLisle, Rupert Hammond-Chambers, Bruce Jacobs, Richard Kagan, Paul Monk, and Randy Schriver, for creative and imaginative perspectives on the Taiwan issue that made this book more than just a collection of conference papers. Heritage interns Tom Chou and Mitsushiro Fujii spent weeks tracking down footnotes. Mike Pillsbury delivered a very exciting peroration on the roots of the Taiwan Relations Act and encouraged this book, but he decided to keep his paper as a chapter in a future book of his own. I encourage all readers to view his presentation at the Heritage Web site.

My most heartfelt thanks go to the editors who have made our collective verbiage readable and corrected typos and inconsistencies throughout. Senior Editor Richard Odermatt gave thoughtful advice on the structure of the text and reviewed the final layout with his usual care, and Senior Copy Editor William Poole saved me from infelicities of expression and helped to make sure that our efforts were expressed in suitably transparent prose.

Publishing Services Director Therese Pennefather gave this project priority in the busy Heritage publishing schedule, and Desktop Publishing Specialist Michelle Smith provided the book's attractive layout. But I want to acknowledge especially the book's superb cover design, which features a photograph of a Japanese Go board done by Andrew Blasko of Editorial Services and my own snapshot of the Formosa Strait portion of the terrestrial globe constructed by Venetian globe maker Vincenzo Coronelli in 1688. Credit for melding the two photos into a powerful cover image goes to Senior Graphic Designer Elizabeth Brewer.

Finally, grateful thanks are due, as always, to the many contributors and other supporters whose unfailing generosity and commitment make all of The Heritage Foundation's work possible.